Value Guide to Advertising Memorabilia

SECOND EDITION

B. J. SUMMERS

COLLECTOR BOOKS
A Division of Schroeder Publishing Co., Inc.

The current values in this book should be used only as a guide. They are not intended to set prices, which vary from one section of the country to another. Auction prices as well as dealer prices vary greatly and are affected by condition as well as demand. Neither the Author nor the Publisher assumes responsibility for any losses that might be incurred as a result of consulting this guide.

ON THE COVER:
Coca-Cola button, $300.00. Beacon Shoes Lighthouse, $75.00. Planter's Peanuts Tin, $35.00. B.Weille & Sons brush, $35.00. Pepsi mileage chart, $35.00. Supp-hose store display, $125.00. Donald Duck Bread painted metal sign, $575.00. Gordon's Tin, $75.00. Yello-Bole store display, $135.00. Paducah Distilleries whiskey jug, $300.00. 7-UP light-up clock, $375.00. Camels 3-D thermometer, $45.00. Pennsylvania Rubber Co. ashtray, $125.00.

Searching For A Publisher?

We are always looking for knowledgeable people considered to be experts within their fields. If you feel that there is a real need for a book on your collectible subject and have a large comprehensive collection, contact Collector Books.

Cover design by Beth Summers
Book design by Sherry Kraus

Collector Books
P.O. Box 3009
Paducah, Kentucky 42002-3009

B.J. Summers
233 Darnell Road
Benton, KY 42025

Printed in the U.S.A. by Image Graphics, Paducah, KY

CONTENTS

DEDICATION

I'm extremely happy to be able to dedicate this book to my new niece, Autumn. Welcome to the world and to the family.

CREDITS

Many thanks to the following for their valuable contributions, either by supplying photographs or allowing their collectibles to be photographed:

Wildflower Antique Mall, Exit 220-Interstate 57 & Rt. 45, Pesotum, IL 61863, 217-867-2704

Serving central Illinois along I-57, this exceptionally clean mall is conveniently located just off Exit 220. It is full of advertising and collectibles and has a better than average supply of Coca-Cola items.

Farmer's Daughter Antiques, 6330 Cairo Rd, Paducah, KY 42001, 502-444-7619

Bill and Jane Miller have one of the neatest shops you'll ever find. The mix of advertising (Bill's specialty), and primitives (Jane's specialty) is a winning combination in everyone's book. Their shop is easily located just a mile off 1-24 at Exit 3. You can't miss the big barn — stop by and talk to one of the friendliest couples in the antique world.

Richard Opfer Auctioneering, Inc., 1919 Greenspring Drive, Timonium, MD 21093, 410-252-5035

Richard Opfer Auctioneering, Inc. provides a great variey of antique and collectibles auctions. Give his friendly staff a call for his next auction catalog.

Charlie's Antique Mall, 303 Main St., P.O. Box 196, Hazel, KY 42049, 502-492-8175

Located in the historic antique community of Hazel, Ky., on Main St., this place has it all. The manager, Ray Gough, has some great dealers with a wide variety of antiques and collectibles and some of the friendliest help you'll find . This border town mall can keep even the pickiest collector busy for the better part of a day.

Gene Harris Antique Auction Center, Inc., 203 South 18th Avenue, P.O. Box 476, Marshalltown, IA 50158, 515-752-0600

If you have been collecting for any time at all, you probably know of this auction house. Seems like there is always an ad in the antique papers for one of their sales. Not only will you find advertising offered but watches and clocks, china, dolls, and almost anything else you can imagine.

Wm. Morford, RD #2 , Cazenovia, NY 13035, 315-662-7625

Wm. Morford has been operating one of the country's better cataloged phone auction businesses for several years. He doesn't list reproductions or repairs that are deceptive in nature. In each catalog is usually a section with items that are for immediate sale. Try out this site and tell him how you got his name and address.

Eric Reinfeld, 87 Seventh Avenue, Brooklyn, NY 11217, 718-783-2313

An avid Whistle and Coca-Cola collector all wrapped into one. Give Eric a call if you're interested in selling or buying advertising relating to these two categories.

Rare Bird Antique Mall, 212 South Main St., Goodlettsville, TN 37072, 615-851-2635

If you find yourself in the greater Nashville, Tenn., area, stop by this collector's paradise. Jon and Joan Wright have assembled a great cast of dealers who run the gamut of collectible merchandise. Step back to an era when the general store was the place to be, and be prepared to invest some well-spent time.

Buffalo Bay Auction Co., 5244 Quam Circle, Rogers, MN 55374, 612-428-8879

A great catalog auction with a good variety of advertising fare. If advertising is your cup of tea, you'll enjoy browsing their catalog with its excellent quality photographs and descriptions.

Twin Lakes Antique Mall, Hwy. 641 North, Gilbertsville, KY, 502-362-2218

Located conveniently in the heartland beside beautiful Kentucky Lake, this new mall is great. Ed and Dee Hanes run a super clean mall in this vacation land with a good selection of general line antiques and collectibles. You'll find a better than average selection of gas collectibles (Ed's hobby).

Affordable Antiques, Inc., 933 S. 3rd St., Paducah, KY 42003, 502-442-1225

Oliver Johnson's building is hard to miss. Situated on the 1-24 downtown loop in Paducah, the large smiley face sign will attract your attention. Oliver has a good general line antique and collectible shop, and he manages to find some of the cleanest and most unusual advertising you'll ever hope to see. If you can't find what you're looking for, Oliver will be happy to help you locate it.

Antiques, Cards and Collectibles, 203 Broadway, Paducah, KY 42001, 502-443-9797

Right on the river in the historic Michael Hardware building, Ray Pelley has three floors filled with antiques and collectibles. Easy to find just off the loop in downtown Paducah. If you need help, Ray, Donna, and Emma are always ready with information and a smile.

Creatures of Habit, 406 Broadway, Paducah, KY 42001, 502-442-2923

A touch of the unusual is the first thing you'll notice when you walk into Natalya and Jack's shop. With an ample supply of out-of-the-ordinary advertising, this is a "must stop" when in the area. Good merchandise and plenty of friendly help are a winning combination.

Collector's Auction Services, Route 2, Box 431, Oakwood Drive, Oil City, PA 16301, 814-677-6070

Mark and Sherry run a great cataloged advertising auction service. With at least two very strong auctions a year, you'll find a fantastic variety of advertising and gas collectibles. Their catalogs are second to none and provide a great reference source. Make sure to give them a call and get involved in their next auction.

Giller Auction House, 405 Jefferson St., Paducah, KY 42001, 502-444-6786

Rolf and Wanda run a good antique auction once a month. They usually have a good supply of furniture and advertising. Give them a call

The Illinois Antique Center, 308 S.W. Commercial, Peoria, IL 61602, 309-673-3354

Overlooking the river in downtown Peoria, this huge warehouse has been remodeled by Dan and Kim and now has a wonderful selection of antiques and collectibles. Always a great source of advertising signs, statues, and memorabilia. You'll find an ample supple of smiling faces and help here. Plan on spending the better part of a day.

Gary Metz's Muddy River Trading Company, 263 Key Lakewood Dr., Moneta, VA 24121, 540-721-2091

Gary probably produces one of the best advertising auctions in this country. While his emphasis is primarily on Coca-Cola and other soda products, he certainly isn't limited to those fields. Gary is probably one of the nicest people you'll ever meet. Give him a call and send for his next catalog to open up a whole new level of collecting.

Pleasant Hill Antique Mall and Tea Room, 315 South Pleasant Hill Rd., East Peoria, IL 61611, 309-694-4040

Bob Johnson and all the friendly staff at this mall welcome you for a day of shopping. And it'll take that long to work your way thru all the quality antiques and collectibles at this mall. When you get tired, stop and enjoy a rest at the tea room where you can get some of the best home cooked food found anywhere. All in all, a great place to shop for your favorite antiques.

Michael and Deborah Summers, Paducah, KY 42001

My brother and sister-in-law are avid collectors, and have been invaluable in helping compile information for this book. Mike and I have spent many days chasing down treasures at auctions.

Bill and Helen Mitchell, 226 Arendall St., Henderson, TN 38340, 901-989-9302

Bill and Helen have assembled a great variety of advertising with special emphasis on Coca-Cola, and they are always searching for new finds. So if you have anything that fits the bill, give them a call or drop them a letter.

Patrick's Collectibles, 612 Roxanne Dr., Antioch, TN 37013, 615-833-4621

If you happen to be around Nashville, Tenn., during the monthly flea market at the state fairgrounds, be certain to look for Mike and Julie Patrick. They have some of the sharpest advertising pieces you'll ever hope to find. And if Coca-Cola is your field, you won't be able to walk away from the great restored drink machines. Make sure to look them up, you certainly won't be sorry.

John and Vicki Mahan, 1407 N. 4th St., Murray, KY 42071, 502-753-4330

John's specialty is porcelain signs, but like most collectors, he's certainly not limited just to signs. He's always looking to buy, sell, or trade, so give him a call .

Chief Paduke Antiques Mall, 300 S. 3rd St., Paducah, KY 42003, 502-442-6799

This full-to-overflowing mall is located in an old railroad depot in downtown Paducah with plenty of general line advertising including good Coke pieces, plus a good selection of furniture. Stop by and see Charley or Carolyn if you're in this area.

One collector's method of displaying part of his collection.

INTRODUCTION

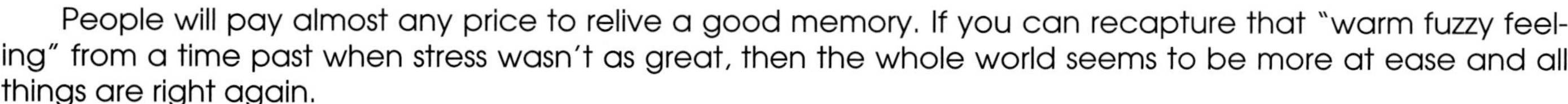

People will pay almost any price to relive a good memory. If you can recapture that "warm fuzzy feeling" from a time past when stress wasn't as great, then the whole world seems to be more at ease and all things are right again.

One way of returning to those thrilling days of yesteryear is to surround ourselves with nostalgic items that evoke those memories. Some collect for investment. Most of us collect so we can be surrounded by objects that will recall pleasant times and relieve stress associated with our day-to-day world.

Advertising art has a magical power. It sells a product or service, and even years later it transforms our surroundings to a simpler place. My office is full of advertising art; my main collecting avenue is Paducah, items and advertising. There's something magical about working in my office while being surrounded by light-up signs, clocks, pre-Prohibition advertising whiskey jugs and bottles, and cardboard signs. It helps me focus on the task at hand, while allowing me to tune out the outside world for a short time.

I do not attempt to set prices in this guide; I simply report what has been paid recently for items. All prices are keyed to allow the reader to know how the price was deduced. If you see a D beside the price, this means a dealer has this item for sale at this price. Similarly, a B is a bid price at auction, while a C is a price given by a collector. Condition is a major factor in establishing value. If I have reported an item with a mint value of $100.00, then it would be overpriced at $100.00 in fair condition. Once below mint condition, value drops drastically. Most items at yard sales and auctions should reflect a value close to wholesale or below. However the key word in that last sentence is SHOULD. But if you have the time and patience, auctions and yard sales can bring great rewards. If you buy from a dealer, please remember the following: this dealer has to make a living selling. He or she does try to buy at a price that will allow a reasonable profit margin. They then have to transport the item, research it, clean it up, place in into inventory, sometimes let it set for years, pay taxes on it, and then have someone offer less than the price that was paid for the item.

However you collect, you have my best wishes. I hope this book helps.

Year	Patent #	Year	Patent #	Year	Patent #	Year	Patent #	Year	Patent #
1836	1	1866	51,784	1896	552,502	1926	1,568,040	1956	2,728,913
1837	110	1867	60,658	1897	574,369	1927	1,612,700	1957	2,775,762
1838	546	1868	72,959	1898	596,467	1928	1,654,521	1958	2,818,567
1839	1,061	1869	85,503	1899	616,871	1929	1,696,897	1959	2,866,973
1840	1,465	1870	98,460	1900	640,167	1930	1,742,181	1960	2,919,443
1841	1,923	1871	110,617	1901	664,827	1931	1,787,424	1961	2,966,681
1842	2,413	1872	122,304	1902	690,385	1932	1,839,190	1962	3,015,103
1843	2,901	1873	134,504	1903	717,521	1933	1,892,663	1963	3,070,801
1844	3,395	1874	146,120	1904	748,567	1934	1,941,449	1964	3,116,487
1845	3,873	1875	158,350	1905	778,834	1935	1,985,878	1965	3,163,865
1846	4,348	1876	171,641	1906	808,618	1936	2,026,516	1966	3,226,729
1847	4,914	1877	185,813	1907	839,799	1937	2,066,309	1967	3,295,143
1848	5,409	1878	198,733	1908	875,679	1938	2,104,004	1968	3,360,800
1849	5,993	1879	211,078	1909	908,436	1939	2,142,080	1969	3,419,907
1850	6,981	1880	223,211	1910	945,010	1940	2,185,170	1970	3,487,470
1851	7,865	1881	236,137	1911	980,178	1941	2,227,418	1971	3,551,909
1852	8,622	1882	251,685	1912	1,013,095	1942	2,268,540	1972	3,631,539
1853	9,512	1883	269,820	1913	1,049,326	1943	2,307,007	1973	3,707,729
1854	10,358	1884	291,016	1914	1,083,267	1944	2,338,081	1974	3,781,914
1855	12,117	1885	310,163	1915	1,123,212	1945	2,366,154	1975	3,858,241
1856	14,009	1886	333,494	1916	1,166,419	1946	2,391,856	1976	3,930,271
1857	16,324	1887	355,291	1917	1,210,389	1947	2,413,675	1977	4,000,520
1858	19,010	1888	375,720	1918	1,251,458	1948	2,433,824	1978	4,065,812
1859	22,477	1889	395,305	1919	1,290,027	1949	2,457,797	1979	4,131,952
1860	26,642	1890	418,665	1920	1,326,899	1950	2,492,944	1980	4,180,867
1861	31,005	1891	443,987	1921	1,364,063	1951	2,536,016	1981	4,242,757
1862	34,045	1892	466,315	1922	1,401,948	1952	2,580,379		
1863	37,266	1893	488,976	1923	1,440,362	1953	2,624,046		
1864	41,047	1894	511,744	1924	1,478,996	1954	2,664,562		
1865	45,685	1895	531,619	1925	1,521,590	1955	2,698,434		

ALCOHOL

Courtesy of Pleasant Hill Antique Mall & Tea Room/Bob Johnson

Amstel light on tap, neon, three colors, near-mint, **$135.00 (D).**

Courtesy of Muddy River Trading Co./Gary Metz

Arrow Beer, matchless body, framed cardboard sign, 22" X 34", excellent, **$250.00 (B).**

Ballantine beer, ask the man for..., light-up advertising clock, 15" X 15", good, **$95.00 (D).**

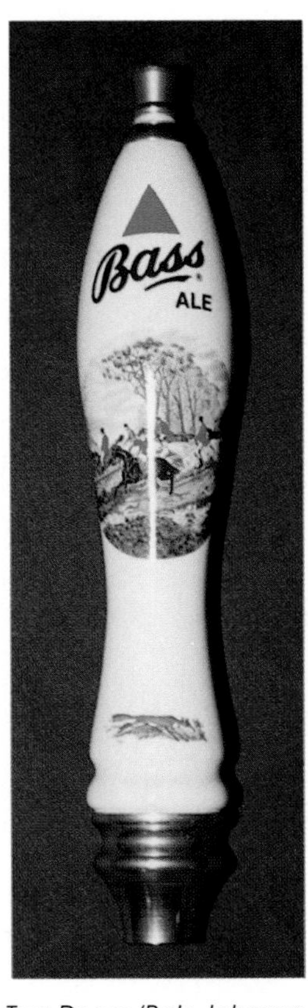

Bass ale, tap handle, features fox hunt scene, excellent, **$25.00 (D).**

Courtesy of Pleasant Hill Antique Mall & Tea Room/Bob Johnson

Bartels Beer, painted metal sign, 18" dia., good, **$125.00 (D).**

Courtesy of B.J. Summers

Blatz at Local Prices, skater statue, good, **$95.00 (C).**

Courtesy of Pleasant Hill Antique Mall & Tea Room/Bob Johnson

Blatz Beer, light-up back bar figure; when lit, bars behind man appear to move, good, **$125.00 (D).**

Courtesy of B.J. Summers

Blatz bottle and can man, Milwaukee's Finest Beer, back bar advertising statue, good, **$125.00 (C).**

Courtesy of Muddy River Trading Co./Gary Metz

Blatz, Milwaukee's most exquisite beer, tin over cardboard with embossed figures, 10½" X 13¾", excellent, **$165.00 (B).**

Courtesy of B.J. Summers

Blatz, man at keg, We Serve The Finest People Everyday, At Local Prices, light-up back bar statue, good, **$95.00 (C).**

Blue Ribbon Bourbon, framed oleograph of cabin beside stream, 48" X 38", excellent, **$550.00 (D).**

Courtesy of Affordable Antiques/ Oliver Johnson

Bock Beer, paper ad, framed, copyright 1925, excellent, **$300.00 (B).**

Courtesy of Pleasant Hill Antique Mall & Tea Room/Bob Johnson

Budweiser Draught Beer, light-up sign featuring pair of hunting dogs, good, **$95.00 (D).**

Courtesy of B.J. Summers

Budweiser, King of Beers, light-up with hitch at bottom, 9½" X 14¾", excellent, **$25.00 (C).**

Courtesy of Affordable Antiques/Olive Johnson

Budweiser, framed lithograph of Custer's last fight, Anheuser Busch, St. Louis, Missouri, U.S.A., 44" X 34", excellent, **$325.00 (D).**

Courtesy of B.J. Summers

Budweiser Draught, light-up advertising sign displaying the team in front of a frosty mug of beer, 16½" dia., excellent, **$55.00 (C).**

Courtesy of Pleasant Hill Antique Mall & Tea Room/Bob Johnson

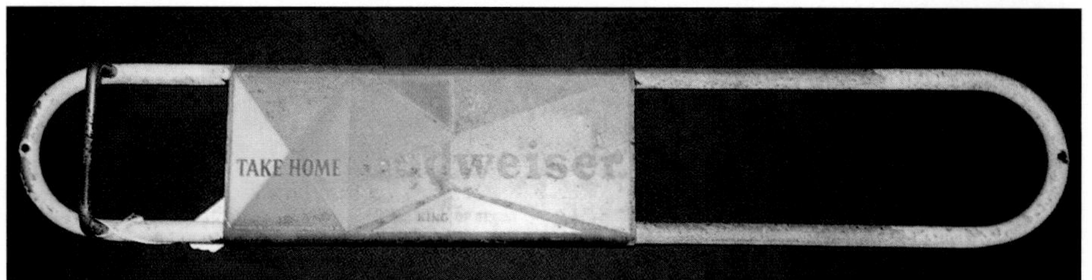

Budweiser, take home, painted metal door push bar; this is in fairly bad shape, but they aren't very common, poor, **$25.00 (D).**

Busch...Beer, western scene light-up clock, 15" X 15", good, **$55.00 (C).**

Courtesy of Muddy River Trading Co./Gary Metz

Consumer's Beer, ask father, artwork of man with glass of beer, embossed tin sign, from Consumers Brewing Co., Mulls Grove, RI, 1940s, 28" X 9¾", excellent, **$225.00 (B).**

Courtesy of Pleasant Hill Antique Mall & Tea Room/Bob Johnson

Dortmunder union, wooden tapper handle, excellent, **$25.00 (D).**

Courtesy of Pleasant Hill Antique Mall & Tea Room/Bob Johnson

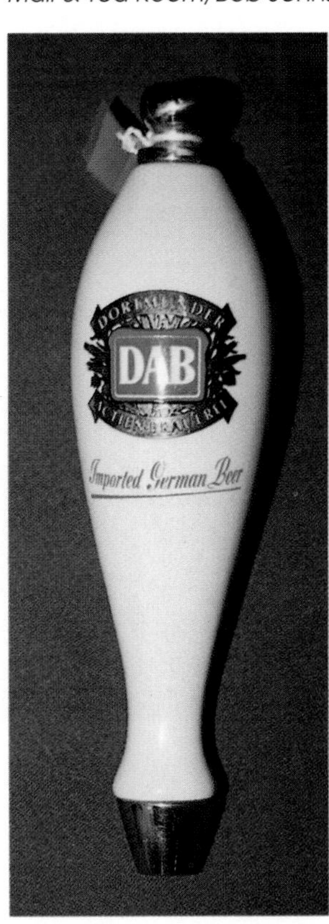

DAB, Imported German Beer, tapper handle, excellent, **$25.00 (D).**

Duquesne Pilsener...The finest Beer in Town, framed print, signed by Walt Otto, Duquesne Brewing Co., Pittsburgh, Pa., 1934, 29" X 32", good, **$125.00 (D).**

Courtesy of Pleasant Hill Antique Mall & Tea Room/Bob Johnson

Falstaff Beer, an old friend!, paper advertising sign, good, **$45.00 (D).**

Courtesy of Pleasant Hill Antique Mall & Tea Room/Bob Johnson

Fox Deluxe Beer serving tray, featuring artwork of hunter with horn, good, **$40.00 (D).**

Gold Seal Champagne, tip tray, manufactured by American artworks, Coshocton, Ohio, 4½" X 6½", excellent, **$50.00 (D).**

Courtesy of Affordable Antiques

Hamm's Beer, Born in the land of sky blue waters, metal and plastic motion light-up sign, great graphics, 31" X 18", excellent, **$225.00 (D).**

Heineken Beer, wooden tapper handle, good, **$10.00 (C)**.

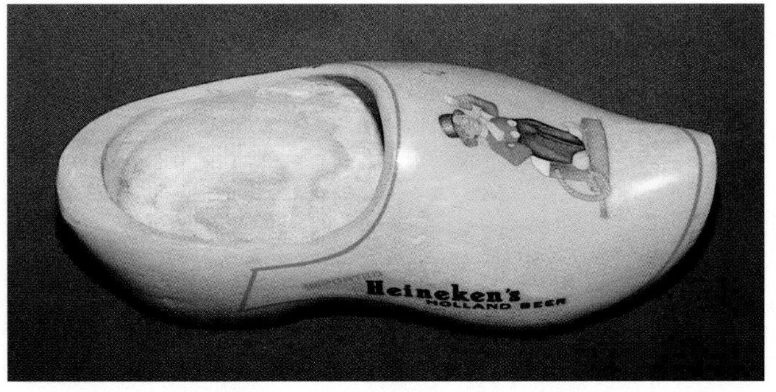

Heineken's Holland Beer, wooden shoe, excellent, **$25.00 (C).**

Courtesy of Richard Opfer Auctioneering, Inc.

I.W. Harper Whiskey, framed print featuring bird dog in front of log cabin with hunting gear on front porch, good strong sign, 24" X 30", near-mint, **$1,000.00 (B).**

Courtesy of B.J. Summers

Johnnie Walker Red, back bar statue, good, **$55.00 (C)**.

James Buchanan & Co. Ltd. scotch whisky distillers, Black & White Scotch Whisky, featuring dogs in field, note spelling of whisky, 23" X 24½", good, **$175.00 (D).**

Korbel Sec California Champagne, painted metal sign, 19" X 13", near-mint, **$200.00 (C).**

Courtesy of B.J. Summers

Löwenbräu, lion, back bar statue with bottle, excellent, **$125.00 (C).**

Courtesy of Pleasant Hill Antique Mall & Tea Room/Bob Johnson

Michelob Classic Dark, tapper handle, excellent, **$15.00 (D).**

Pleasant Hill Antique Mall & Tea Room/Bob Johnson

Michelob Light, tapper handle, with skier on top, excellent, **$20.00 (D).**

Labatt's, porcelain serving tray, 16" X 12", excellent, **$65.00 (D).**

Courtesy of Pleasant Hill Antique Mall & Tea Room/Bob Johnson

Miller Genuine Draft, light-up, three-dimensional advertising of bottle in ice block, excellent, **$55.00 (D).**

Courtesy of B.J. Summers

Miller High Life, light-up advertising sign, "Buy it now" with bottle and can on each side of message, good, **$55.00 (C).**

Courtesy of Pleasant Hill Antique Mall & Tea Room/Bob Johnson

Miller High Life, neon, new, excellent, **$125.00 (C).**

Moosehead Beer, tin advertising sign, excellent, **$25.00 (D).**

Courtesy of Richard Opfer Auctioneering, Inc.

Muchlebach's, die cut tin litho match holder, shaped like bottle, "special brew," 7" H, good, **$180.00 (B).**

Courtesy of Pleasant Hill Antique Mall & Tea Room/Bob Johnson

Old Kentucky's Boss, whiskey bottle with paper label, good, **$10.00 (D).**

Courtesy of Pleasant Hill Antique Mall & Tea Room/Bob Johnson

Pabst Blue Ribbon, back bar statue featuring boxer in ring with bottle, excellent, **$125.00 (D).**

Pabst Blue Ribbon Beer, advertising cardboard poster, framed, waiter in uniform carrying a tray of beer and glasses, older version, 26½" X 36", excellent, **$675.00 (C).**

Courtesy of B.J. Summers

Pabst Blue Ribbon Beer, menu board, new, excellent, **$35.00 (D).**

Courtesy of B.J. Summers

Pabst Blue Ribbon...Old Time Beer Flavor, light-up motion train, good, **$155.00 (C).**

Courtesy of Pleasant Hill Antique Mall & Tea Room/Bob Johnson

Pabst Blue Ribbon, serving tray, Pabst Brewing Company, Milwaukee, Wisc., excellent, **$12.00 (D).**

Pickwick Ale, advertising, painted tin over cardboard, Copyright Hoffenreffer & Co., Inc., 23" X 6½",fair, **$55.00 (C).**

Pickwick Ale, "Ale that is Ale," round serving tray, Copyright Hoffenreffer & Co., Inc., artwork of ale barrels being drawn by team of horses, 12" dia., excellent, **$100.00 (C).**

Courtesy of Buffalo Bay Auction Co.

R. Brand & Co. Fine Whiskeys and Wines...Toledo, O., tin litho advertising sign with artwork of young woman in period dress, good strong image and message, 1800s, 17" X 23", excellent, **$1,318.00 (B)**.

Courtesy of B.J. Summers

Roanoke Rye, Thompson, Wilson & Co., Distillers, Paducah, Ky., framed paper litho, still has good colors, professionally restored, in original frame, 1900s, 14" X 19", excellent, **$1,000.00 (C).**

Courtesy of B.J. Summers

Rehkopf's Special, Straight Kentucky Whiskey, Paducah, Ky., 1 qt. stone jug, excellent, **$325.00 (C).**

Schell's Carbonated Mead, prohibition advertising sign for August Schell Brewing Co., New Ulm, Mn., great artwork of woman with peacock, 16¼" X 33", near-mint, **$1,350.00 (B).**

Schenley, Please Pay When Served, ad sign, good, **$25.00 (C).**

Courtesy of Pleasant Hill Antique Mall & Tea Room/Bob Johnson

Schlitz, bottle flashlight, good, **$35.00 (D).**

Courtesy of Pleasant Hill Antique Mall & Tea Room/Bob Johnson

Schlitz, salt & pepper set, good, **$10.00 (D).**

Courtesy of Muddy River Trading Co./Gary Metz

Schmidt's, Drink Malta, embossed tin sign featuring artwork of bottle at left of sign, 1930s, excellent, **$170.00 (B).**

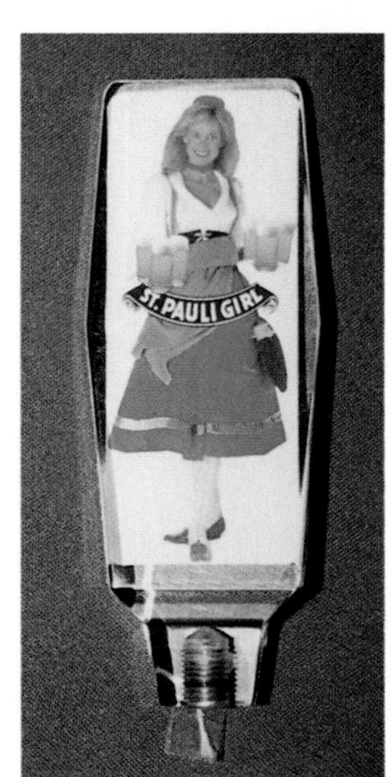

St. Pauli Girl, tapper handle, featuring girl with mugs of beer, excellent, **$15.00 (D).**

Courtesy of Pleasant Hill Antique Mall & Tea Room/Bob Johnson

Schmidt's, bronze bartender with embossed lettering, 7¾" H, excellent, **$175.00 (C).**

Standard Ale, framed cardboard advertisment, with artwork of delivery truck, Standard Brewing Co., Inc., Rochester, N. Y., 16" X 12½", excellent, **$100.00 (C).**

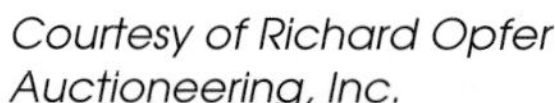
Courtesy of Richard Opfer Auctioneering, Inc.

Stegmaier Brewing Co., tin litho match holder, 5" H, good, **$110.00 (B).**

Sterling Beer...Mellow, metal figural bell that rings when her hands are squeezed together, 4¾" X 14¾", good, **$75.00 (C).**

Courtesy of Richard Opfer Auctioneering, Inc.

Sunny Brook Pure Rye, tin match holder with great litho of rye bottle, 5" H, good, **$110.00 (B).**

Tech Beer, Too good to forget, self-framing painted metal advertising sign, Pittsburgh Brewing Co., Pittsburgh, Pa., artwork of hunting scene, 26½" X 18½", good, **$125.00 (D).**

Turnbull's Standard Scotch Whisky, Offices-51 High Street, HAWICK, artwork of bottle in center, embossed painted tin, note spelling of whisky, 24½" X 18", good, **$85.00 (C).**

West Virginia Pilsner Beer, cardboard advertising poster, featuring artwork of woman and glass of beer, 14" X 22", good, **$75.00 (C).**

Courtesy of B.J. Summers

Wiedemann Fine Beer, 3-D plastic sign with trumpeter swan flying over wetlands, 16" X 18", good, **$45.00 (C).**

NOT PICTURED:

Akron Brewing Co., Akron, Ohio, litho decal of factory scene on wood, 1930s, 36" X 24", near-mint, **$210.00 (B).**

Anheuser Busch 5¢, stoneware dispenser by Cardley & Hayes, NY, good strong lettering and color, 1919, near-mint, **$125.00 (B).**

Anteek Beer, composition back bar statue in likeness of bartender with product name on apron, 22" tall, excellent, **$275.00 (D).**

Augustiner Beer, properly aged painted tin sign, 20" X 13¾", excellent, **$45.00 (C).**

Bailey's Pure Rye, round metal tip tray with product bottle and shot glass on tray center, "Used medicinally & Socially," 4¼" dia., excellent, **$140.00 (B).**

Baltimore American Ale & Beer 10¢, painted tin sign, 35¾" X 18", good, **$85.00 (C).**

Barbarossa Premium Beer, embossed paper hanging tavern sign, artwork of Merlin and elves in cameo, 10½" X 13½", near-mint, **$50.00 (B).**

Barclay's Lager, tin litho advertising sign with artwork of man with glass of product, 1910, 14" X 21", excellent, **$75.00 (B).**

Bartel's Lager, Ale & Porter, Syracuse, NY, with artwork of man with large tankard of product, 4⅛" dia., excellent, **$100.00 (B).**

Bartholomay B...Beers, Ales & Porter...in Kegs & Bottles, round metal tip tray with artwork of woman on large bird, 4¼" dia., excellent, **$110.00 (B).**

Beck's Bottled Beer, round metal tip tray with artwork of eagle on red, white, and blue shield in center of tray, 4⅛" dia., good, **$140.00 (B).**

Beefeater Gin...The imported One, wood and composition back bar statue, 8½" X 17", excellent, **$95.00 (D).**

Black Label Beer, die cut cardboard in image of man carrying case of product, three-dimensional, 110" X 23", near-mint, **$75.00 (D).**

Blatz, alto-plaster ad sign of F. Scott Fitzgerald in German pub, Blatz Old Heidelberg, 1933, 42¾" X 27¾", excellent, **$175.00 (B).**

Blatz, bottle man holding mug of beer with one hand and advertising pennant in other hand, plastic and glass construction, 6¾" X 15½", excellent, **$125.00 (D).**

Blatz...Blatz can (barrel) man holding mug of beer, metal and plastic bar statue, 6½" X 10½", excellent, **$125.00 (D).**

Blatz...Old Heidelberg...better because it's ester aged, metal serving tray, 13¼" X 10½", good, **$105.00 (D).**

Blatz Pilsner Beer, die cut easel back cardboard store advertising sign in shape of bottle of product, 1947, 7" X 27", near-mint, **$25.00 (B).**

Bock Beer Hangers from Donaldson Litho Co., Newport, Ky., generic sign for retail trade, graphics of serving girl with tray of product, 18½" X 26½", near-mint, **$330.00 (B).**

Brandy Wine, Seminole Flavor Co., Chattanooga, TN, paper sign with artwork of woman riding on eagle, 1939, 22" dia., near-mint, **$75.00 (B).**

Budweiser Beer, light-up cash register light and sign, 10¼" X 8¼", excellent, **$45.00 (D).**

Budweiser...Enjoy DuBois...DuBois Brewing Co., Dubois, PA, metal back with glass front light-up clock, 15" dia., excellent, **$225.00 (D).**

Budweiser...The New..You've waited 7 years for this...served everywhere, paper litho mounted on cardboard with mug in hand graphics, 1920s, 21" X 11", good, **$41.00 (B).**

Budweiser/King of Beers, light-up wall sign with plastic convex cover, 15" X 20", excellent, **$95.00 (C).**

C. Pfeiffer Brewing Co...Detroit, Mich., round metal tip tray, with graphics of product bottle in tray center, 4" dia., excellent, **$100.00 (B).**

Campbell & Co.'s Edinburgh Ales, framed advertising sign, 28½" X 55½", excellent, **$35.00 (C).**

Cardinal Beer...The Beer with the Real Hop Flavor, round metal tip tray with graphics of red-haired woman with bouquet of flowers, 4⅛" dia., excellent, **$110.00 (B).**

Central Brewing Co., Highest Grades of Pure Lager, Ales & Porter, round metal tip tray with artwork of horse in center of tray, 4½" dia., excellent, **$150.00 (B).**

Chas. D. Kaier Co. Ltd...Mahanoy City, Pa., round metal tip tray with product bottle in center of tray, 4⅛" dia., excellent, **$55.00 (B).**

Christian Feigenspan Brewing Co., metal serving tray with artwork of woman with red ribbon in hair, 13¼" dia., excellent, **$75.00 (D).**

Chum's...Scranton Distributing Co., round metal tip tray with graphics of man in tux seated at table with product and large dog, 4⅛" dia., excellent, **$375.00 (B).**

Consumer's Beer...Ask Father, tin advertising sign with artwork of man with white hair holding glass of product, 27¾" X 9¾", excellent, **$55.00 (B).**

Cooks Beer, metal over cardboard advertising sign with artwork of woman with long gloves, 1936, 18" X 29", fair, **$195.00 (D).**

CV...Please Pay When Served, embossograf of mother dogs and pups, Terre Haute Brewing Co., 16½" X 10½", excellent, **$35.00 (B).**

Diamond State Brewery, Wilmington, Delware, tin litho deep dish serving tray with graphics of old man with stein and dog, 12" dia., excellent, **$35.00 (B).**

DuBois Budweiser beer, light-up sign, metal back with curved glass front, 11" X 9¾", excellent, **$175.00 (C).**

Duquesne Brewing Company...Duke Beer, metal back curved front glass advertising light-up clock, 16" X 16", excellent, **$55.00 (D).**

Duquesne Pilsner, metal and glass light-up sign, 24" X 6", excellent, **$125.00 (C).**

Erlanger Beer...Classic 1893, 13" X 10½", excellent, **$15.00 (D).**

Falls City Beer, It's pasteurized, it's bitter free, paper 6-pack take-out bag with handles, 7¾" X 9¾", excellent, **$10.00 (D).**

Falstaff Beer...An old Friend, horizontal painted metal sign featuring artwork of medieval man with stein being served by waitress, 17½" X 15", good, **$100.00 (D).**

Falstaff...Enjoy Beer, two-piece painted metal sign, 17½" X 15", excellent, **$105.00 (D).**

Finotti, paper calendar with tear sheets at bottom with artwork of pretty girl sitting next to globe with message in center, 1961, excellent, **$35.00 (C).**

Fort Pitt Special Beer, cardboard litho advertising sign with ball player artwork, 26" X 18", near-mint, **$875.00 (B).**

Fred Krug Brewing Co., 50th Anniversary plate, with artwork of factory on one side and artwork of Mr. Krug on other side, 1909, near-mint, **$85.00 (B).**

Frederick's Premium Beer... Brewed with pure artesian well water, round metal serving tray with artwork of bottle in center, 13¼" dia., excellent, **$85.00 (D).**

Gallagher & Burton Whiskey, tip tray, "I am well preserved you see, many thanks to G & B", 4½" dia., near-mint, **$40.00 (B).**

Gallaher & Burton Whiskey, round metal tip tray with artwork of older gentleman with bottle of product, 4¼" dia., excellent, **$35.00 (B).**

Genesee Beer, tin on cardboard ad sign with two people sitting on product box, 14½" X 7", excellent, **$50.00 (B).**

George H. Goodman Company, Incorporated, 1-gal. whiskey crock, with message in outline box on front, cream, excellent, **$155.00 (C).**

Goebel Bantam Beer...Enjoy, die cut cardboard rooster "tootin" his own horn, 9" X 11", excellent, **$30.00 (B).**

Grain Belt Brewing Co., litho on canvsas depicting wilderness scene of hunters, horses, wolves and deer, Minneapolis, 31" X 26", near-mint, **$65.00 (B).**

Green River...The Whiskey Without a Headache, ink blotter with graphics of old black man and sway back horse with jug of product on saddle, 9¼" X 4", excellent, **$71.00 (B).**

Green River Whiskey, full figure back bar statue of elderly black man and sway-backed horse carrying whiskey, 14" X 10½" X 4", near-mint, **$485.00 (B).**

Griesedieck Bros...Premium Light...Beer...It's De-Bitterized, round metal frame advertising clock with message in center of face, 15" dia., good, **$135.00 (D).**

Hanlen Bros...Harrisburg, PA...The Old Reliable Liquor Dealers, round metal tip tray with artwork of horse's head in tray center, 4⅛" dia., excellent, **$130.00 (B).**

Harvard Brewing Co., tin litho sign featuring artwork of woman enjoying cocktail in room overlooking garden courtyard, 36" X 45", excellent, **$1,750.00 (B).**

Heineken's Imported Holland Beer, tin litho over cardboard, with Holland graphics in left lower corner, 1950s, excellent, **$45.00 (B).**

Hyroler Whiskey...Louis J. Adler & Co., round metal tip tray with artwork of man in dress attire and top hat, 4¼" dia., excellent, **$45.00 (B).**

Jacob Ruppert, oval serving tray, 1930s, 10¾" X 14½", good, **$85.00 (C).**

John Dewar & Sons, Old World scene cardboard ad in original oak frame, 31¼" X 22¼", excellent, **$25.00(D).**

King's Puremalt...good for insomnia...strengthening...heathful, oval tip tray with graphics of product bottle in tray center, 6⅛" L, excellent, **$120.00 (B).**

Korbel Sec Champagne, beveled edge tin over cardboard, self-framing, with artwork of woman with grapes and product bottle at right of artwork, 19" X 13", near-mint, **$365.00 (B).**

Krueger Beer & Ale in bottles and keg-lined cans, 10" X 15", excellent, **$150.00 (B).**

Lehnert's Beer...Drink...Made in Catasauqua, Pa., round metal tip tray with graphics of large dog sporting eyeglasses and smoking a cigar, 4¼" dia., excellent, **$300.00 (B).**

Liberty Beer...In Bottles Only, American Brewing Co., round metal tip tray with Indian logo in center of tray, 4⅛", excellent, **$160.00 (B).**

Lieber's Gold Medal Beer, tip tray, featuring graphics of product bottle in center of tray, 5" dia., excellent, **$55.00 (B).**

Lily...A Beverage...Rock Island Brewing Co., Rock Island, Illinois, metal tip tray featuring graphics of product bottle in center with sandwich and glass of product, 6½" L, excellent, **$110.00 (B).**

Meyer Brewing Co., Compliments of...Bloomington, Ill., round tip tray with image of young woman, same image as is found on Old Reliable Coffee tip tray, 4¼" dia., excellent, **$201.00 (B).**

Miller High Life...The champagne of bottled beer, with lady on crescent moon, round metal serving tray, 12" dia., excellent, **$50.00 (D).**

Monroe Beer, round metal tip tray with banner across the globe, 4⅛" dia., excellent, **$40.00 (B).**

Monticello Special Reserve..It's All Whiskey, oval metal tip tray with graphics of Monticello along with men on horseback, 6¼", excellent, **$65.00 (B).**

Moose Beer..."Better Than Ever," painted wooden sign, 15" X 6⅞", good, **$95.00 (C).**

Moosehead...Imported on tap, neon wall sign with facsimile of moose in neon, excellent, **$175.00 (D).**

National Ales, Brew'g Co., Syracuse, NY, heavy enamel porcelain match striker, 4" X 6", excellent, **$500.00 (B).**

National Beer...The Best in the West, round metal tip tray with artwork of cowboy riding horse with bottle of product, 4½" dia., excellent, **$625.00 (B).**

Neuweiler's Beer...Watch the place awhile..., cardboard advertising sign with artwork of two men in bar, 17¼" X 13¾", excellent, **$45.00 (C).**

Nikolai, dancing Russian figural back bar statue, composition, excellent, **$75.00 (D).**

Northampton Brewing Co...Lager Beer, round metal tip tray with artwork of hand holding 3 bottles of product, 4⅛" dia., excellent, **$140.00 (B).**

Obermeyer & Leibmann's...Bottled Beer, beer push cart with big iron wheels and product message on sides, 43" tall, excellent, **$1,500.00 (B).**

Old Barbee, Vienna Art Plate, graphics of old man pouring product and women conversing beside log house, Louisville distillery, 1908, 10" dia., near-mint, **$594.00 (B).**

Old Boone Whiskey...Thixton, Millett & Co., Louisville, Ky., round metal tip tray with graphics of log cabin distillery, 4⅛" dia., excellent, **$210.00 (B).**

Old Crow, composition advertising figural backbar display, 3½" X 11½", excellent, **$75.00 (D).**

Old Crow, figural whiskey decanter complete with cane and spats, excellent, **$40.00 (C).**

Old Dutch Beer, embossed die cut store advertising sign with man holding mug of product, excellent, **$55.00 (B).**

Old Hickory Distillery...Madisonville, Ky., advertising crock jug, 1-gal., excellent, **$150.00 (C).**

Old Overholt Whiskey, oleograph canvas in wood frame with artwork of man with bottle of product and a fishing rod, Old Overholt rye, 1913, 27½" X 38½", excellent, **$350.00 (D).**

Old Reading Beer...Traditionally Pennsylvania Dutch, round metal serving tray, 12" dia., excellent, **$35.00 (D).**

Old Style...Brewed with water from when the earth was pure, plastic light-up sign, 15" X 10¼", excellent, **$25.00 (D).**

Pabst Beer, sign with artwork of Spanish-American war heroes around table celebrating with product, 1899, excellent, **$610.00 (B).**

Pabst Blue Ribbon Beer...at popular prices, painted tin sign with artwork of beer can with message at top, 26" X 60", excellent, **$95.00 (C).**

Pabst Extract, cardboard and paper calendar with graphics of woman with yellow scarf, 1917, 7¼" X 36", near-mint, **$380.00 (B).**

Pabst Extract, yard-long American Girl, in long dress with top strip, bottom strip missing, 1914, 35½" L, excellent, **$100.00 (B).**

Pearless Majestic...American Brewing Co., Phil., round metal tip tray with see, hear, and speak no evil monkeys artwork, 4¼" dia., excellent, **$185.00 (B).**

Peter Doelger...Bottled Beer, round metal tip tray with eagle image in center, 4⅛" dia., excellent, **$160.00 (B).**

Pittsburgh Brewing Company...From, cardboard advertising sign, 40½" X 22", excellent, **$65.00 (C).**

Plymouth Dry Gin...Coates...Original, with artwork of monk with product bottle, 4⅛" dia., excellent, **$40.00 (B).**

Popel-Giller Co. Inc., High Grade Bottled Beer, round metal tip tray with artwork of woman with glass of product and bouquet of flowers, 4¼" dia., excellent, **$90.00 (B).**

Red Seal Bottlers Extracts, litho on heavy paper with artwork of woman wearing red hat and red dress, St. Louis, Mo., business, 11½" X 16½", good, **$125.00 (B).**

Rienzi Beer...In Bottles Only...Bartholomay Brewery.. Rochester, NY, round tip tray with artwork of man on white horse with product bottle, 4⅛" dia., excellent, **$130.00 (B).**

Rolling Rock, The Premium Beer, advertising glass sign, easel back, cobalt, excellent, **$125.00 (C).**

Royalty Club Whiskey....A. Friedman Co...Sole Distributers, framed painted glass, 31" X 21", excellent, **$55.00 (D).**

Ruhstaller's Lager...Best Beer Brew...Sacramento, Cal., round metal tip tray with serving maid carrying steins of product, 4¼" dia., excellent, **$170.00 (B).**

Scheidt Brewery, poster, paper litho with artwork of Admiral Dewey and other Naval Commanders with battleship scenes in background, 23½" X 33", excellent, **$1,250.00 (B).**

Schlitz, neon sign in original wood crate, three color, red, blue, and green, 1930s, 17" X 29", near-mint, **$490.00 (B).**

Seagram's 7, glass serving pitcher with handle with logo embossed on side, 8" X 7", excellent, **$15.00 (D).**

Standard Brewing Co...tru age...nine months old beer, round metal serving tray, 12" dia., excellent, **$65.00 (D).**

Stegmaier Beer...The Home of..., oval metal tip tray with graphics of factory, 6⅛" L, excellent, **$65.00 (B).**

Stegmaier Brewing Co...Wilkes Barre, Pa., round metal tip tray with factory scene, 4¼" dia., excellent, **$140.00 (B).**

Stegmaier Brewing Co...Wilkes Barre, Pa., round metal tip tray with artwork of hand holding 4 bottles of product, 4⅛" dia., excellent, **$150.00 (B).**

Stegmaier's...We Serve...Gold Metal Beer, tin litho ad sign featuring cone top can and short neck bottle of product, excellent, **$72.00 (B).**

Tech Beer...None Better...Pittsburgh Brewing Co., metal tip tray with artwork of product bottle in center, 6⅝", excellent, **$80.00 (B).**

The Columbus Brewing Co...Select Pale Beer, round metal tip tray with image of middle-aged woman in center, 4⅛" dia., excellent, **$75.00 (B).**

The Penna. Bottling & Supply Co. Inc., round metal tip tray with product bottles in tray center, 4⅛" dia., excellent, **$50.00 (B).**

The Pilsener Brewing Co...Cleveland, Ohio, round metal tip tray with bottle and glass of product, 4¼" dia., excellent, **$90.00 (B).**

Tivioli Brewing Co...Detroit, round metal tip tray, with product bottle in center, 4⅛" dia., excellent, **$80.00 (B).**

Torrey's Original Old Mt. Vernon Ale, round metal tip tray with graphics of product bottle in tray center, 3⅝" dia., excellent, **$40.00 (B).**

Turnbulls Standard Scotch Whisky, embossed tin litho with image of product bottle, 12½" X 18", excellent, **$135.00 (B).**

Urbana Wine Co...Gold Seal...Champagne, metal tip tray with artwork of product bottle in tray center, 6⅝", excellent, **$45.00 (B).**

W. Schneider...Wholesale Wine & Liquor Co., crock jug, 1-gal., brown over cream, excellent, **$100.00 (D).**

Walter's Pilsner Beer...Time for, light-up advertising clock with artwork of brown bear in center spotlight, reverse painted glass, 15" dia., near-mint, **$293.00 (B).**

West End Brewing Co., Utica, New York, tin litho tray with graphics of Lady Liberty standing in center between beer keg and eagle, 13" dia., good, **$163.00 (B).**

White Top Champagne, round metal tip tray with product bottle artwork on tray center, 4⅛" dia., excellent, **$35.00 (B).**

Windsor...Supreme, figural head pitcher, excellent, **$25.00 (D).**

Yuengling's...Beer, Porter and Ale, round metal tip tray with graphics of eagle with wooden keg, 4¼" dia., excellent, **$50.00 (B).**

Courtesy of Muddy River Trading Co./Gary Metz

Buick, Bangor, Mich., embossed tin dealer sign, 1920s, 19½" X 13½", good, **$210.00 (B).**

Buss Auto Fuses, Why Be Helpless, tin advertising sign, featuring man in front of older period car in headlights of oncoming car, 8½" X 7½", excellent, **$75.00 (C).**

Courtesy of Illinois Antique Center/Kim & Dan Phillips

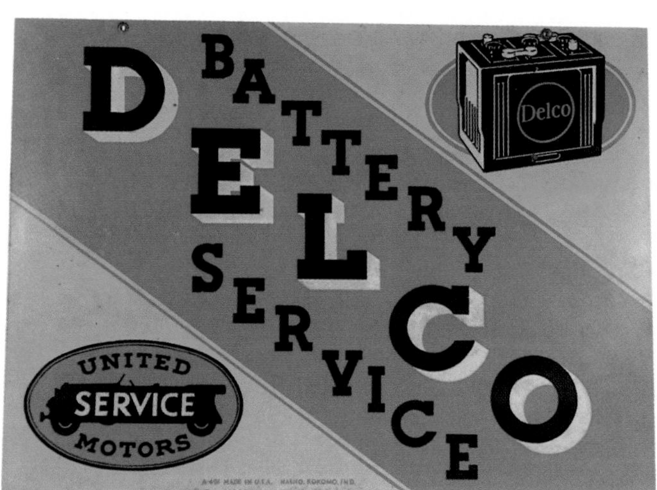

Delco...Battery Service, United Service Motors, painted metal advertising sign, with battery art-work in upper right corner, 30" X 22", excellent, **$175.00 (C).**

Dixie Gasoline, Oils, Power to Pass, oval double sided sign on original stand, 24" X 46", fair, **$450.00 (D).**

Courtesy of Affordable Antiques/Oliver Johnson

Gulf, Heating Oils, three-dimensional sign on hanging arm, good graphics with sign in flames, excellent, **$295.00 (D).**

Kelly Tires, painted metal flange sign, with the Kelly girl waving from older model touring car, 24" dia., excellent, **$1,850.00 (C).**

Mobil Oil...Pegasus, die cut porcelain horse, 36" tall, red, excellent, **$900.00 (C).**

Courtesy of Antiques Cards & Collectibles/Ray Pelly

Pennsylvania Rubber Co., Jeannette, PA, non-skid with CV logo, ashtray in vaseline glass, excellent, **$125.00 (D).**

Courtesy of Illinois Antique Center/Kim & Dan Phillips

Pennzoil...Safe Lubrication, with early brown bell in center, metal lollipop sign with original heavy embossed stand, 1920s, good, **$675.00 (D).**

Courtesy of Affordable Antiques

Phillips 66 Tires Batteries, light-up double bubble advertising clock, great color, 18" dia., near-mint, **$700.00 (D).**

Courtesy of Wm Morford Investment Grade Collectibles

Red Seal, automotive ignition battery advertising sign, tin over cardboard, strong colors, 27" X 19", excellent, **$1,500.00 (B).**

Red Crown Gasoline, circular porcelain sign with crown logo in center, 42" dia., excellent, **$875.00 (C).**

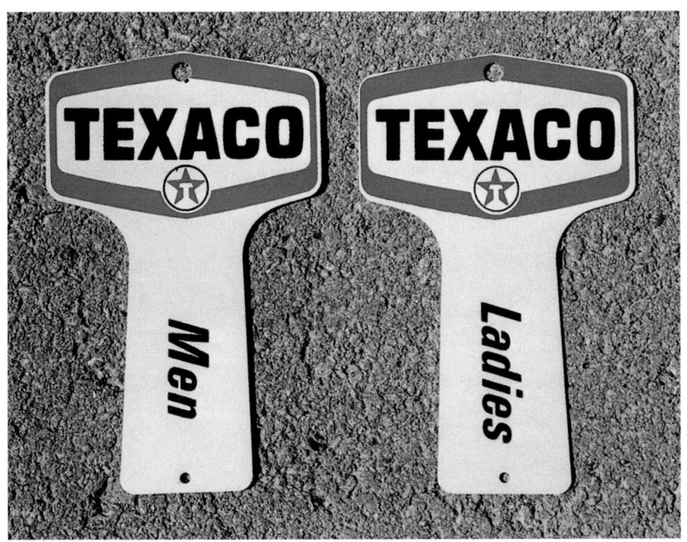

Texaco, restroom key tags, NOS, 3½" X 5½", near-mint, **$50.00 (C).**

Courtesy of Riverview Antique Mall

Trojan T Gasoline, porcelain sign, 28" X 22", good, **$425.00 (D).**

Tracto Motor Oil, embossed painted metal sign, 35" X 11", excellent, **$50.00 (C).**

Courtesy of Rare Bird Antique Mall-Jon & Joan Wright

Union 76 Certified Service Truck, toy truck in original box, has steerable wheels, with original decals, NOS, 24½" X 9½" X 9½", excellent, **$200.00 (D).**

Courtesy of Riverview Antique Mall

Vauxhall, sales and service porcelain sign, double sided, 42" X 27", excellent, **$450.00 (D).**

NOT PICTURED:

AC Spark Plug Cleaning Station, tin sign, showing artwork of donkey in bath tub at top center of sign with spark plug message below, 1945, 11" X 15½", red, black & yellow, excellent, **$225.00 (D).**

AC Spark Plugs, metal sign advertising AC method of cleaning, with artwork of donkey in bath tub, cost 5¢, vertical rectangle, black & yellow, good, **$95.00 (D).**

Aetna Automobile Insurance, painted tin sign, 24" X 12", black lettering on orange, fair, **$75.00 (C).**

Amalie...Pennsylvania Motor Oil, dial-type scale thermometer, metal body with glass front, 9" dia., excellent, **$85.00 (C).**

Amalie...Pennsylvania Motor Oil, light-up clock, metal body with glass face, 15" dia., excellent, **$235.00 (C).**

American cloth sleeve patch, 3" X 2⅜", excellent, **$10.00 (C).**

American Motor Hotel Association/Member, porcelain sign with sunburst in center containing AMHA initials, 1951, 20" X 25", excellent, **$225.00 (D).**

Amoco, winter lubricants, cloth service station banner, featuring silhouette artwork of car driving up hill in winter weather, 37½" X 35", good, **$125.00 (C).**

Auto-Lite, authorized electric motometer owen dyneto service, porcelain sign, 35¾" X 25½", excellent, **$175.00 (C).**

Barns-Dall, Be Square To Your Engine, porcelain pump sign with "B square" logo in center and message around edges, 3" dia., excellent, **$150.00 (C).**

Bayerson Oil Works, calendar with artwork of two lions and at bottom on original frame is the message, 1914, excellent, **$75.00 (D).**

Blue Crown Spark Plugs, store display, has plug on top of electrical display that fires when button on box is pushed, never used, 9" X 8¾" X 5", near-mint, **$210.00 (B).**

Boston Tire & Rubber Co...Automobile, Bicycle, and Carriage Tires, round metal tip tray with artwork of pretty girl with bouquet of flowers, 4¼" dia., good, **$200.00 (B).**

Buick...Motor Cars, vertical porcelain thermometer with dealer address at bottom, 1915, 7¼" X 27", white on blue, excellent, **$300.00 (C).**

C.P.W. Motor Car Enamel, cardboard poster showing man with older model touring car, 17¾" X 21¾", excellent, **$195.00 (C).**

Cadillac Service, plastic clock with Cadillac logo in center, 12" dia., excellent, **$175.00 (D).**

Carter Carburetor, light-up advertising piece of iron construction with product name on milk glass globe, 13½" X 27½", red, excellent, **$575.00 (C).**

Chevrolet Motor Cars, calendar with great graphics of early touring car in front of house with large porch, 1920, fair, **$175.00 (C).**

Chevron Supreme Gasoline, cloth sleeve patch, 2¾" dia., good, **$10.00 (C).**

Chrysler, MoPar Parts, metal painted flange sign, 23¾" X 16¾", black, orange on yellow, excellent, **$215.00 (D).**

Citgo, cloth sleeve patch, 2⅜" sq., excellent, **$10.00 (C).**

D-X, metal reflective license plate add-on, 5½" X 4", excellent, **$25.00 (D).**

DuPont Denatured Alcohol...Anti Rust Anti-Freeze, painted metal thermometer with scale in vertical arrow, messages at top and bottom, 8" X 38½", black, orange and red, excellent, **$95.00 (D).**

Esso "Fat Man," plastic bank, NOS, 5" tall, near-mint, **$100.00 (B).**

Esso, plastic figure bank with product name on front, 6½" tall, red, excellent, **$95.00 (C).**

Esso...Put a tiger in your tank, plastic service station advertising banner, with artwork of Esso tiger, 42" X 83", excellent, **$135.00 (D).**

Esso...watch your savings grow, square embossed glass advertising block, excellent, **$55.00 (D).**

Eveready Mazda Automobile Lamp Kit, metal case with spare lamps, product graphics on both sides, NOS, excellent, **$30.00 (D).**

Eveready Prestone, gallon metal can with original paper information sheet for car and radiator tag, 1-gal., excellent, **$175.00 (D).**

Firestone Cycle Tires...For Sale here, painted metal sign, 22" X 11½", excellent, **$225.00 (C).**

Firestone...Tires, Batteries, Spark Plugs, Brake Lining and Accessories, square advertising clock with lettering in center, 15¼" X 15¼", orange, white and dark blue, good, **$155.00 (D).**

Firestone Tires...Most miles per dollar...Butternut Valley Hdwe. Co...Gilbertsville, N.Y., painted tin sign, 35½" X 11½", excellent, **$125.00 (D).**

Firestone Tires, paper calendar with bottom tear sheets, great graphics of early touring car on winding road in forest, 1928, excellent, **$175.00 (D).**

Fisk...Red Tops, paper advertisment showing older model touring car with kids looking at product on car, 12½" X 17", excellent, **$85.00 (D).**

Francisco Auto Heater...Summer Here all the Year, with great graphics of people in cut-away touring car on snow-covered roads at night, self-framing, 40" X 18", excellent, **$575.00 (D).**

Freeman...Headbolt Engine Heater, painted metal thermometer with messages to right of vertical scale, rolled edges, 6" X 15", good, **$95.00 (D).**

Getty, cloth sleeve patch, 4½" X 2⅞", good, **$10.00 (C).**

Gilmer, super-service moulded rubber fan belt, cardboard product box, excellent, **$425.00 (C).**

Goodrich...Batteries, Tires, Accessories, porcelain advertising sign, self-framing, 60" X 20½", excellent, **$175.00 (D).**

Goodrich...You'll get more and quicker heat with this ..hot water heater, paper advertising with artwork of early model auto heater, 57" X 34", excellent, **$25.00 (D).**

Goodyear...Tires, metal framed glass front light-up sign with fleet foot at top center, good, **$65.00 (D).**

Goodyear Tires, wooden painted thermometer with tire surrounding the earth at top, dealer message at bottom, vertical scale, 3¼" X 11½", good, **$65.00 (D).**

Gulf, cloth sleeve patch, 2½" X 2¼", good, **$12.00 (C).**

Gulf, plastic letters on metal strip, blue, excellent, **$115.00 (C).**

Gulf, round plastic light-up sign with lettering across center, 31" dia., excellent, **$165.00 (D).**

Gulf, service station attendant's summer hat, NOS, Brokfield Uniforms, 6¾", near-mint, **$95.00 (D).**

Gulf...That Good Gasoline, At the sign of the orange disc, with artwork of early touring car driving up hill, porcelain sign, 27½" X 60", fair, **$750.00 (C).**

Harley-Davidson, 75th anniversary bullet pencil, 1978, excellent, **$50.00 (C).**

Havoline Marine Oil...it makes a difference...Havoline Oil Company, New York City, tin litho paperweight made to resemble a 1-gal. oil can, filled with sand, 1½" X 2½" X 1", excellent, **$1,550.00 (B).**

Hood Tires, wooden thermometer with Hood man with stop flag at top center over vertical scale, Hood tires message in circle at bottom, 4" X 15", orange, white and black, good, **$325.00 (C).**

Hudson...Rambler...Sales...Service, porcelain advertising sign, 1940s, 42" X 30", excellent, **$500.00 (C).**

Humble Gasoline, celluloid advertising knife sharpening stone with product message on back, 1⅝" X 2⅞", excellent, **$110.00 (B).**

Hygrade Products Co., New York, NY, fuel pump rebuild kits, metal with lift front door, with original parts inside, 12¾" X 15" X 12¾", excellent, **$195.00 (D).**

Illinois Farm Bureau, Illinois Agricultural Mutual Insurance Co., porcelain license plate attachment, 3¾" X 4½", excellent, **$85.00 (C).**

Indian Gas...Indian Refining Co., Incorporated, die cut hanging sign, held by metal brackets over round extension arm, double sided, 45" X 36", good, **$575.00 (C).**

Indian Gasoline, porcelain advertising sign, with artwork of Indian gas logo at top of message, Indian Refining Co., New York, New York, 1940s, 12" X 18", good, **$165.00 (C).**

Indianapolis Speedway, silk checkered flag, 17" X 17", excellent, **$85.00 (C).**

Jenny Gasoline, linen finish playing cards with artwork of early service station and car on each card with original box, full deck, excellent, **$130.00 (B).**

John Deere...Farm Implements, double sided porcelain hanging advertising sign with artwork of JD logo at center top, 72" X 23¾", excellent, **$950.00 (D).**

Kendall Motor Oil...The Dealer Sign of Quality, vertical embossed painted metal sign, with logo at top of message, good, **$95.00 (C).**

Lee Tires, metal framed glass front light-up sign, 32" X 7½", excellent, **$165.00 (D).**

Mack...Leading Gasoline Truck of America, celluloid pocket mirror, 2½" X 3⅛", excellent, **$550.00 (B).**

Mansfield Tires...Becker Texaco Service, plastic round light-up advertising clock with metal ring around glass clock face, excellent, **$225.00 (D).**

Marathon Oil Co., pocket knife, excellent, **$20.00 (C).**

Master Trucks Inc., Chicago, USA, cast iron ink well with embossed lettering, 7" X 5½" X 2¾", excellent, **$210.00 (B).**

Merrill...Transport Company, dial-type thermometer with the outside resembling a tire, 15" dia., excellent, **$250.00 (D).**

Michelin Man, molded ashtray, with Michelin Man standing in ashtray, 1940s, 6" X 4¾", excellent, **$85.00 (C).**

Mobil, attendant's summer hat, all original, excellent, **$175.00 (C).**

Mobil, cloth sleeve patch, 3⅛" X 1¼", good, **$10.00 (C).**

Mobil oil...follow the magnolia trail, large shop calendar with fishing scene on front in center of message, 1933, excellent, **$95.00 (C).**

Mobile, playing cards with original leather carrying case, near-mint, **$20.00 (C).**

Mobilgas, enameled cloisonné uniform badge with Pegasus over name, screw-on attachment, ⅝" X 1⅝", excellent, **$375.00 (B).**

Mobilgas...Friendly Service, porcelain thermometer with Pegasus at top center, vertical scale, 4¼" X 34½", excellent, **$250.00 (C).**

Mobilgas...Special, porcelain die cut gas pump sign with artwork of Pegasus at top of message, 1947, 12" X 12", excellent, **$115.00 (C).**

Mobilgas, tin toy Ford tanker truck, 1940s, 2½" X 9", red & white, good, **$225.00 (C).**

Mobiloil, Magnolia trail calendar with great graphics of ocean scene at sunset in center of message, 1933, excellent, **$95.00 (C).**

Mobiloil...Vacuum Oil Company, porcelain thermometer with vertical scale, Pegasus at top in shield, 8" X 23", white, red, and blue, excellent, **$225.00 (C).**

Mobil Service, advertising shop clock with Pegasus in center of face, 13" dia., excellent, **$165.00 (C).**

Monroe...the ultimate in shock absorbers...America rides...Monroe, light-up advertising clock, good, **$115.00 (D).**

Nash...Authorized service, porcelain advertising sign, 42" X 42", excellent, **$500.00 (C).**

Nash...P.K. Williams, plastic dial-type thermometer with calendar tear sheet receptacle at bottom, no sheets, 7½" X 15", excellent, **$15.00 (C).**

Oilzum...America's Finest Oil, double sided painted tin sign with artwork of Oilzum Man at lower left, 60" X 36", good, **$1,800.00 (C).**

Oilzum Motor Oil...Choice of Champions, light-up advertising clock with Oilzum Man in center, 14½" dia., excellent, **$1,100.00 (C).**

Oilzum Motor Oil...Choice of Champions, square advertising clock, 16" sq., excellent, **$175.00 (D).**

Oilzum...The Choice of Champion Race Drivers, painted tin therrmometer, artwork of Oilzum Man to left of vertical scale, message at top & bottom, 7½" X 15", excellent, **$450.00 (C).**

Pennzoil...Get Protection Reserve...Motor Oil, dial-type thermometer, with message in center, metal body, glass front, 12" dia., excellent, **$145.00 (C).**

Pennzoil...Safe Lubrication, oval porcelain sign with bell in center, 62" X 35", black & orange on yellow, good, **$155.00 (C).**

Pennzoil...Sound Your Z, vertical painted metal sign with logo at bottom, good, **$105.00 (D).**

Phillips 66, match holder, tin with message on front, Delzell Service, Stevens Point, WI, phone 1276, 3" X 3" X 6", near-mint, **$52.00 (B).**

Phillips 66...Phillips Petroleum Co., Chicago Division, silver anniversary pocket mirror, 1955, 3½" dia., excellent, **$130.00 (C).**

Phillips 66, porcelain shield sign, 29" X 29", good, **$175.00 (C).**

Pontiac...Authorized Service, porcelain sign with Indian head logo in center of sign, 41½" dia., excellent, **$325.00 (C).**

Prestone Anti-Freeze...You're set-safe-sure, porcelain vertical scale thermometer, rolled sides and corners, with messages at top & bottom, 1940s, 8¾" X 36", good, **$125.00 (D).**

Prosper Lambert Automobiles, oval metal serving tray with scalloped edges, graphics of man in early auto, product message on reverse side, 5", good, **$500.00 (B).**

Purolator, oil rack complete with top sign, 1950s, good, **$125.00 (C).**

Quaker State Motor Oil...Certified Guaranteed, round top double sided porcelain drive way sign with logo at top of sign, 26½" X 29", good, **$95.00 (D).**

Recommended Hotel, AAA, porcelain neon, double sided, hanging sign, 48" X 31½", red, white & blue, excellent, **$425.00 (C).**

Richfield...here soon, paper poster with artwork of man in early model race car, 39½" X 54½", good, **$225.00 (C).**

Schrader Tire Gauge, store display in shape of gauge with hinged top to store tire gauges, 6" X 14¾", excellent, **$175.00 (C).**

Shaler Rislone...The Oil Alloy, painted metal thermometer, vertical scale with artwork of product can to left of scale, 9½" X 25", excellent, **$45.00 (C).**

Shell, cloth sleeve patch, 2" sq., fair, **$8.00 (C).**

Shell...for fuel oil with foa-5x, decal for use on home heating drums, NOS, near-mint, **$10.00 (D).**

Shell Tootsie Toy, pressed steel tanker truck, 1¾" X 6", yellow, fair, **$65.00 (C).**

Sinclair, illuminated metal & glass clock with Dino, 1950s, excellent, **$500.00 (D).**

Sinclair, Marx, Toy tanker truck, 18½" long, red & white on green, excellent, **$675.00 (C).**

Sinclair Pennsylvania Motor Oil, porcelain gas pump sign with artwork of Dino at bottom of message, 11" dia., good, **$250.00 (C).**

Skelly-Hood, snow dome, plastic and glass advertising dome for Skelly and Hood tires with advertising bill board inside dome, 4" X 3" X 3", excellent, **$130.00 (B).**

Socony Gasoline, paper calendar with artwork of attendant beside visible pump, no tear sheets left, 1928, fair, **$95.00 (C).**

Sta Cool Oil...Keeps The Motor Cool, tin oil can with product label on front and back, 1-gal., excellent, **$35.00 (C).**

Standard Oil Co. of New York...Socony Motor Oil...Heavy, die cut porcelain sign, 8" X 9½", excellent, **$575.00 (C).**

Standard Oil Company of N.Y...Polarine oil and greases for motors, porcelain sign, 12" X 22", good, **$275.00 (C).**

Standard Oil Company of New York...Socony Oils, aircraft with artwork of airplane in center of message, porcelain, 30" X 20", good, **$375.00 (C).**

Standard Oil Company...perfection kerosene, with artwork of oil lamp at lower center of message, painted tin, 18" X 14", excellent, **$95.00 (C).**

Studebaker Batteries, light-up clock, metal body with glass front, logo at top center with message at lower center, 15¼" sq., excellent, **$175.00 (C).**

Sunoco, cloth sleeve patch with dia.mond with arrow, 2¾" X 2", excellent, **$10.00 (C).**

Super-X...Steel oil ring...Dry As A Bone, papier-maché likeness of bone with product message on front, rare piece, 24" long, excellent, **$225.00 (C).**

Texaco, cloth sleeve patch with star in circle at bottom of patch, lettering in black, 2¼" X 2", good, **$10.00 (C).**

Texaco...Exclusive Texaco dealer offer, motorized plastic toy tanker with original cardboard box, 5" X 26½", excellent, **$200.00 (C).**

Texaco Fire Chief Gasoline, porcelain sign, 18" X 12", excellent, **$225.00 (C).**

Texaco Fire Chief hat, promotional celluloid hat with reflective front shield, 5" X 11", excellent, **$55.00 (C).**

Texaco fire chief, plastic fireman's hat with large white shield on front with product message, 8" tall, white on red, excellent, **$75.00 (C).**

Texaco, metal body, glass front dial-type thermometer with dealer info around outside face, 12" dia., excellent, **$325.00 (D).**

Texaco, round cloth sleeve patch with green "T" in star, 2½" dia., excellent, **$10.00 (D).**

Texaco, service station attendant's metal pinback badge featuring artwork of Texaco Scotties, 3¼" X 3¼", excellent, **$525.00 (B).**

Texaco, watch fob, embossed metal fob with Texaco star, 1¼" X 1⅜", excellent, **$240.00 (B).**

The Texas Company...Petroleum and its Products, die cut paper calendar with Texaco logo at top, bottom tear sheets complete, 1922, excellent, **$195.00 (C).**

Thomas A. Edison, Edison-Splitdorf Corporation, spark plug in original cardboard box, good, **$12.00 (D).**

Tydol Flying A, cloth banner with Flying A giant putting wings on older model car, 79" X 34", excellent, **$135.00 (C).**

Vacuum Oil Company, Gargoyle Mobiloil "E" metal oil can with paper label, 1-gal., **$35.00 (C).**

Valentine & Co...why drive a shabby car...refinish with Valentine's Colors..., celluloid vertical thermometer, 5½" X 20", near-mint, **$145.00 (C).**

Vanderbilt Premium Tread..., round light-up advertising clock with logo in center of face, 1958, 14½" dia., excellent, **$135.00 (D).**

Veedol...it's time to change to warm weather..., cloth banner, with artwork of bird on clothesline and artwork at lower right, 58" X 36", excellent, **$135.00 (C).**

Waynesboro Motor Club, AAA, Spring Water, porcelain sign, 9¾" X 12", red, blue & black, good, **$175.00 (C).**

Westinghouse Mazda Lamps for automobiles, metal store cabinet with logo on end, 1929, black on orange, excellent, **$295.00 (D).**

White Rose...Quick Starting, tin litho advertising bank with artwork of the Enarco kid with board, 3½" X 2⅛", excellent, **$210.00 (B).**

Whiz Patch Outfit, extra heavy metal store display with artwork of man repairing tire on older model car, near-mint, **$425.00 (C).**

Willys-Overland Company...Dollar for Dollar Whippet Product of.., porcelain sign, 36" X 24", cream on red, good, **$325.00 (C).**

Wolf's Head Motor Oil...We sell, painted metal curb sign with logo in lower right, with original cast base with raised letters, 59" dia., red, white, and green, excellent, **$350.00 (C).**

Wynn's Friction Proofing, round plastic shop clock, red & white, excellent, **$115.00 (D).**

Zero Flo...Pours at 35° below, paraffin base motor oil, painted tin sign, 28" X 20", white, orange & black, excellent, **$155.00 (C).**

Phinney-Walker, Clocks For Automobiles..., 15" X 20", cardboard. **$375.00 (B).**

Courtesy of Richard Opfer Auctioneering, Inc.

Allyn & Blanchard Co., tin litho match holder, 7" H, excellent, **$320.00 (B).**

Courtesy of Muddy River Trading Co./Gary Metz

Arbuckles Ground Coffee..."It smells Good, Daddy," embossed tin sign featuring artwork of man with paper and girl with cup of coffee, 27" X 11", excellent, **$475.00 (B).**

Courtesy of Pleasant Hill Antique Mall & Tea Room/Bob Johnson

Beech-Nut Coffee, tin with key wound top, 1-lb., fair, **$12.00 (D).**

Courtesy of Richard Opfer Auctioneering, Inc.

Blanke's Coffee, tin litho store bin with great graphics of horseback rider on front, 24¾" H, excellent, **$600.00 (B).**

Courtesy of Pleasant Hill Antique Mall & Tea Room/Bob Johnson

Bliss Coffee, key wound tin, 1-lb., fair, **$15.00 (D).**

Courtesy of Richard Opfer Auctioneering, Inc.

Blue Parrot Coffee, tin with great colors and artwork of parrot on limb, extremely rare piece, 6" H, excellent, **$5,000.00 (B).**

Courtesy of Pleasant Hill Antique Mall & Tea Room/Bob Johnson

Borden's Instant Coffee, jar with screw top, featuring paper label, 5-oz., excellent, **$7.00 (D).**

Butter-Nut specially mellowed coffee, "The Delicious Coffee," with key wound top, Paxton and Gallagher Co., Omaha, Nebraska, 1-lb., excellent, **$20.00 (D).**

Courtesy of Pleasant Hill Antique Mall & Tea Room/Bob Johnson

Chase and Sanborn Drip Grind Coffee, tin, key wound lid, 1-lb., fair, **$15.00 (D).**

Courtesy of Pleasant Hill Antique Mall & Tea Room/Bob Johnson

Gamble's Super Quality Coffee, glass jar, Gamble Stores, Minneapolis, 1-lb, excellent, **$15.00 (D).**

Courtesy of Pleasant Hill Antique Mall & Tea Room/Bob Johnson

Gold Star Coffee, David G. Evans Coffee Co., St. Louis, glass jar, 3-lb., good, **$35.00 (D).**

Courtesy of Pleasant Hill Antique Mall & Tea Room/Bob Johnson

Golden Wedding Coffee, key wound vaccum pack can, 1- lb., good, **$35.00 (D).**

Courtesy of Pleasant Hill Antique Mall & Tea Room/Bob Johnson

Hills Bros. Coffee, glass jar, 1-lb., excellent, **$15.00 (D).**

Courtesy of Richard Opfer Auctioneering, Inc.

Hoffmann's Old Time Coffee, tin with great graphics on front, 4¼" H, excellent,

Courtesy of Richard Opfer Auctioneering, Inc.

Hoffmann's Old Time Roasted Coffee, grinder with litho tin front with wood frame on cast iron, 13½" H, excellent, **$1,200.00 (B).**

Courtesy of Richard Opfer Auctioneering, Inc.

Hy-Quality Coffee, die cut paper litho on cardboard, hanging sign of woman in swing drinking coffee, 36½" H, excellent, **$900.00 (B).**

Johnson's Log Cabin tin litho store bin, resembles log cabin, 24" X 18" X 28", excellent, **$2,750.00 (B).**

Courtesy of Pleasant Hill Antique Mall & Tea Room/Bob Johnson

Kaffee Hag Coffee, metal vaccum pack tin with key wound lid, 1-lb., good, **$40.00 (D).**

Courtesy of Richard Opfer Auctioneering, Inc.

Lion Coffee, store bin featuring lion pulling chariot on lift-top lid, 32¼" H, excellent, **$450.00 (B).**

Courtesy of Rare Bird Antique Mall–Jon & Joan Wright

Courtesy of Pleasant Hill Antique Mall & Tea Room/Bob Johnson

McLaughlin's Manor House Coffee, tin with key wound lid, 1-lb, fair, **$8.00 (D).**

Courtesy of Pleasant Hill Antique Mall & Tea Room/Bob Johnson

Millar's Magnet Coffee, F.B. Millar & Co, Chicago, Denver, 1-lb., good, **$25.00 (D).**

Old Judge Coffee, store paper sample cup with graphics of product can on front, 2½" X 2½", excellent, **$4.00 (D).**

Courtesy of Muddy River Trading Co./Gary Metz

Old Reliable Coffee...Always Good, tin sign, 1910s, 6½" X 9", excellent, **$350.00 (B).**

Courtesy of Rare Bird Antique Mall–Jon & Joan Wright

Old Southern Coffee, Larkin Co., Buffalo, NY, tin litho container with slip lid, features artwork of woman in chair with cup of product, 1-lb., excellent, **$75.00 (D).**

Courtesy of Pleasant Hill Antique Mall & Tea Room/Bob Johnson

Peak Coffee, packed for Independent Grocers Alliance Dist. Co., Chicago, Ill., excellent, **$35.00 (D).**

Courtesy of Pleasant Hill Antique Mall & Tea Room/Bob Johnson

Radiant Coffee, tin with key wound lid, Chris Hoerr & Sons, Peoria, Ill., 1-lb., fair, **$20.00 (D).**

Courtesy of Pleasant Hill Antique Mall & Tea Room/Bob Johnson

Richelieu Coffee, Sprague, Warner & Company, Chicago, Ill., U.S.A., with screw-on lid, 1-lb., good, **$35.00 (D).**

Courtesy of Richard Opfer Auctioneering, Inc.

Scull's Coffee, tin store bin, featuring great stenciled and litho graphics, 21½" H, excellent, **$925.00 (B).**

Courtesy of Richard Opfer Auctioneering, Inc.

White House Coffee, "The Very Highest Quality," tin litho match holder, featuring graphics of the White House, 5" H, good, **$375.00 (B).**

NOT PICTURED:

Acme Brand Coffee, American Stores Co., tin litho with embossed slip lid, graphics of polka dot banner around bottom, 1-lb., excellent, **$84.00 (B).**

Aladdin...The Wonderful Coffee, tin litho can with artwork of Aladdin lamp in center of product message, 3-lb., excellent, **$170.00 (B).**

Aunt Nellie's Coffee, tin litho key wind container, 1-lb., excellent, **$266.00 (B).**

Beech-Nut Brand Coffee, key wound tin litho container with graphics of product leaf in oval on front, 1-lb., excellent, **$65.00 (D).**

Bethelem Extra Fancy Rio Coffee, John Bird Co., Maine, store bin, Three Cow logo at top left inside star, 1900s, 10" X 17", good, **$155.00 (B).**

Bird Brand Steel Cut Coffee, tin litho with small canister top, graphics of colorful bird on perch, good, **$97.00 (B).**

Blue Bonnet Coffee, key wind tin litho container with graphics of woman in blue hat on front, 1-lb., excellent, **$348.00 (B).**

Blue Bonnet Coffee, tin litho can with artwork of red-haired woman wearing blue hat, key wound lid, 1-lb., excellent, **$1,700.00 (B).**

Borden's Instant Coffee, jar with screw top, featuring paper label, 5-oz., excellent, **$7.00 (D).**

Bouquet Roasted Coffee, Tracy & Co., Syracuse, NY, paper litho on tin with slip lid, 1-lb., near-mint, **$60.00 (B).**

Breakfast Call Coffee, tin litho coffee can, Independence Coffee Co., Denver, Colo., 4⅛" X 5⅞", excellent, **$60.00 (B).**

Bursley's Coffee, tin litho key wind container, 1-lb., excellent, **$30.00 (B).**

Cafe Empire Blend Coffee, tin litho can, 4⅜" X 5½", excellent, **$70.00 (B).**

Cambridge Coffee Whole Bean, tin litho can, 3½" X 7¼", excellent, **$210.00 (B).**

Campbell Brand Coffee, tin litho pail with wire handles, graphics of camels on desert, 4-lb., excellent, **$75.00 (B).**

Casewell's National Crest Coffee, key wind tin litho container, 1-lb., excellent, **$30.00 (B).**

Chase & Sanborn, tin store bin with embossed lettering "Old Gov't Java" on front with litho birds, flowers, and stems, 1880s, 13" X 14" X 19", good, **$420.00 (B).**

Cheerio Coffee, key wound tin litho coffee can with artwork of singing bird, 5" X 4", good, **$190.00 (B).**

Chef Coffee, tin litho key wound can with artwork of chef on front, rare piece, Lee & Cady, Detroit, 1-lb., excellent, **$500.00 (B).**

Club Lake Coffee, paper litho on tin can with graphics of lake and club house, 3-lb., good, **$65.00 (D).**

Commonwealth Brand Coffee, Warranted Pure, with litho of White House on front, slip lid, 1-lb., excellent, **$80.00 (B).**

Country Club Coffee, tin litho key wind container, 1-lb., excellent, **$25.00 (B).**

Cupid Coffee, paper litho on tin container from Excelsior Mills, E.B. Millar Co., Chicago, with graphics, naturally, of Cupid grinding coffee, 1900s, 3¾" X 6¾", excellent, **$175.00 (B).**

Denison's Coffee...Ask for, pennant, felt with message, 25", near-mint, **$82.00 (B).**

Devotion Coffee, key pry lid tin litho with graphics of couple ready for devotion, 1-lb., excellent, **$109.00 (B).**

Diamond D Coffee, Dwinell-Wright Company, New York, N.Y., cardboard container, 1-lb., excellent, **$25.00 (D).**

Dilworth's Golden Urn Coffee, tin litho container with screw-on lid, 1-lb., excellent, **$200.00 (B).**

Donald Duck High Grade Pure Coffee, key wind lid, tin litho with graphics of Donald Duck on front, 1-lb., excellent, **$797.00 (B).**

Dutch Girl Coffee...Roasted and Packed by The Eureka Coffee Co., Buffalo, NY, cardboard can with tin top and bottom, with artwork of Dutch girl on front, 3" X 6½" X 4¼", excellent, **$130.00 (B).**

Dutch Java Blend Coffee, die cut cardboard litho with artwork of young boy holding basket, 6¾" X 8½", excellent, **$190.00 (B).**

Dutch Java Coffee, pocket mirror, "Secret of Happiness" message on back, 2" dia., excellent, **$55.00 (B).**

Farmers Pride Brand Steel Cut Coffee, tin coffee can with paper label of small child and man with cup of coffee, 4⅛" X 6", excellent, **$300.00 (B).**

Folger's Golden Gate Steel Cut Coffee, tin can with paper label with artwork of ships in San Francisco Bay, hard to find item, 2½-lb., 6" X 6", excellent, **$90.00 (B).**

Folgers Coffee, pull string cardboard container that holds free puzzle,"Free when you buy Folger's Vacuum or Flaked Coffee," ship graphics on front, 2¾" X 3½", near-mint, **$25.00 (D).**

French Marker Coffee and Chicory, tin litho key wind container, 1-lb., excellent, **$25.00 (B).**

Gill's Hotel Special Coffee and Chicory, key wind tin litho container, 1-lb., excellent, **$37.00 (B).**

Grand Union Coffee, key wind tin litho container, 1-lb., excellent, **$60.00 (B).**

Harvest Queen Coffee, key wind tin litho container with graphics of crown on front, 1-lb., excellent, **$37.00 (B).**

Hills Bros. Coffee...Coffee hungry folks prefer..., roll down paper over cloth sign with artwork of early scene in cabin around table with product, 61½" X 42", excellent, **$375.00 (B).**

Hills Bros. Coffee, Drip Grind Coffee, tin container with artwork of Hills man drinking product on front, 20-lb., 9½" X 9½" X 13", excellent, **$30.00 (D).**

Hinz's Eagle Brand Coffee, paper label on tin container with slip lid, 1-lb., near-mint, **$30.00 (B).**

Holland House Coffee, key wind tin litho container, 1-lb., excellent, **$25.00 (B).**

Honeymoon Keen Cut Breakfast Coffee, key wind tin litho container with graphics of loving couple sitting on crescent moon, 1-lb., excellent, **$71.00 (B).**

Hotel McAlpin Coffee, tin litho container with small canister-type lid on top, graphics of hotel scene, 1910, 6" X 11", excellent, **$55.00 (B).**

IGA Deluxe Coffee, key wind tin litho container with eagle graphics on front, 1-lb., excellent, **$25.00 (B).**

Isbrandtsen Red Label, key wind tin litho container with graphics of large ship on front, 1-lb., excellent, **$75.00 (B).**

Jam-Boy Coffee, tin litho pry-type lid with graphics of young man at table with cup of product, 1-lb., excellent, **$352.00 (B).**

Johnson's Peacemaker Coffee, die cut cardboard in image of store bin, 13½" X 14", excellent, **$455.00 (B).**

Kaffee Hag Coffee, tin litho key wind, unopened container, 1-lb., excellent, **$37.00 (B).**

Kellogg's Supreme Quality Coffee, tin litho key wind container, 1-lb., excellent, **$28.00 (B).**

King Cole Coffee, tin litho with pry lid with graphics of king holding cup of product, 1-lb., excellent, **$484.00 (B).**

Lady Hellen Coffee, pry lid paper label on tin container, 1-lb., excellent, **$110.00 (B).**

Levering's Coffee, paper litho on cardboard with advertising message and product image on back and a checker board on reverse side, 1910s, 4¾" X 9½", excellent, **$75.00 (C).**

Log Cabin Coffee, Shaffer Stores, Altona, PA, tin litho key wound coffee can showing great graphics of cabin in clearing in woods, 1-lb., 4" X 5", excellent, **$1,550.00 (B).**

London House Coffee, Silver Banner, tin litho container, key wind container, 1-lb., excellent, **$44.00 (B).**

Lucky Cup Coffee, tin key wind top with graphics of steaming cup of coffee with horseshoe, 1-lb., excellent, **$33.00 (B).**

Manbru Coffee, Schreiber Products Corporation, Buffalo, NY, tin litho with screw lid, 1-lb., excellent, **$25.00 (B).**

Marvel Brand Coffee and Food Products, display case decal with great graphics of product in front of window scene, 1925, 8½" X 11", excellent, **$80.00 (B).**

Maxwell House Coffee, cardboard string hung ad sign with 1920s coffee container artwork, 1920s, excellent, **$325.00 (B).**

Maxwell House Coffee...Good to the Last Drop, celluloid advertising sign with graphics of upturned coffee cup, 12" X 6", excellent, **$125.00 (B).**

Maxwell House Coffee, Good to the Last Drop, heavy paper sample cup with artwork of tilted coffee cup on front, 2½" X 2½", excellent, **$3.00 (D).**

Maxwell House Coffee...since 1892, oval metal serving tray, 15" X 12½", excellent, **$20.00 (D).**

May-Day Coffee...You'll Like The Flavor, tin litho container, key wind and unopened, 1-lb., near-mint, **$34.00 (B).**

McLaughlins Columbian Coffee, tin litho container with graphics of sailing ship on side, pry-type lid, 1-lb., excellent, **$74.00 (B).**

Millar's Home Blend Coffee, key wind tin litho container, 1-lb., near-mint, **$37.00 (B).**

Mohican Coffee, tin litho container with slip lid and artwork of Indian in full headdress on front, 1-lb., good, **$40.00 (D).**

Morning Glow Coffee, tin litho coffee can featuring artwork of ship, 5" X 4", excellent, **$170.00 (B).**

Morning Joy Pure Coffee, key wound tin litho can with artwork of singing bird in front of sunrise, 5" X 3½", excellent, **$250.00 (B).**

Morton House Coffee, tin litho screw lid container, 1-lb., excellent, **$61.00 (B).**

Old Plantation Steel Cut Coffee, heavy paper bag with graphics of black man with sack of product in front of paddle wheeler, 1-lb., excellent, **$15.00 (B).**

Old Reliable Coffee...A Real Breakfast, Always The Same, Always Good, with graphics of breakfast scene and product box, trolley car sign, cardboard, 21" X 11", near-mint, **$97.00 (B).**

Old Reliable Coffee...Guaranteed Pure, round metal tip tray with artwork of Russian man and package of product, 4¼" dia., excellent, **$100.00 (B).**

Old Reliable Coffee, metal tip, tray with image of pretty woman with flower in hair, 4¼" dia., near-mint, **$143.00 (B).**

Old Reliable Coffee...Welcome as April showers, trolley car sign with artwork of man with cup of coffee, 21" X 11", excellent, **$175.00 (D).**

Olympian Coffee, tin litho pry lid container, 1-lb., excellent, **$88.00 (B).**

Our Jewel Roasted Coffee, Ericsson's Mills, New York, tin litho with knob handle top, graphics of young child in cameo on front, scarce, 1-lb., good, **$159.00 (B).**

Palace Brand Coffee, tin litho, slip lid container with graphics of Winter Carnival Ice Palace, from Atwood & Co., Minneapolis, 3-lb., good, **$236.00 (B).**

Pickwick Coffee, tin litho coffee can with artwork of Mr. Pickwick on front, 3-lb., excellent, **$90.00 (B).**

Quality Inn Coffee, tin key wound litho, can with good graphics of horseback travelers arriving at inn, 1-lb., 5" X 4", excellent, **$250.00 (B).**

R-KAO Coffee, For Lovers of True Flavor, tin litho container with slip lid, scarce item, 1-lb., excellent, **$85.00 (B).**

Red Gate Mocha and Java Coffee, cardboard advertising sign, framed, excellent, **$101.00 (B).**

Red Spot Coffee, embossed tin door push bar, 19¾" X 2¾", near-mint, **$60.00 (B).**

Red Wolf Steel Cut Coffee, tin litho container with wire handle, graphics of wolf in oval on front, 6-lb., excellent, **$200.00 (B).**

Royal Blend High Grade Roasted Coffee, Granger & Co., Buffalo, NY, paper litho on cardboard with crown graphics on lid and front, trolley on reverse, 1-lb., excellent, **$45.00 (B).**

Sally Clover Coffee, tin litho screw lid container, 1-lb., near-mint, **$45.00 (B).**

San Marto Coffee, tin litho screw lid with graphics of Joan of Arc on front, 1-lb., near-mint, **$85.00 (B).**

Sanita Malt Coffee, paper litho ad sign with art of two small girls at table, 10" X 15", excellent, **$44.00 (B).**

Serv-us Brand Coffee, tin litho with screw-on lid, graphics of steaming cup of product, 1-lb., excellent, **$80.00 (B).**

Special Combination Coffee from Sears-Roebuck & Co., Chicago, Illinois, tin litho container with wire bail handle, 10-lb., black on green background, excellent, **$80.00 (B).**

Square Deal Coffee, tin litho container with artwork of hands shaking in agreement, 4" X 6", good, **$375.00 (B).**

Star Cup Coffee, key wound tin litho coffee can with great graphics of a king drinking a cup of coffee, 1-lb., excellent, **$190.00 (B).**

Strong Heart Coffee, round coffee tin can with paper label bearing artwork of colorful Indian, 5¼" X 4¼", excellent, **$300.00 (B).**

Strong Heart Coffee, tin litho can with screw on lid, graphics of Indian in center on front, 1-lb., excellent, **$467.00 (B).**

Sun Flower Brand Steel Cut Coffee, tin litho coffee can with pry-type lid, artwork of large sunflower on front, 1-lb., 5¼" X 3¾", excellent, **$1,100.00 (B).**

Sunny Brook Coffee, silk-screen print on tin sign with graphics of water featured in center, 20" X 14", excellent, **$80.00 (B).**

Swansdown Coffee, tin litho coffee can with artwork of swan, 4¼" X 6¼", excellent, **$825.00 (B).**

Swell Brand Coffee, tin litho pry lid container with graphics of large steamship on front, 1-lb., excellent, **$187.00 (B).**

The Chimes Coffee, paper litho on cardboard container with pry lid, with graphics of stage with curtains drawn, 1-lb., excellent, **$77.00 (B).**

The Morey Mills Mocha & Java Coffee, Denver, Colo., tin litho hinged lid coffee can with artwork of moon and star on front, 1900s, 6" X 6¾" X 3¾", excellent, **$170.00 (B).**

Timur Coffee, tin litho pry lid container, with graphics of Arabian-type rider on horseback, 1-lb., near-mint, **$1,210.00 (B).**

Tudor Coffee, paper litho on tin container with graphics of mansion on mountain, 1-lb., excellent, **$88.00 (B).**

Universal, tin litho container with graphics of Uncle Sam-like figure, slip lid, 1-lb., excellent, **$163.00 (B).**

Wak-em-up coffee, tin litho coffee can with artwork of Indian in full headdress, 7½" X 8¾", excellent, **$450.00 (B).**

Wedding Breakfast Coffee, Behring-Stahl Coffee Co., St. Louis, Mo., features graphics of wedding party, 1-lb., excellent, **$35.00 (D).**

Weideman Boy Brand Coffee, key wound tin litho can with trademark image of Weideman Coffee, 1-lb., 5" X 4", excellent, **$190.00 (B).**

White Lilac Coffee, tin litho can, Consolidated Tea Co., Inc., New York, rectangular with artwork of lilacs in bloom on front, 4¼" X 6" X 2⅞", excellent, **$450.00 (B).**

Wigwam Brand Coffee, tin litho with pry lid and graphics of Indian silhouette on front, 1-lb., excellent, **$75.00 (B).**

MISCELLANEOUS

Courtesy of Riverview Antique Mall

A.A. Godkin Chemist, brass sign for drug store, 72" X 9", excellent, **$275.00 (B).**

ABC Oil Burners, die cast metal sign, 11" X 8", near-mint, **$150.00 (B).**

Courtesy of Richard Opfer Auctioneering, Inc.

A. Hussey & Co., tin litho match holder, die cut, good graphics, "while others think we work", 7" H, excellent, **$1,550.00 (B).**

Acme Cowboy Boots, neon sign, neon on painted metal, 20¼" X 12½", near-mint, **$750.00 (B).**

Alexander poster, "The man who knows," 28¼" X 42", red, black & white litho, excellent, **$85.00 (D).**

Alliance Coffee/For Coffee Contentment Serve Alliance Coffee, with man in chef's wear tipping a cup of coffee, die cut cardboard, 1910, 12½" X 16⅛", excellent, **$255.00 (C).**

American Eagle Fire Insurance Company, New York, painted tin sign with wood frame, 20½" X 26½", near-mint, **$875.00 (D).**

Courtesy of Riverview Antique Mall

American Express Money Orders Sold Here, porcelain flange sign, 16" X 13", white lettering on blue background, excellent, **$225.00 (D).**

American Express Co. Agency, raised lettering heavy porcelain sign, 18½" X 16½", excellent, **$1,550.00 (B).**

Courtesy of Wm. Morford Investment Grade Collectibles

Courtesy of Richard Opfer Auctioneering, Inc.

American Hat Works Co. Inc., porcelain advertising sign, 40¼" L, excellent, **$375.00 (B).**

Courtesy of Creatures of Habit

American Negro Exposition/Chicago Coliseum, framed, 7-color screened print, 1940, excellent, **$175.00.**

Courtesy of Riverview Antique Mall

American Ingot Iron Road Culverts, embossed painted metal sign, 20" X 5½", white lettering on blue, excellent, **$85.00 (D).**

Arm & Hammer Soda, framed cardboard litho advertising sign, copyright 1908 by Church & Dwight Co., signed by Robin Snipe, 14½" X 11½", good, **$70.00 (D).**

American Stores Co., advertising sign, entitled "The Younger Generation", 14¼" X 18¼", excellent, **$90.00 (D).**

Courtesy of Muddy River Trading Co./Gary Metz

Aunt Jemima Flour, curved porcelain sign, hard-to-find piece, manufactured by Burdick in Chicago, good, **$6,000.00 (B).**

Courtesy of Riverview Antique Mall

Authorized DeLaval Dealer, on metal arm, good, **$350.00 (B).**

Courtesy of Muddy River Trading Co./Gary Metz

Authorized Gulf Dealer, porcelain advertising sign, 1930s, 40" X 9", good, **$130.00 (B).**

B.F. Goodrich, "Litentufs," Lite in weight, tuf to wear out, cardboard sign, with artwork of rubber footwear, 14" X 19½", excellent, **$35.00 (D).**

Courtesy of Pleasant Hill Antique Mall & Tea Room/Bob Johnson

Baker's Breakfast Cocoa...Walter Baker & Co. Ltd., Dorchester, Mass., round metal tip tray with great graphics of farm house and woman with tray of product, 6" dia., excellent, **$190.00 (B).**

Courtesy of Muddy River Trading Co./Gary Metz

Barber Shop, two sided porcelain flange sign, 24" X 12", red, white, & blue, near-mint, **$190.00 (B).**

Courtesy of Muddy River Trading Co./Gary Metz

Barber Pole, porcelain pole, 6" X 29", red, white & blue, excellent, **$275.00 (B).**

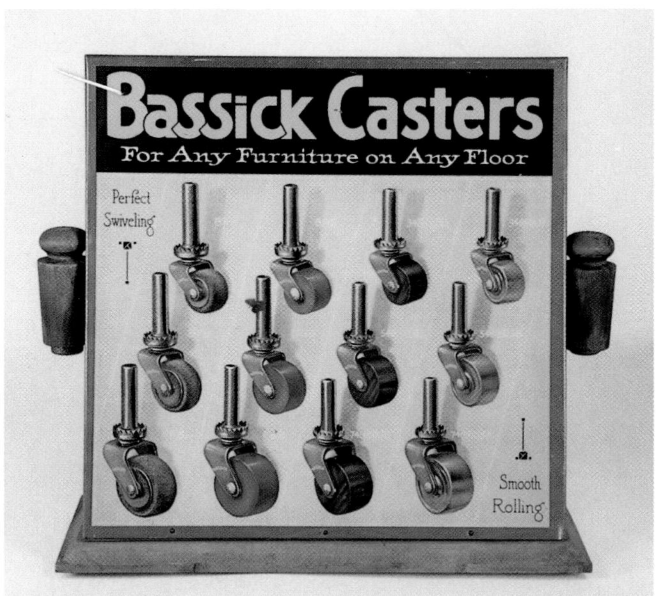

Bassick Casters, wooden display, metal and wood construction with casters on front, 13"W X 12¾" X 4¾"D, excellent, **$30.00 (B).**

Courtesy of Creatures of Habit

Beacon Shoes...Lighthouse on Rock, with product name beaming out from light source, composition construction, 6¼" X 10½", excellent, **$75.00 (D).**

Courtesy of Richard Opfer Auctioneering, Inc.

Belle Plains Candy Kitchen, framed embossed die cut calendar, 1916, excellent, **$110.00 (B).**

Bennett's Metal Polish, tin litho match holder, with artwork of metal polish can on front, 5"H, good, **$325.00 (B).**

Berry Brothers Varnishes, When You See Varnishes and Hard Oil Finish, painted tin sign with embossed lettering, The Tuscaro Adv. Co., Coshocton, Ohio, 27½" X 19½", fair, **$150.00 (D).**

Bickmore, Easy-Shave Cream, die cut cardboard, featuring artwork of man applying product to shaving brush, 13" X 21", excellent, **$25.00 (C).**

Bissell's Carpet Sweeper, floor display unit, 23" X 59", fair, **$55.00 (B).**

Courtesy of Muddy River Trading Co./Gary Metz

Bit-O-Honey, embossed tin sign, great graphics, 20" X 9", excellent, **$650.00 (B).**

Courtesy of Riverview Antique Mall

Borax Extract of Soap, for washing everything, painted metal sign, 24" X 7", good, **$65.00 (D).**

Courtesy of Richard Opfer Auctioneering, Inc.

Born Steel Range, tin litho match holder with great graphics of early kitchen range, "Oven Heats In 10 Minutes", 5" H, good, **$380.00 (B).**

Brach's Candy, stand-up rabbit advertising prop with hat pegs, 48" H, excellent, **$25.00 (C).**

Courtesy of Riverview Antique Mall

Brattleboro Steam Laundry, thermometer on painted wood, 9¼" X 18", good, **$395.00 (D).**

Courtesy of Richard Opfer Auctioneering, Inc.

Bull Frog Shoe Polish, tin litho advertising sign with likeness of frog, double sided, 17¾" X 13", good, **$4,000.00 (B).**

Courtesy of Muddy River Trading Co./Gary Metz

Butter Krust Bread, die cut porcelain advertising sign, 1930s, 14" X 18½", excellent, **$2,100.00 (B).**

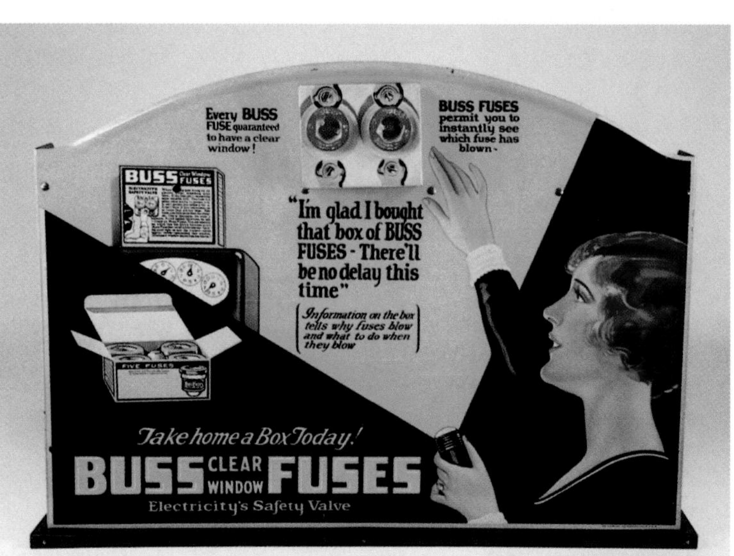

Buss Clear Window Fuses, metal display with great graphics, 1920s, 18¼" X 13¼" X 5", excellent, **$110.00 (B).**

Campbell's Soup, porcelain thermometer, features facsimile of tomato soup can with dial-type thermometer in center of can, great graphics, 7"W X 12"H X 1¼"D, near-mint, **$2,100.00 (B).**

Courtesy of Muddy River Trading Co./Gary Metz

Courtesy of Riverview Antique Mall

Canadian National Telegraph and Cable Office, porcelain flange sign, excellent, **$365.00 (D).**

Carter the Great, framed cardboard poster by the Otis Lithograph Co., Cleveland, Ohio, made in U.S.A/,4630-M, 42" X 78", excellent, **$500.00 (B).**

Courtesy of Riverview Antique Mall

Careystone Asbestos Shingles, painted embossed metal sign, 29" X 11½", excellent, **$65.00 (D).**

Case, cast iron advertising eagle, 57½" tall, good, **$2,400.00 (C).**

Ceresota Flour, match holder, barrel-style with image of young boy on top of barrel, with original box, 3" X 6", near-mint, **$500.00 (B).**

Courtesy of Richard Opfer Auctioneering, Inc.

Ceresota, prize bread flour, tin litho match holder, featuring graphics of young boy cutting loaf of bread, 5" H, good, **$330.00 (B).**

Courtesy of Richard Opfer Auctioneering, Inc.

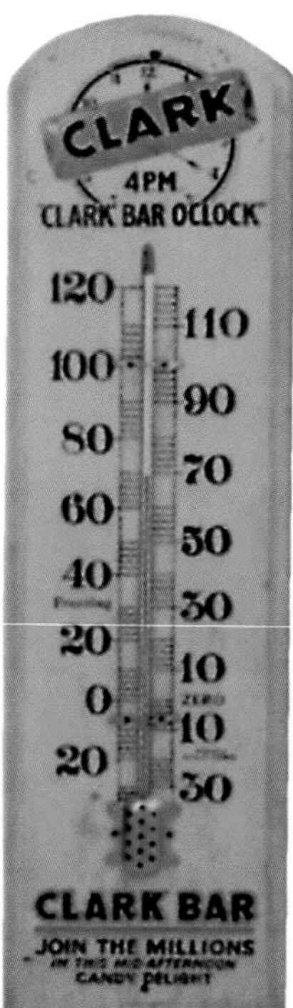

Clark Bar, thermometer, painted wood, with clock, bar clock figure at top, 19" H, excellent, **$325.00 (B).**

Courtesy of Muddy River Trading Co./Gary Metz

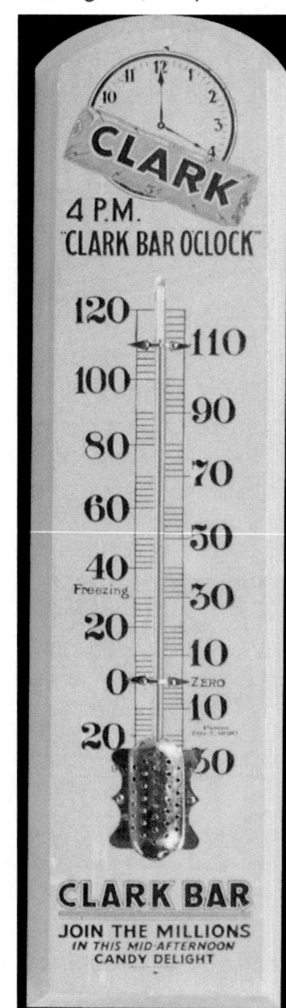

Clark Bar, Clark Bar, join the millions, wooden thermometer, 1920s, 5½" X 21½", near-mint, **$1,550.00 (B).**

Courtesy of Muddy River Trading Co./Gary Metz

Clark's Teaberry Gum, That mountain tea flavor, sign, 11¾" X 8¾", excellent, **$350.00 (B).**

Cleveland and Buffalo...The Great Ship Seeandbee...C&B Line, oval metal tip tray with graphics of ship at sea, 6¼"L, good, **$300.00 (B).**

Courtesy of Rare Bird Antique Mall–Jon & Joan Wright

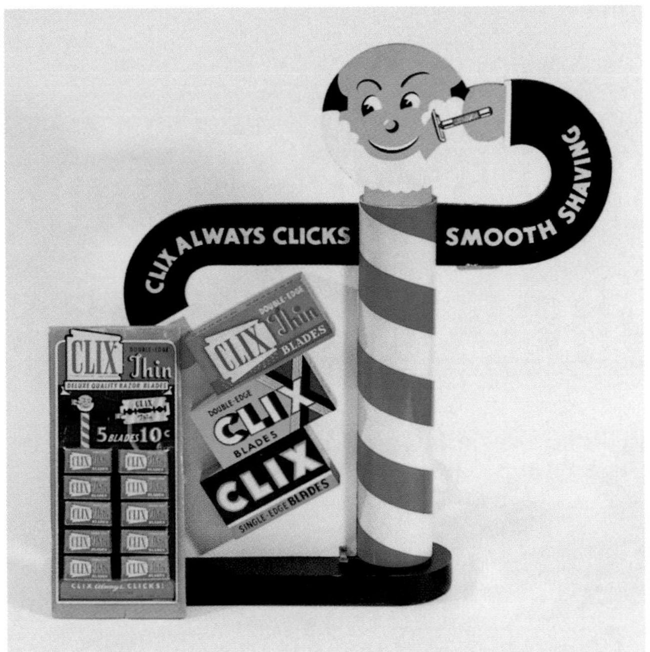

CLIX, Clix Always Clicks Smooth Shaving, barber shop three-dimensional razor blade display, barber pole lights up, 17½" X 26", near-mint, **$375.00 (D).**

Colman's Mustard, wooden store display box, "Grand Prix Highest Award, Paris 1900", 1900s, 21"W X 4"H X 12¼"D, fair, **$20.00 (B).**

Courtesy of Richard Opfer Auctioneering, Inc.

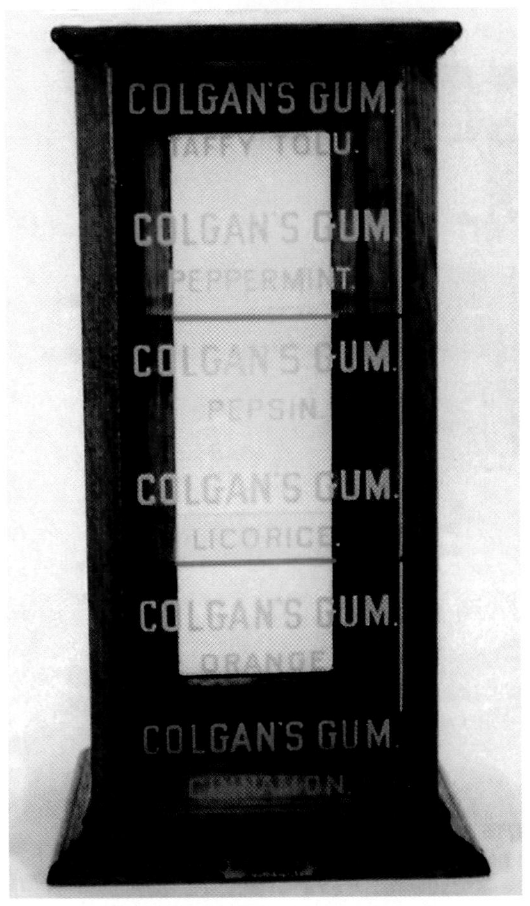

Colgan's Orange Gum, wood and etched glass display cabinet, 17½" T, excellent, **$1,500.00 (B).**

Courtesy of Richard Opfer Auctioneering, Inc.

Collins & Co. Axe, advertising sign, embossed tin on cardboard, 20" H, near-mint, **$50.00 (B).**

Courtesy of Pleasant Hill Antique Mall & Tea Room/Bob Johnson

Crazy Water Crystals, Just add it to your drinking water, cardboard advertising sign with easel back, 9¾" X 13½", excellent, **$55.00 (D).**

Courtesy of Muddy River Trading Co./Gary Metz

Dairy Made Ice Cream serving tray, you're sure it's pure, great graphics of young girl eating ice cream, 10½" X 13½", excellent, **$325.00 (B).**

Courtesy of Riverview Antique Mall

Cream Buying Station, Swift & Company, double sided porcelain sign, 41½" X 14½", white on blue, good, **$195.00 (D).**

Courtesy of Richard Opfer Auctioneering, Inc.

Dagget & Rasmsdells, display cabinet with great colorful tin litho front, scarce, 10½" H, excellent, **$1,300.00 (B).**

Courtesy of Michael and Debbie Summers

Daisy Brand, One of America's Finest Dairies, light-up reverse painted glass sign, featuring small child on limb with birds singing the praises, 1950s, excellent, **$275.00 (C).**

Courtesy of Buffalo Bay Auction Co.

Dairylea Ice Cream, die cut advertising fan with great graphics of cow jumping over the moon, ice cream cone handle, near-mint, **$155.00 (B).**

Courtesy of Muddy River Trading Co./Gary Metz

Damascus Ice Cream, die cut porcelain advertising sign, 1920s, 18" X 17", excellent, **$1,400.00 (B).**

Defense Bonds, this year give a share in America, framed poster with artwork of Santa Claus promoting bonds and stamps, 24" X 30", excellent, **$85.00 (C).**

Courtesy of Buffalo Bay Auction Co.

Deering IHC, paper litho calendar featuring graphics of young woman with horse, initials carved into fence post, full calendar pad, 1912, 13¼" X 23¼", near-mint, **$440.00 (B).**

Courtesy of Riverview Antique Mall

DeSoto Hotel Bath House, metal reflective advertising sign with applied lettering, "Fire Proof, Hot Springs, Ark.," 28" X 20", good, **$165.00 (D).**

Courtesy of Richard Opfer Auctioneering, Inc.

DeKalb Hybrid Corn, embossed painted tin sign, St. Thomas Metal Signs, Ltd., St. Thomas, Ont., featuring winged corn logo, 19¼" X 13¼", excellent, **$175.00 (B).**

DeLaval Cream Separators, tin litho advertising sign with great graphics and strong colors, 29½" X 40½", near-mint, **$2,700.00 (B).**

Courtesy of Richard Opfer Auctioneering, Inc.

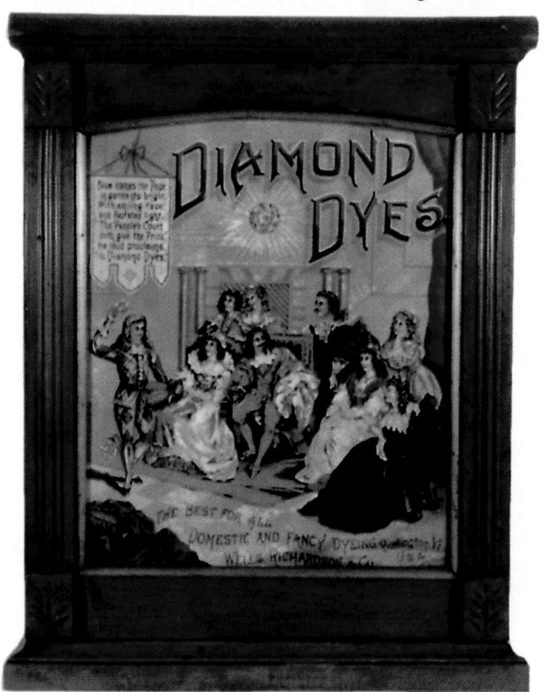

Diamond Dyes, advertising cabinet with tin litho front featuring artwork of the Page in The Peoples court, 27"H, excellent, **$700.00 (B).**

Courtesy of Richard Opfer Auctioneering, Inc.

Diamond Dyes, cabinet with tin litho front of little girl, 20"H, excellent, **$1,300.00 (B).**

Courtesy of Wm. Morford Investment Grade Collectibles

Diamond Dyes, rare double sided die cut advertising sign, excellent, **$1,600.00 (B).**

Courtesy of Muddy River Trading Co./Gary Metz

Diamond Dyes, wooden cabinet with embossed tin sign door, "The Standard Package Dyes of the World," excellent, **$650.00 (B).**

Courtesy of Richard Opfer Auctioneering, Inc.

Diamond Dyes, wooden display cabinet with embossed tin litho front, great graphics show woman dying fabric at table, 29½"H, excellent, **$2,400.00 (B).**

Courtesy of Richard Opfer Auctioneering, Inc.

Diamond Dyes, wooden display cabinet, with rare tin litho advertising on front door, by Wells and Hope Co., 30½" H, excellent, **$2,300.00 (B).**

Courtesy of Muddy River Trading Co./Gary Metz

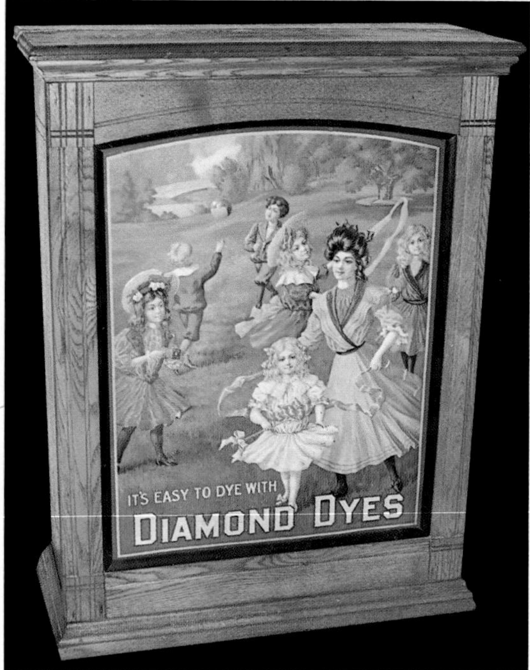

Diamond Dyes, wooden dye cabinet with embossed tin sign on door, "It's easy to dye with...," 23"W X 30"H X 10"D, excellent, **$775.00 (B).**

Courtesy of Muddy River Trading Co./Gary Metz

Donaldson Litho Company, salesman sample featuring advertising for fair at Newport, Ky., Aug., 5, 6, 7, 8, 1913, great graphics, 1913, 20" X 30", near-mint, **$290.00 (B).**

Courtesy of Riverview Antique Mall

Diehl's Bread Sold Here "It's Thoroughly Baked," porcelain sign, 24" X 12", excellent, **$185.00 (B).**

Courtesy of Riverview Antique Mall

Domestic Sew Machines, neon light-up store sign, on metal base, with domestic oil cans, excellent, **$465.00 (D).**

Courtesy of Muddy River Trading Co./Gary Metz

Butterfly Quality Bread, door push, porcelain on aluminum, frame, 1930s, good, **$170.00 (B).**

Courtesy of Muddy River Trading Co./Gary Metz

Butter-Nut Bread, door push, porcelain, good, **$175.00 (B).**

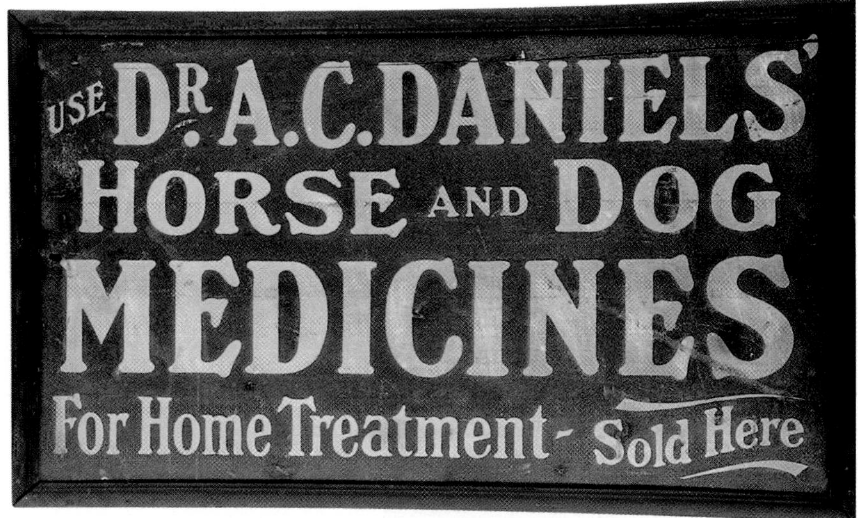

Dr. A.C. Daniels' Horse and Dog Medicines, wooden sign with wood frame, 30½" X 18¼", good, **$400.00 (B).**

Courtesy of Richard Opfer Auctioneering, Inc.

Dr. Pierce's Favorite Prescription, litho paper advertising sign, in girlhood, womanhood, and motherhood, For Sale Here, great colorful graphics, 11¼" X 48", good, **$1,200.00 (B).**

Courtesy of Muddy River Trading Co./Gary Metz

Dr. Pierce's Prescription, decal on window glass, features woman in a flared glass with a glass holder, 1890s, good, **$2,400.00 (B).**

Drummond's Horse Shoe, die cut cardboard sign, in frame, 17" X 21", excellent, **$170.00 (B).**

Courtesy of Richard Opfer Auctioneering, Inc.

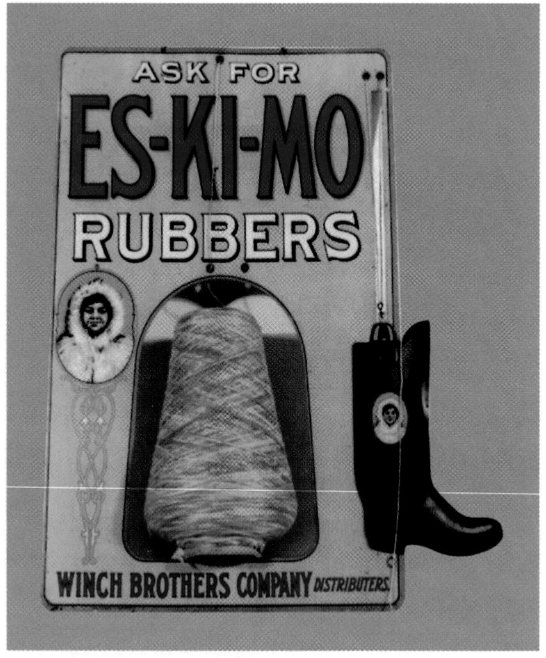

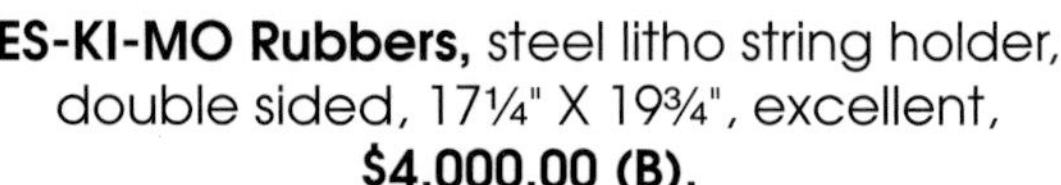

ES-KI-MO Rubbers, steel litho string holder, double sided, 17¼" X 19¾", excellent, **$4,000.00 (B).**

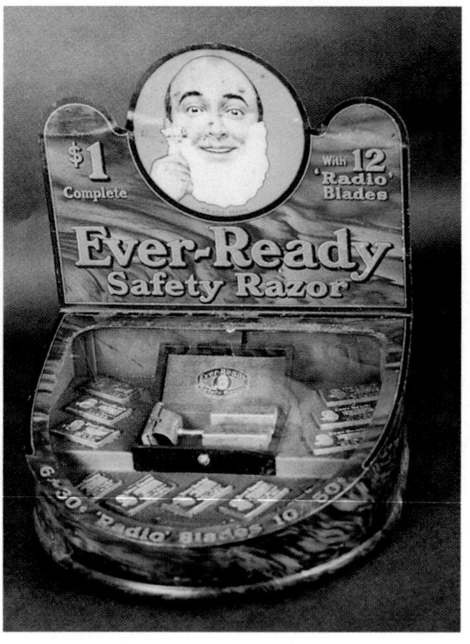

Ever-Ready Safety Razor, countertop display, tin litho with glass and wood, still contains early razor blades, 9½" X 11½", excellent, **$1,100.00 (B).**

Courtesy of Muddy River Trading Co./Gary Metz

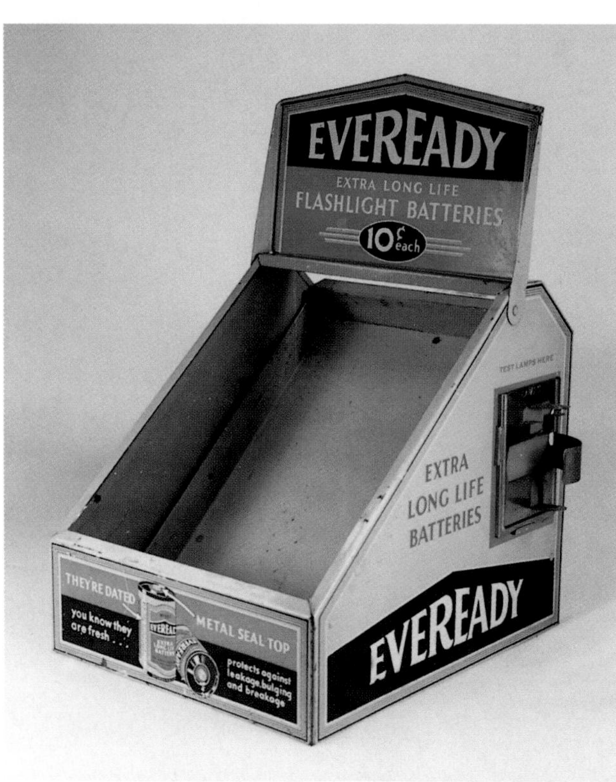

Eveready battery display, extra long life flashlight batteries, metal with glass front, 9"W X 14"H X 10½"D, good, **$75.00 (B).**

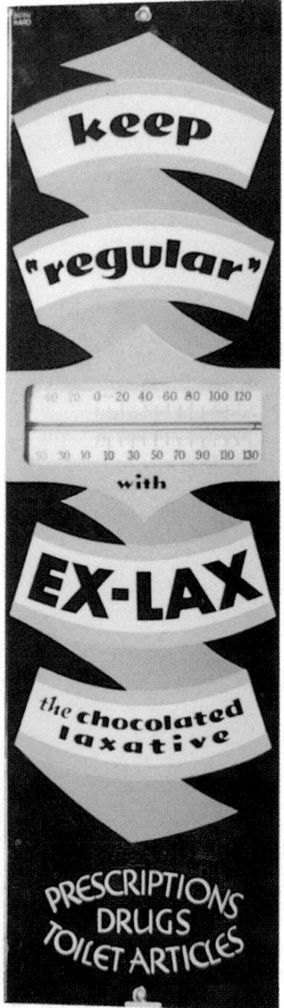

Ex-Lax, porcelain thermometer with unusual horizontal scale, "Keep regular with Ex-Lax, the chocolated laxative," great graphics, 10" X 36" X 1", excellent, **$550.00 (B).**

Ferry's Seeds, framed advertising poster, "A word to the wise...The best that grow," 27" X 36", excellent, **$425.00 (B).**

Courtesy of Wm. Morford Investment Grade Collectibles

Ferris Corset, tin litho self-framing advertising sign, artwork of two girls, 16½" X 22½", near-mint, **$2,300.00 (B).**

Courtesy of Rare Bird Antique Mall–Jon & Joan Wright

Florsheim Shoe...for the man who cares, Shoes For Men, neon store display with pair of men's shoes over neon, Art Deco style, near-mint, **$395.00 (D).**

Courtesy of Wm. Morford Investment Grade Collectibles

Free Land Overalls, heavy porcelain advertising sign, 30" X 10", excellent, **$475.00 (B).**

Courtesy of Old Homeplace Antiques–Jackie Thomas

Flying Red Horse, first aid kit by Mobilgas-Mobiloil, 3¼" X ¾" X 2¾", good, **$150.00 (D).**

Courtesy of B.J. Summers

General Electric Lamps, They stay brighter longer, general store lamp tester, with original early lamps, with message on reverse painted glass, good, **$450.00 (D).**

Genesee Plating Works...Compliments of..., Rochester, NY, earlier cast iron figural match safe with hinged lid over match pocket, 4⅜" X 8½", excellent, **$625.00 (B).**

Courtesy of Riverview Antique Mall

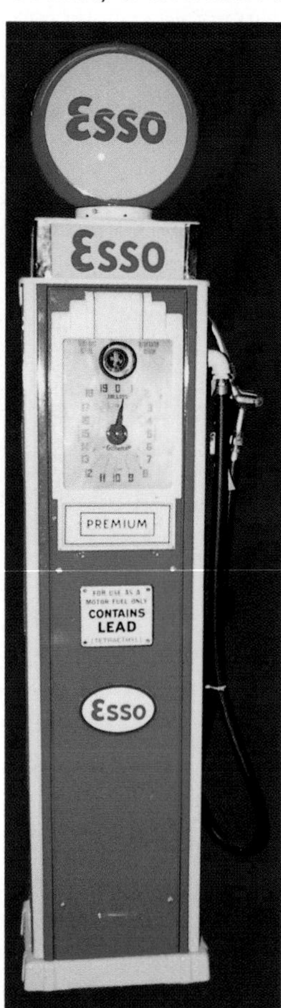

Gilbarco, clock face pump restored as an Esso pump, great example of the Art Deco influence, near-mint, **$2,650.00 (D).**

Courtesy of Riverview Antique Mall

Gold Bell, gift stamps advertising store sign, painted metal, 19½" X 28", good, **$165.00 (D).**

Courtesy of Muddy River Trading Co./Gary Metz

Gold Dust Washing Powder, round string hung double sided cardboard advertising sign, 6½" dia., excellent, **$120.00 (B).**

Courtesy of Richard Opfer Auctioneering, Inc.

Gold Seal Boots and Overshoes, double sided tin litho advertising sign, featuring artwork of boots and shoes, 18¼" L, good, **$170.00 (B).**

Courtesy of Riverview Antique Mall

Golden Shell Motor Oil, double sided driveway sign, 26½" X 34½", good, **$325.00 (D).**

Courtesy of Muddy River Trading Co./Gary Metz

Gollam's Lebanon Ice Cream, We Serve, painted metal double sided sidewalk sign, 1940s, excellent, **$250.00 (B).**

Courtesy of Riverview Antique Mall

Goodrich Tires, supplies porcelain flange sign, 18" dia., white lettering on blue background, good, **$265.00 (D).**

Goodrich Sport Shoes, advertising die cut cardboard poster featuring artwork of Indian, framed, 26" X 41", excellent, **$260.00 (B).**

Courtesy of B.J. Summers

Gordon's Potato Chips, can with Gordon's delivery truck at top, metal, 7½" X 11½", red and cream, excellent, **$85.00 (C).**

Grand Old Party...1856 to 1908, round tip tray with artwork of Taft & Sherman in center of tray under graphics of White House, great strong graphics, 4⅛" dia., excellent, **$85.00 (B).**

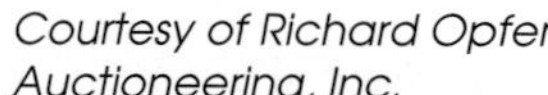
Courtesy of Richard Opfer Auctioneering, Inc.

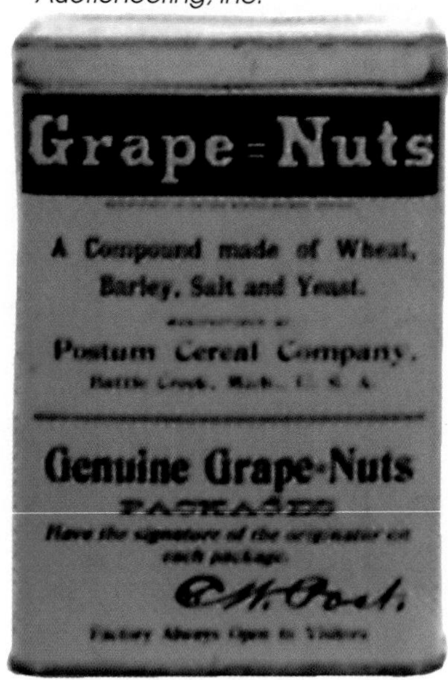

Grape Nuts, Postum Cereal Company, cereal tin, 5½" H, excellent, **$140.00 (B).**

Great Majestic Ranges, gesso bas-relief advertising sign with graphics of woman cooking on product, great details, 1915, 37" X 49" X 4¼", excellent, **$3,000.00 (B).**

Courtesy of Antiques Cards & Collectibles/Ray Pelly

Grape-Nuts...To school well fed on...There's a reason, self-framing tin sign with little girl walking with St. Bernard, 20¼" X 30¼", excellent, **$1,350.00 (D).**

Gypsy Hosiery...George H. Buschmann, Owensville, Mo., round metal tip tray with gypsy camp scene and gypsy woman inset in center, 6" dia., excellent, **$210.00 (B).**

Courtesy of Buffalo Bay Auction Co.

H.M. Pentz, Glen Hope, Penn Milling Specialist, paper die cut calendar of young lady with large hat, full monthly pad, 1913, 14" X 23", near-mint, **$363.00 (B).**

Hair Bobbing, Ladies & Children Our Specialty, porcelain advertising sign, 24" X 12", good, **$350.00 (B).**

Courtesy of Richard Opfer Auctioneering, Inc.

H. Sandmeyer & Co, tin litho match holder, Peoria, Ill., Golden Anniversary Hardware, 5" H, good, **$110.00 (B).**

Courtesy of John and Vicki Mahan

Headlight Overalls, porcelain store advertising sign, featuring train with light, "Agency for..." 32" X 10", good, **$300.00 (C).**

Hartford Fire Insurance Company, advertising with artwork of deer in center, painted metal flange sign, 1950s, 18" X 28", good, **$325.00 (B).**

Courtesy of Buffalo Bay Auction Co.

Heinz 57 Varieties, die cut string holder, double sided, hard-to-find item, 17" X 14" X 7", excellent, **$5,400.00 (B).**

Courtesy of Muddy River Trading Co./Gary Metz

Hemmer's Ice Cream, serving tray, "Rich and Delicious" with artwork of ice cream products in center of tray, 1920s, 13" X 13", good, **$170.00 (B).**

Hendlers Ice Cream, paper litho advertising sign, framed, 20" X 29", fair, **$625.00 (B).**

Courtesy of Affordable Antiques

Hershey's Krackel Milk Chocolate, case box that held 24 bars, 1-lb., 5 oz., excellent, **$7.00 (D).**

Hitchner Cookie Store, bin cover, metal and glass, 10¼" X 10½", fair, **$15.00 (B).**

Courtesy of Muddy River Trading Co./Gary Metz

Honey-Fruit Gum, "Nothing Like It, Delightful Flavor," tin over cardboard advertising sign, manufactured by Franklin-Caro Company in Richmond, Va., 16¼" X 9", excellent, **$1,300.00 (B).**

Hiram's General Store, punch board, 12½" X 15", good, **$70.00 (B).**

Courtesy of Illinois Antique Center/Kim & Dan Phillips

Hollywoodglo...The screenstar loveliness use, tri-fold cardboard advertising with early motion picture cameras and actress, good, **$45.00 (D).**

Courtesy of Rare Bird Antique Mall–Jon & Joan Wright

Howdy Doody Washington Apples, plastic bag, NOS with graphics of Howdy Doody and friends on front, 3-lb., excellent, **$15.00 (D).**

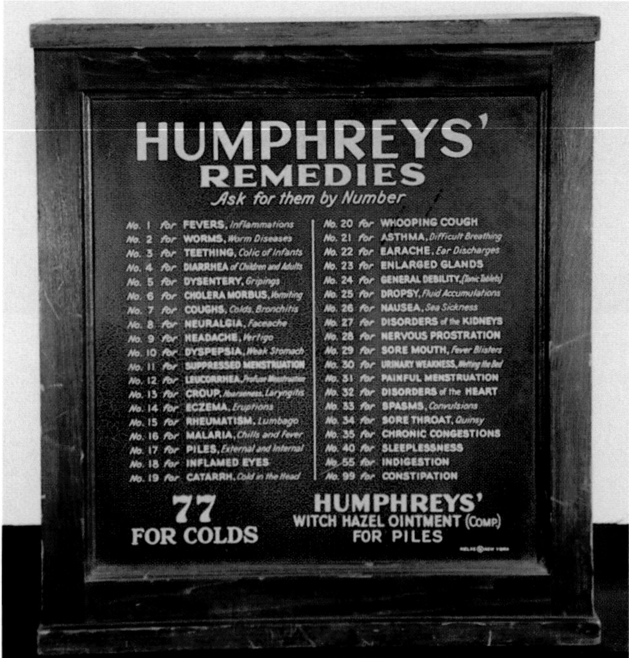

Humphreys' Remedies, store display wooden cabinet with metal front, 18"W X 21"H X7¼"D, excellent, **$250.00 (B).**

Courtesy of Riverview Antique Mall

Ideal Bread, rack sign, painted metal, "Ideal for every meal," 40" X 17½", fair, **$195.00 (D).**

Courtesy of B.J. Summers

Ideal...Quality chekd Dairy Products, plastic light-up advertising clock, 15½" dia., good, **$135.00 (C).**

Courtesy of Pleasant Hill Antique Mall & Tea Room/Bob Johnson

Illinois Valley...Ice Cream, metal and plastic light-up sign, excellent, **$155.00 (D).**

Ingersoll Watches, metal store display case, brown metal with woodgrain look, manufactured by the H.D. Beach Co., Coshocton, Ohio, U.S.A., 9½"W X 14¼"H X 6"D, good, **$100.00 (B).**

Courtesy of Chief Paduke Antique Mall

Keen Kutter...Safety Razor, cardboard ad with artwork of man shaving, "Always Ready To Shave...The Razor That Fits The Face", good graphics, 20¾" X 10¾", excellent, **$75.00 (D).**

Courtesy of Muddy River Trading Co./Gary Metz

Kellogg's Toasted Corn Flakes, hanging cardboard advertising sign, "A Hit and A Miss" featuring artwork of girl eating cereal, Look for this Signature,W.K. Kellogg, 1915, 10½" X 15½", good, **$250.00 (B).**

Courtesy of Riverview Antique Mall

Kerr-Views Milk, porcelain bottle shaped advertising sign, "From our own herd," 19" X 48", good, **$1,850.00 (D).**

Courtesy of Richard Opfer Auctioneering, Inc.

Kellogg's Toasted Corn Flakes, double sided sheet steel flange sign, with great graphics of small girl in basket, 13½" X 19½", excellent, **$3,400.00 (B).**

Kellogg's Toasted Corn Flakes...Fine With Berries, Peaches or Bananas, cardboard store sign, featuring artwork of young girl with product box, 1915, 11" X 20", near-mint, **$550.00 (B).**

Courtesy of Riverview Antique Mall

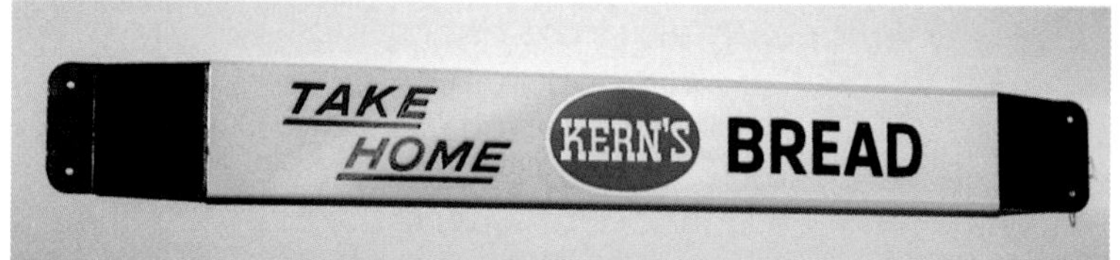

Kern's Bread, porcelain door push bar, "Take Home..." 27" X 3", excellent, **$135.00 (D).**

Courtesy of Chief Paduke Antique Mall

Kirchhoff's Bread, door push, heavy metal and adjustable, used on screen doors before the days of air conditioning, good, **$60.00 (D).**

Courtesy of Muddy River Trading Co./Gary Metz

Kirk's Pancake Flour, embossed painted tin sign, with artwork of chef carrying serving tray, 1930s, 20" X 14", good, **$225.00 (B).**

Courtesy of Richard Opfer Auctioneering, Inc.

Kirkman's Borax Soap, die cut tin litho match holder, featuring woman doing wash in wooden tub, 7" H, near-mint, **$5,700.00 (B).**

Courtesy of Wm. Morford Investment Grade Collectibles

"Kis-Me," die cut easel back embossed cardboard advertising sign for Kis-Me chewing gum, hard to find, 6½" X 10½", excellent, **$1,550.00 (B).**

Koken Shop, advertising porcelain barber sign, originally held light bulbs on the outside of sign, rare find, 31" dia., good, **$1,800.00 (B).**

Kum-Seald, handkerchief wood and glass display with glass front, back opens for refilling, 22"W X 12"H X 8"D, excellent, **$140.00 (D).**

Courtesy of Rare Bird Antique Mall–Jon & Joan Wright

Lance, glass store jar with crossed lances on front & back with hard-to-find metal Lance bottom, 1940s, excellent, **$175.00 (D).**

Courtesy of Muddy River Trading Co./Gary Metz

Lenox Soap, porcelain advertising sign, 10" X 6", good, **$120.00 (B).**

Courtesy of Richard Opfer Auctioneering, Inc.

Libby's rolled ox tongues, paper litho under glass, framed, excellent, **$425.00 (B).**

Lions International, porcelain sign, 30" dia., good, **$20.00 (B).**

Courtesy of Riverview Antique Mall

Look Better, Feel Better, porcelain barber pole, 7½" X 48", red, white & blue, good, **$350.00 (D).**

Courtesy of Creatures of Habit

Lolita Talcum Powder, tin oval container with artwork of "Lolita" on front, 4¼" X 7" X 9", excellent, **$145.00 (D).**

Lipton's Tea...Always Satisfactory, double sided die cut tin litho store string dispenser, 13¾" X 19½", excellent, **$1,512.00 (B).**

Lowe Brothers Paints for all purposes, porcelain advertising store sign, 27¾" X 19¾", good, **$45.00 (B).**

Courtesy of Muddy River Trading Co./Gary Metz

Luden's Chewing Gum, change receiver, featuring artwork of gum packages in center, 1920s, 11" dia., good, **$180.00 (B).**

Courtesy of Riverview Antique Mall

Marx Old Style Bread, Famous for Flavor, features artwork of bread wagon being pulled by oxen, 36" X 24", excellent, **$450.00 (B).**

Courtesy of Old Homeplace Antiques–Jackie Thomas

Master Locks display, Strength Security Padlock, metal, 5½" dia., good, **$25.00 (D).**

Courtesy of Muddy River Trading Co./Gary Metz

Mansfield's Pepsin Gum, automatic clerk dispenser with advertising tag on top, 6½"W X ½"D X 11½"H, excellent, **$400.00 (B).**

Master Feeds, We sell ..., oval porcelain store sign, 26½" X 16", excellent, **$75.00 (B).**

Mazda Lamps, cardboard store display, "How are you fixed for Mazda lamps ?" featuring artwork of display being held by bellman, fair, **$55.00 (D).**

Mazda Lamps, store display, "How are you fixed for lamps?" with artwork of box of National Mazda Lamps over message, good, **$65.00 (D).**

Courtesy of Muddy River Trading Co./Gary Metz

Meadow Gold Ice Cream, Please Pay When Served, masonite display board, manufactured by Kay Displays, 11" X 16", excellent, **$55.00 (B).**

Courtesy of Richard Opfer Auctioneering, Inc.

Mennen, tin litho flange advertising sign, with great graphics of young child holding Mennen's product, 22¾" W X 14¼" H, excellent, **$1,250.00 (B).**

Courtesy of Muddy River Trading Co./Gary Metz

Mentholatum, A.A. Hyde, die cut cardboard advertising display with nurse showing the many uses for the product, 31" X 43", near-mint, **$190.00 (B).**

Michigan Bell Telephone, porcelain flange sign, 11¾" X 11", excellent, **$250.00 (B).**

Courtesy of Wm Morford Investment Grade Collectibles

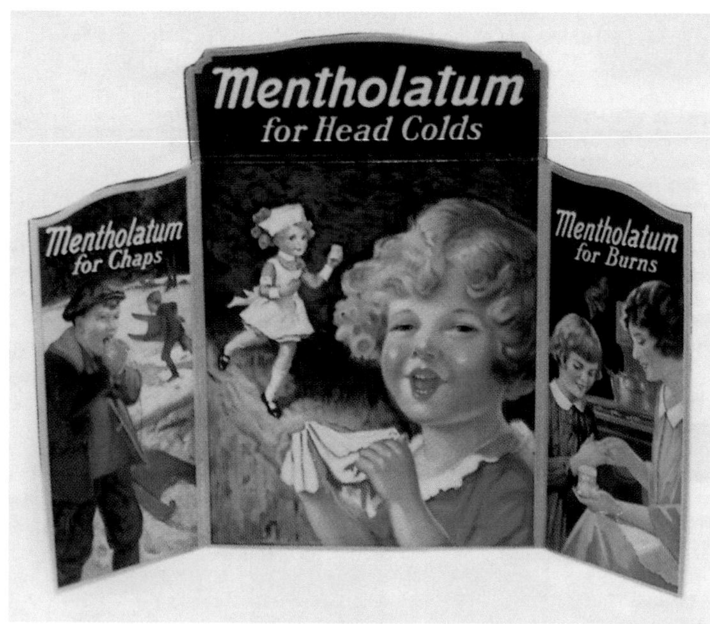

Mentholatum, cardboard tri-fold drugstore window display, great graphics and strong colors, 48" X 35", excellent, **$625.00 (B).**

Merrick...Six Cord Soft Finish Spool Cotton, wood and glass cabinet, with product message on front glass, good, **$1,250.00 (D).**

Midwest Ice Cream, porcelain store advertising sign, featuring a bonnet-clad lady with a serving tray, 20" X 30", good, **$245.00 (D).**

Courtesy of B.J. Summers

Midwest Milk, light-up clock, metal body with reverse painted glass front cover, 15½" X 15½", white and red, excellent, **$175.00 (C).**

Courtesy of Richard Opfer Auctioneering, Inc.

Milwaukee Harvesting Machines, Always Reliable, tin litho match holder, great graphics of worker with bandana and wide brimmed hat, 5½" H, excellent, **$350.00 (B).**

Courtesy of Creatures of Habit

Mojud Supp-hose, three-dimensional store advertising with woman in yellow outfit sitting in ladder-back chair, plastic, excellent, **$175.00 (D).**

Miller's Finer, Flavor-Rich Milk, Delicious Ice Cream, reverse painted glass sign front, fair, **$45.00 (D).**

Courtesy of Chief Paduke Antique Mall

Mr. Peanut, costume, excellent, **$500.00 (B).**

Courtesy of Buffalo Bay Auction Co.

Munsing Wear...Perfect Fitting...Union Suits, die cut tin litho with graphics of children playing with mother, excellent, **$3,100.00 (B).**

Courtesy of Muddy River Trading Co./Gary Metz

MunsingWear, cardboard easel back store display featuring artwork of kids on early model car, "joy riding in Munsingwear," 8½" X 11", excellent, **$160.00 (B).**

Courtesy of Muddy River Trading Co./Gary Metz

MunsingWear, easel back cardboard store advertising display, featuring artwork of small red-haired girl, "Miss Particular," 1910, 8½" X 11", near-mint, **$65.00 (B).**

Courtesy of Muddy River Trading Co./Gary Metz

MunsingWear, easel back cardboard store advertising featuring little girl with chalkboard,"Munsing Union Suits in all styles – for all ages", 1910, 8½" X 11", excellent, **$95.00 (B).**

Courtesy of Riverview Antique Mall

Nanty-Glo, sign advertising Edelstein's for clothing, arrow-shaped painted arrow, 5" X 20", excellent, **$65.00 (D).**

Courtesy of B.J. Summers

New Era Dairy, Velvet Rich, Ice Cream, plastic front light-up clock, has metal back, good, **$95.00 (C).**

Nabisco National Biscuit Company, store bin cover, gold metal frame with glass cover, "Patented March 13, 1923" embossed on side, excellent, **$25.00 (B).**

Courtesy of Affordable Antiques

New Era... Ice Cream, neon light-up store sign, 24¾" X 14¾", good, **$375.00 (D).**

New York Central-Hudson Type locomotive, printed in the U.S.A, H.O. Bailey Studios, 1934, 29" X 14", good, **$110.00 (B).**

Niagara Shoes, store advertising sign, tin over cardboard, "for youthful feet," featuring artwork of Niagara Falls, 9" X 19", excellent, **$100.00 (B).**

Courtesy of Richard Opfer Auctioneering, Inc.

None Such, clock, pumpkin-shaped, paper litho, embossed in pie tin, 9½" H, excellent, **$925.00 (B).**

Northern Navigation Division Ticket and Information sign, Canadian National Route, graphics of steamship at dock, celluloid over metal, 8" X 9", excellent, **$650.00 (B).**

Notary Public, celluloid over metal sign bonded by Hartford Accident and Indemnity Company with artwork of the Hartford deer in lower center, 8¾" X 4½", good, **$25.00 (B).**

Courtesy of B.J. Summers

NuGrape Soda, light-up advertising clock, featuring convex glass front, by Swihart, 1940s, 13" X 14", good, **$175.00 (C).**

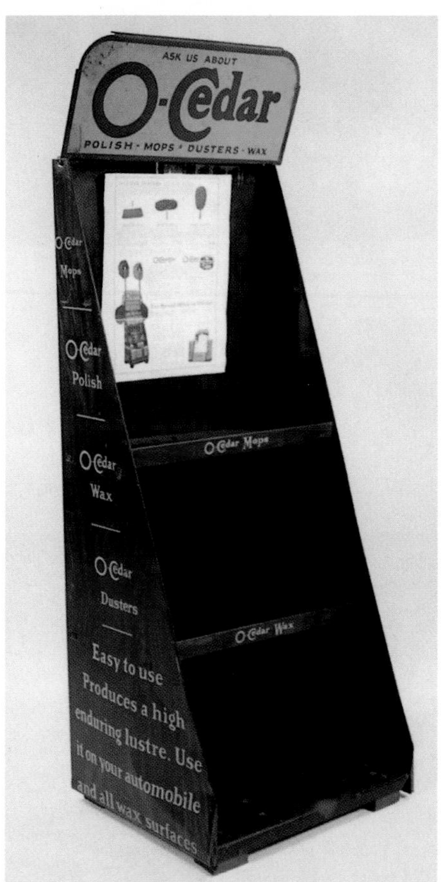

O-Cedar, store display rack, metal with woodgrain look, featuring advertisment from 1925, 1920s, 14"W X 40½"H X 11½"D, good, **$120.00 (B).**

Courtesy of Morford Auctions

Nutriola Blood & Nerve Food, early cardboard sign with great graphics, 14" X 18", excellent, **$975.00 (B).**

Courtesy of B.J. Summers

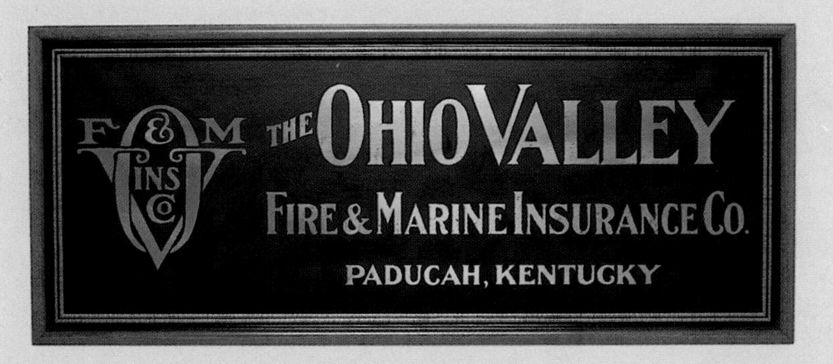

Ohio Valley Fire & Marine Insurance, advertising sign, solid brass with embossed lettering and copper flashing on front, from Paducah, Kentucky, framed and restored, 24" X 9", excellent, **$375.00 (C).**

Courtesy of Richard Opfer Auctioneering, Inc.

Old Dutch Cleanser, double sided tin litho advertising sign, good strong colors, 12¾" L, near-mint, **$160.00 (B).**

Courtesy of Richard Opfer Auctioneering, Inc.

Old Judson, tin litho match holder, J.C. Stevens, 518 Delaware St., Kansas City, MO, USA, 5" H, excellent, **$200.00 (B).**

Onondaga Brand Glass, flange painted metal advertising sign, featuring artwork of Indian in center, 18½" X 13½", excellent, **$200.00 (B).**

Courtesy of Richard Opfer Auctioneering, Inc.

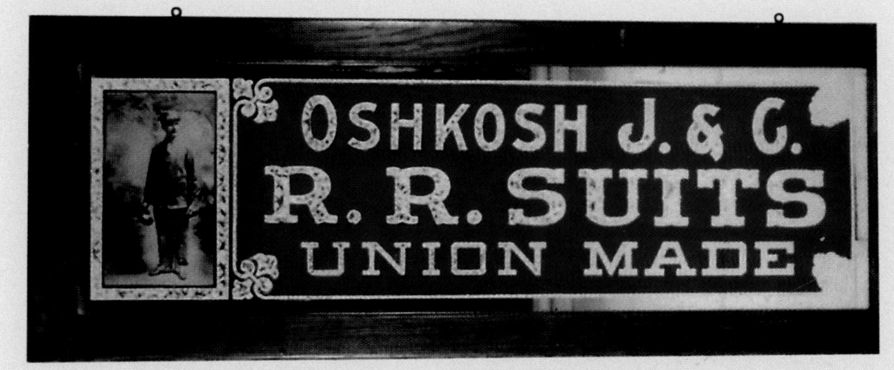

Oshkosh R.R. Suits, Union Made, reverse painted glass in wood frame, featuring good graphics of oil worker at left side of sign, 48¼" X 18½", excellent, **$3,800.00 (B).**

Parker Pen, light-up display, wood and glass with original key, 20½" X 9" X 9", excellent, **$85.00 (B).**

Courtesy of Muddy River Trading Co./Gary Metz

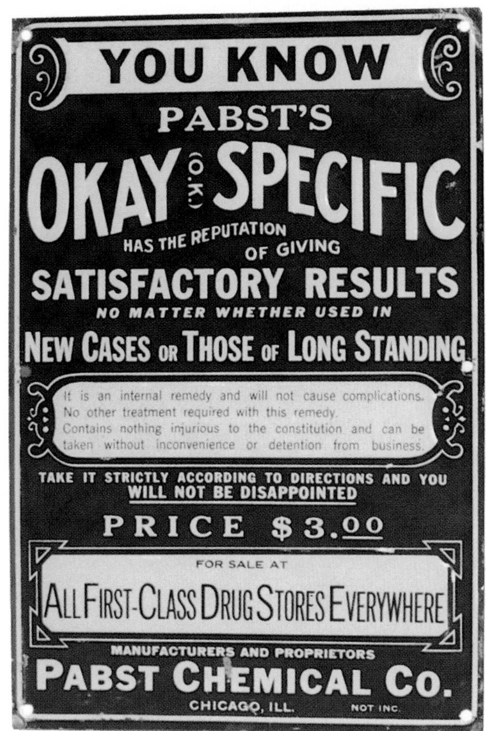

Pabst's Okay Specific Medicinal Remedy, embossed tin sign, 6" X 9", excellent, **$85.00 (B).**

Patterson Sargent Paint, die cut porcelain advertising sign "For Better Results," 33" X 24", near-mint, **$75.00 (B).**

Courtesy of Muddy River Trading Co./Gary Metz

Peerless Weighing Machine Co., curved porcelain penny scale sign, "Did you weigh yourself today," 5½" X 9", good, **$170.00 (B).**

Courtesy of Muddy River Trading Co./Gary Metz

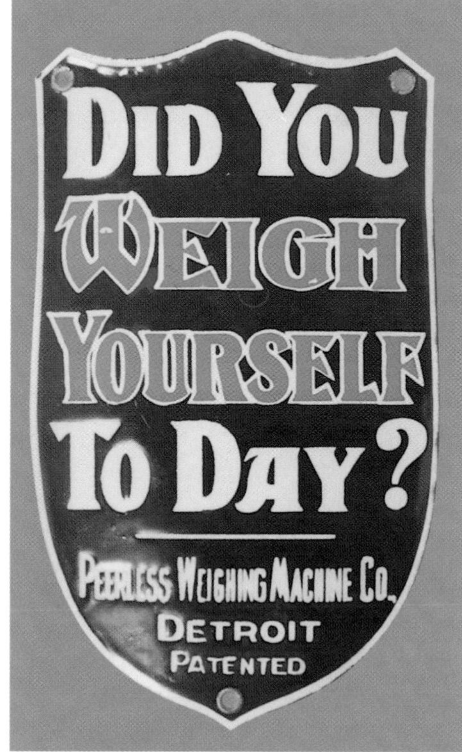

Peerless Weighing Machine Co., curved porcelain sign off penny scale, "Did you weigh yourself today," 5½" X 9", excellent, **$230.00 (B).**

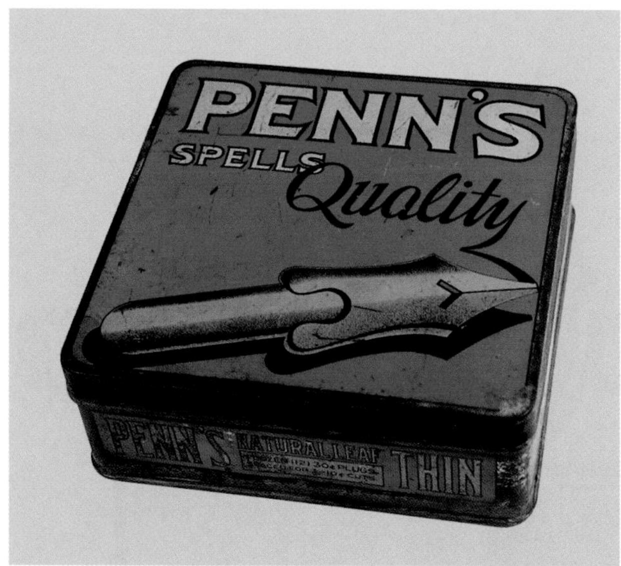

Penn's Spells Quality, tin box, metal with hinged lid, 6½" W X 2½"H X 6½"D, good, **$330.00 (B).**

Philco, die cut cardboard standup advertising sign, featuring Don McNeil of the "Breakfast Club" showing all the features of the refrigerator, 1940s, 32" X 64", good, **$15.00 (B).**

Courtesy of Riverview Antique Mall

Philip Morris, painted metal sign featuring the Philip Morris boy holding a metal cigarette pack, 1940s, 27" X 15", fair, **$195.00 (D).**

Pittston Gazette, porcelain advertising sign, manufactured by Ing-Rich, Beaver Falls, Pa., "Bright, Clean, Newsy," 16" X 8", excellent, **$100.00 (B).**

Courtesy of Muddy River Trading Co./Gary Metz

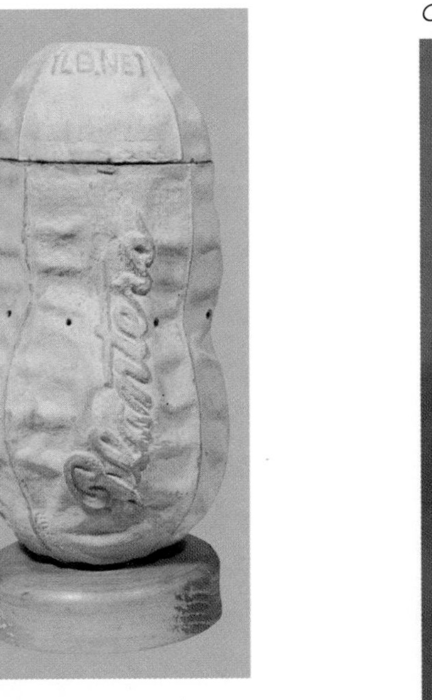

Planters Peanut, container, shaped to resemble a peanut, 11" long, good, **$35.00 (B).**

Courtesy of Muddy River Trading Co./Gary Metz

Planters Peanut, glass barrel jar, with original lid featuring peanut-shaped handle, excellent, **$200.00 (B).**

Courtesy of Muddy River Trading Co./Gary Metz

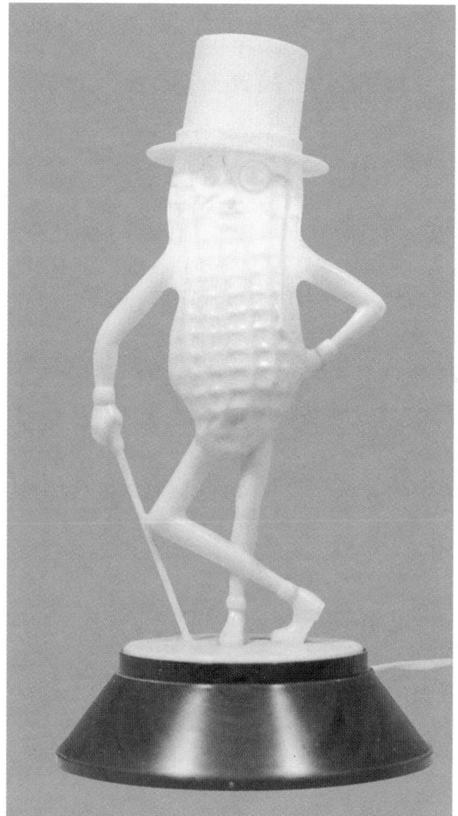

Planters Mr. Peanut, plastic night light, 10" tall, excellent, **$250.00 (B).**

Courtesy of Muddy River Trading Co./Gary Metz

Planters Peanuts, wax-coated box, good, **$40.00 (B).**

Courtesy of Muddy River Trading Co./Gary Metz

Planters Peanuts, square can of salted nuts, 1920s, 1-lb., good, **$90.00 (B).**

Courtesy of Creatures of Habit

Polaroid Land Camera, light-up display sign with clock in left side of display, 1960s, good, **$125.00 (D).**

Courtesy of Richard Opfer Auctioneering, Inc.

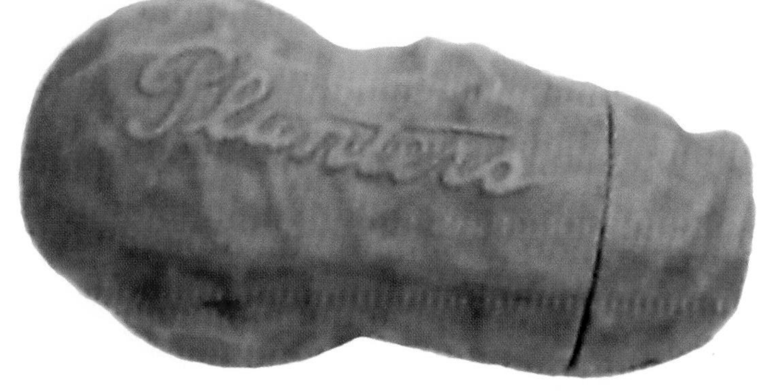

Planters Pulp Peanut, advertising display with Planters name on two sides, 10¼", excellent, **$70.00 (B).**

Courtesy of Riverview Antique Mall

Postal Telegraph, double sided porcelain flange sign, "The International System", 29½" X 16", excellent, **$325.00 (D).**

Courtesy of B.J. Summers

Prairie Farms, Milk, Ice Cream, round light-up clock, plastic front cover on plastic base, good, **$115.00 (C).**

Courtesy of Morford Auctions

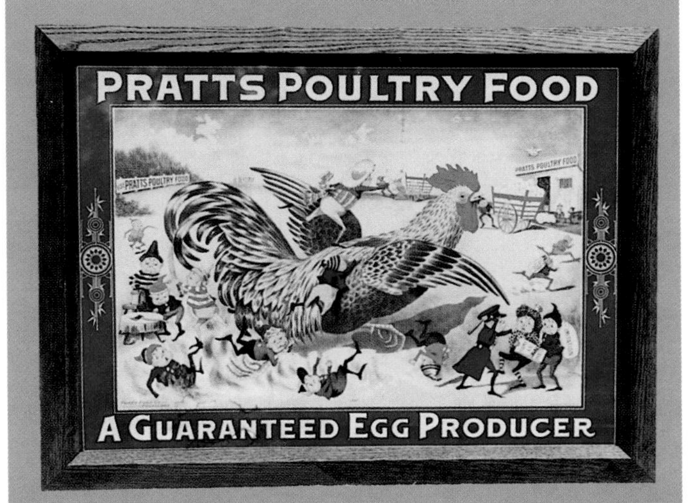

Pratts Poultry Food, A Guaranteed Egg Producer, framed paper litho, 21" X 28", excellent, **$675.00 (B).**

Pratt & Lambert Paint, double sided porcelain sign, 36" X 24", excellent, **$75.00 (B).**

Courtesy of Richard Opfer Auctioneering, Inc.

Primley's California Fruit and Pepsin Chewing Gum, display case with oak framing and etched glass, 18¼", excellent, **$525.00 (B).**

Courtesy of Riverview Antique Mall

Public Telephone, Bell System Connections, double sided porcelain flange sign, white on blue, poor, **$295.00 (D).**

Courtesy of Riverview Antique Mall

Public Telephone, The Lincoln Telephone and Telegraph Company, porcelain flange sign, 16" dia., excellent, **$345.00 (D).**

Pulver's Kola-Pepsin Chewing Gum, two piece cardboard box with great graphics of vending machine on both sides, 6⅞" X 5¼5" X 1⅜", good, **$3,000.00 (B).**

Courtesy of Richard Opfer Auctioneering, Inc.

Putnam Dyes, wooden store display box featuring General Putnam litho on outside cover, also litho on inside cover, strong colors, with original dye packages, excellent, **$350.00 (B).**

Courtesy of Riverview Antique Mall

Rain Dears, self-framed painted metal sign, "Finest Plastic Rainboots," 25" X 9½", excellent, **$45.00 (D).**

RCA Radiola Dealer, porcelain scroll advertising sign, 14½" X 19", fair, **$70.00 (B).**

RCA Victor Records Oleograph, pictures early Nipper at phonograph, "His Master's Voice", framed, 30" X 24", excellent, **$550.00 (B).**

Courtesy of Muddy River Trading Co./Gary Metz

Red Goose Shoes, telechron light-up clock with goose in center, 1930s, excellent, **$400.00 (B).**

Courtesy of Riverview Antique Mall

Red Top steel posts, painted metal sign, 18" X 24", good, **$85.00 (D).**

Courtesy of Richard Opfer Auctioneering, Inc.

Reliance Baking Powder, tin litho match holder, graphics of woman working in kitchen, 5¾" H, good, **$425.00 (B).**

Courtesy of Richard Opfer Auctioneering, Inc.

REX Flintkote Roofing, "For all roofs," tin litho match holder, great graphics of barn with message on roof, 5" H, good, **$350.00 (B).**

Courtesy of Muddy River Trading Co./Gary Metz

Rochester Journal, advertising sign, made of embossed tin, "inspiring-new-complete/make it a daily visitor to your home", 1920s, 20" X 5", excellent, **$95.00 (B).**

Ridenour-Johnson Hardware Co. Advertisement, framed cardboard litho, copyright 1922, 1920s, 16" X 26½", good, **$70.00 (B).**

Roe Feeds, painted metal sign, 7" X 12", excellent, **$85.00 (D).**

Courtesy of Muddy River Trading Co./Gary Metz

Ryzon, The Perfect Baking Powder, double sided tin sign with artwork of baking powder can, arm hung, 1940s, 12" X 16", excellent, **$475.00 (B).**

S.M. Hess & Brother, advertising calendar, by Hayes Litho Co., "manufacturers of rich grade fertilizers," 1907, 15" X 22¼", fair, **$140.00 (B).**

Courtesy of Richard Opfer Auctioneering, Inc.

Sauer's, flavoring and extracts, wood case clock with reverse painting and lettering, 42½" H, excellent, **$1,550.00 (B).**

Courtesy of Muddy River Trading Co./Gary Metz

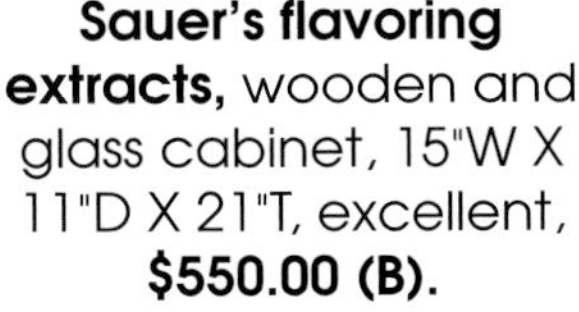

Sauer's flavoring extracts, wooden and glass cabinet, 15"W X 11"D X 21"T, excellent, **$550.00 (B).**

Courtesy of Morford Auctions

Scudder's Brownie Brand Confection Butter Maple Flavor, can featuring Brownie characters, 1½-lb., excellent, **$240.00 (B).**

Roszell's Sealtest... Homogenized Milk, plastic and neon sign, excellent, **$175.00 (D).**

Courtesy of Chief Paduke Antique Mall

Search Light, American Diamond Matches, with 1913 award on back, "In American Factories, By American Workers, For American Home Use," box, good, **$3.00 (D).**

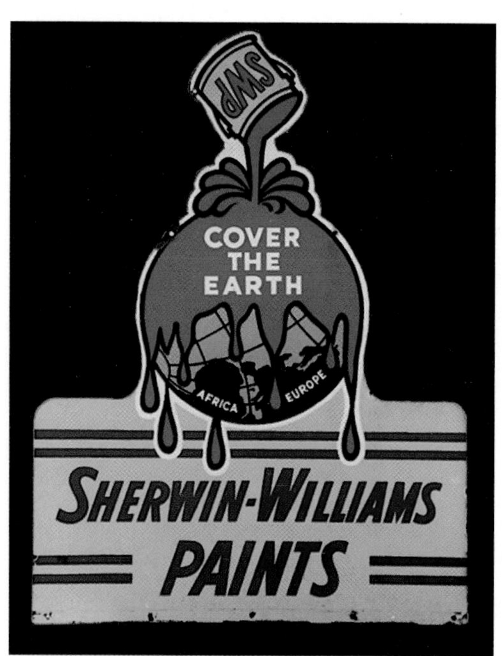

Sherwin-Williams Paints, Cover the Earth, painted metal sign, good, **$175.00 (C).**

Courtesy of Muddy River Trading Co./Gary Metz

Serve it and you please all, with artwork of neopolitan ice cream in center, round, porcelain, 18" dia., excellent, **$800.00 (B).**

Courtesy of Richard Opfer Auctioneering, Inc.

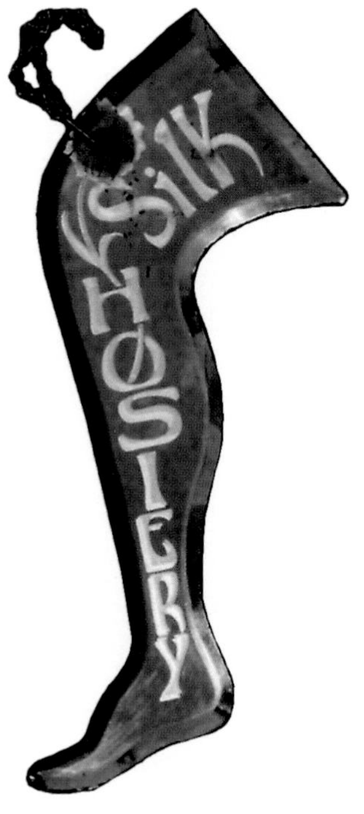

Silk Hosiery, advertising mirror, acid etched figural hanging sign, 13" H, good, **$625.00 (B).**

Courtesy of Richard Opfer Auctioneering, Inc.

Slade's Spices and Baking Powder, advertising litho paper sign with likeness of small girl with flowers, 20" X 25¾", good, **$475.00 (B).**

Courtesy of B.J. Summers

Southern Bell Telephone and Telegraph Co./American Telephone & Telegraph Co., milk glass globe, at one time these hung at Bell business offices, getting to be a hard item to find, blue lettering and bell on white, near-mint, **$875.00 (C).**

Close-up of artwork

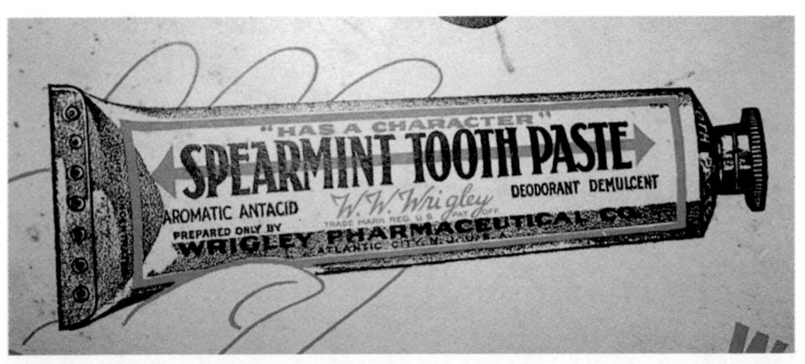

Spearmint Toothpaste, W.W. Wrigley, heavy cardboard advertising sign, 24" X 18", fair, **$45.00 (D).**

Courtesy of Courtesy of Chief Paduke Antique Mall

Spitting on Sidewalks Prohibited, painted metal sign, 9¾" X 7", black lettering on light background, fair, **$110.00 (B).**

Courtesy of Riverview Antique Mall

Standard Oil Products, porcelain sign, 30" X 20", white on blue, good, **$235.00 (D).**

"Steamro" Red Hots, porcelain advertising sign, 17¼" X 2¼", good, **$180.00 (D).**

Courtesy of Muddy River Trading Co./Gary Metz

Squire's Ham's, "John P. Squire & Company, Boston," embossed self-framing tin sign, artwork of sitting pig in center of sign, 1906, 20" X 24", excellent, **$300.00 (B).**

Courtesy of Richard Opfer Auctioneering, Inc.

Sunny Brook Pure Rye Bourbon, advertising tin litho match holder featuring artwork of whiskey bottle, good graphics, 5"H, good, **$130.00 (B).**

Sunbeam Bread, door push with bread loaf cut out in center of door bar, used before air-conditioning on screen doors to protect screens, 1950s, 30" X 15", excellent, **$275.00 (B).**

Courtesy of Muddy River Trading Co./Gary Metz

Sunbeam Bread, sign, artwork of loaf of bread with girl, "reach for...it's batter-whipped," 1950s, 6" X 3", excellent, **$400.00 (B).**

Superior Pickles, glass jar with hard-to-find paper label, 1860, 13¾" H, good, **$60.00 (C).**

Courtesy of Richard Opfer Auctioneering, Inc.

Teaberry Gum, litho tin with great graphics on all sides and on both the inside and outside of the lid, good strong colors, 6¾" L, excellent, **$225.00 (B).**

Courtesy of B.J. Summers

Telephone, light-up sign for pay station booths, metal frame and plastic message, 19½" X 5¾", excellent, **$165.00 (C).**

The Dreadnoughts, advertising poster, "greatest perch and gymnastic-act," with graphics of acrobatics and photos in spotlights, 39" X 52", excellent, **$100.00 (B).**

The Brunswick Bakle-Collender Co., cardboard framed advertisment featuring a scene from the National Bowling Association International Tour in Madison Sq. Garden 5/24-6/12, 1909, 1909, 37" X 28", excellent, **$1,200.00 (B).**

The Foster Hose Supporters, celluloid litho on cardboard advertising sign, featuring artwork of woman with garter belt, 17" H, near-mint, **310.00 (B).**

Courtesy of Richard Opfer Auctioneering, Inc.

"The Girl on the Barge," heavy paper window card from the Unique Theatre, 14" X 22", good, **$25.00 (D).**

The Navy...I want you, cloth backed recruiting poster signed by artist, Howard Chandler Christy, with artwork of girl in uniform, 1917, 26½" X 41", excellent, **$325.00 (C).**

Courtesy of Pleasant Hill Antique Mall & Tea Room/Bob Johnson

The Old Settler, general store box, will clear black water in a few hours, 10-oz., fair, **$7.00 (D).**

The Orange Candy Kitchen Ice Cream & Candy, framed die cut litho advertising calendar, featuring artwork of little boy and kittens, 1911, 14½" X 18½", good, **$60.00 (B).**

The Royal Tailors, die cut painted tin stand-up advertising sign, great graphics, 19½" X 9", excellent, **$450.00 (D).**

Courtesy of Richard Opfer Auctioneering, Inc.

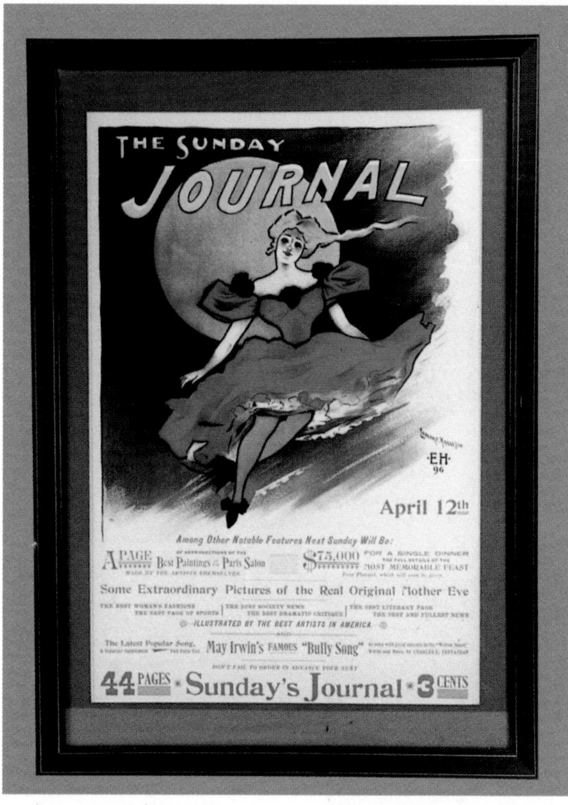

The Sunday Journal, matted and framed, signed by Liebler & Morse Lith, E.H. 96, April 12, great graphics, 17½" X 25½", good, **$25.00 (B).**

Jersey-Creme, At Founts, The Perfect Drink, In Bottles, tin tray, nice litho with girl in period dress, 12" dia., excellent, **$300.00 (B).**

Tintex, painted tin sign, tints as you rinse, artwork of woman tinting clothes, 21¼" X 23", fair, **$50.00 (C).**

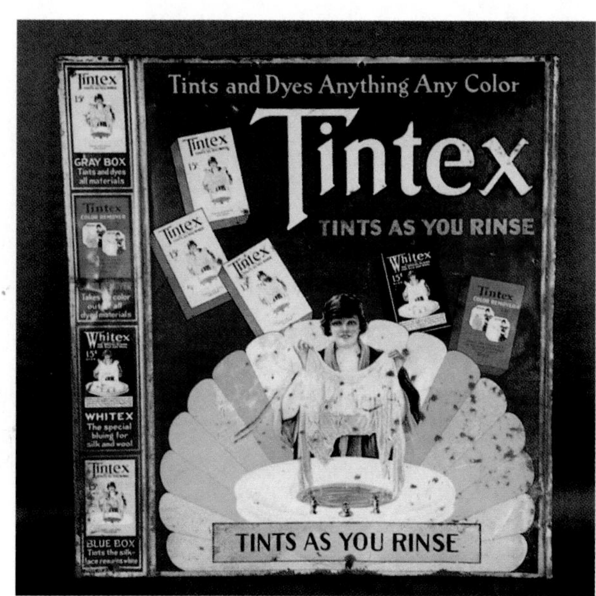

Courtesy of Wildflower Antique Mall

Tom's Toasted Peanuts, metal advertising thermometer, excellent, **$45.00 (D).**

Courtesy of Muddy River Trading Co./Gary Metz

Tom's Toasted Peanuts, store jar with Tom's lid, excellent, **$65.00 (B).**

Courtesy of Riverview Antique Mall

Tree Brand Shoes, Battreall Shoe Co., metal flange sign, double sided, excellent, **$950.00 (D).**

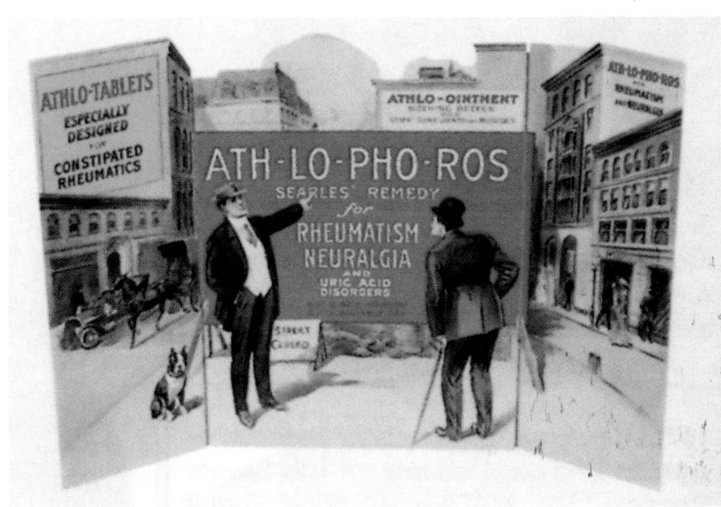

Ath-Lo-Pho-Ros Rheumatism and Neuralgia Remedy, three-piece window display, 20¼" X 18¾", near-mint, **$275.00 (B).**

Courtesy of B.J. Summers

U.S. Army, I Want You, porcelain double sided recruiting sign designed to fit in metal sidewalk frame, 25" X 38", excellent, **$275.00 (C).**

U.S. Postage Stamps, dispenser with porcelain front and metal back, by Automatic Dispenser Company, Los Angeles, CA, 8"W X 19½"H X 4½"D, excellent, **$100.00 (C).**

Courtesy of Richard Opfer Auctioneering, Inc.

Tubular Cream match holder, The Pet of the Dairy, great image of woman with child at separator, 6¾" H, excellent, **$375.00 (B).**

U. S. Quality Enameled Ware, curved glass light-up store advertising sign, featuring enamel steam pot likeness in center, 7" X 13½", excellent, **$550.00 (B).**

Courtesy of Muddy River Trading Co./Gary Metz

Courtesy of Buffalo Bay Auction Co.

Uncle Sam Stock Medicine Co., Quincy, Ill., U.S.A., heavy paper with patriotic images of Statue of Liberty and naval ships returning home, great item, 1919, 15" X 20", near-mint, **$225.00 (B).**

Courtesy of B.J. Summers

Union Farmer's Gin...phone 32, Portageville, Mo., vertical scale thermometer in country scene with silhouettes in foreground, 10¼" X 8¼", excellent, **$45.00 (C).**

Union Shop, celluloid window sign for Bakery and Confectionery Workers, 12" X 7", excellent, **$10.00 (D).**

Courtesy of Richard Opfer Auctioneering, Inc.

Universal Stoves and Ranges, advertising match holder with good strong litho on tin, 5" H, excellent, **$240.00 (B).**

Courtesy of Muddy River Trading Co./Gary Metz

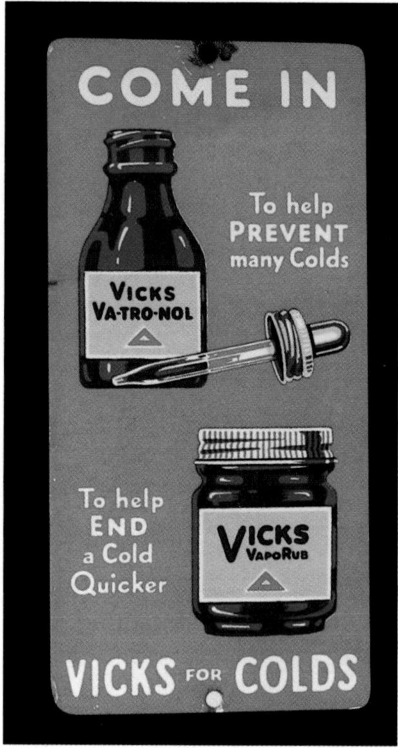

Vicks, porcelain door push plate with artwork of Va-tro-nol, and VapoRub, 3¾" X 7¾", excellent, **$130.00 (B).**

Courtesy of Muddy River Trading Co./Gary Metz

Wagner's Ice Cream, tin advertising sign featuring artwork of different ice cream products on a wooden serving tray, 1920s, 19½" X 13½", good, **$250.00 (B).**

Courtesy of Riverview Antique Mall

Watertite Paints & Enamels, painted embossed metal sign, 24" X 12", good, **$135.00 (D).**

Weather-Bird Shoes, neon and porcelain advertising sign in the shape of a rooster weather vane, 17" X 25½", excellent, **$1,700.00 (D).**

Courtesy of Richard Opfer Auctioneering, Inc.

Wells, Richardson & Co., advertising sign, chromo-litho paper on canvas backing with embossed frame, advertising lactated foods for infants and invalids, good rare piece, 25½" X 34¾", good, **$500.00 (B).**

Courtesy of Riverview Antique Mall

Western Union Telegrams may be telephoned from here, porcelain flange advertising sign, 22" X 12", good, **$225.00 (D).**

Western Union Telegraph here, porcelain advertising sign with side mounting tab, 25" X 16¾", white and yellow on dark blue, excellent, **$155.00 (C).**

Courtesy of Riverview Antique Mall

Wildroot, ask for, embossed painted metal sign featuring a barber pole at right of message, 28" X 10", good, **$95.00 (D).**

Courtesy of Muddy River Trading Co./Gary Metz

Williams Bread, porcelain and wrought iron door push bar, good, **$230.00 (B).**

Courtesy of Riverview Antique Mall.

Wisconsin Engines, embossed painted metal dealer sign, 30" X 24", good, **$235.00 (D).**

Courtesy of Muddy River Trading Co./Gary Metz

Wonder Orange, drink, embossed tin advertising sign, featuring spotlight on oranges at left of message, 1930s, 19½" X 13½", good, **$225.00 (B).**

Courtesy of Wm. Morford Investment Grade Collectibles

Worcester Elastic Stocking & Truss Co., celluloid advertising pocket mirror, great graphics of partially naked woman, excellent, **$400.00 (B).**

Courtesy of Richard Opfer Auctioneering, Inc.

Walk Over Shoes, double sided sheet steel flange sign, 13½" X 19½", excellent, **$600.00 (B).**

Courtesy of Wm. Morford Investment Grade Collectibles

Wrigley's Doublemint, General Store, double sided porcelain sign, 30" X 9", fair, **$2,400.00 (B).**

Courtesy of Muddy River Trading Co./Gary Metz

Wurlitzer, bubbling display advertising sign, limited edition, great presentation piece, 1990, excellent, **$425.00 (B).**

Yeast Foam, paper advertising poster featuring great graphics of young girl at table in front of a stack of "Buckwheat Cakes," 10" X 15", excellent, **$125.00 (C).**

Courtesy of Richard Opfer Auctioneering, Inc.

Zeno, carved wooden display case, oak and glass, 15¼" H, excellent, **$675.00 (B).**

NOT PICTURED:

A.C. Huff Music Store...High Grade Pianos, round metal tip tray with artwork of pretty woman in tray center, 4⅛" dia., excellent, **$90.00 (B).**

A.F. Movitt Prescription Druggist, die cut cardboard calendar from Chicago, IL, with artwork of young girl with flowers, 11½" X 17", excellent, **$181.00 (B).**

A&P, wooden tea bin with slanted lid and A&P logo in front and lid in old red paint, excellent, **$210.00 (B).**

ABC Chewing Gum, featuring artwork of the A.B.C. bathing girl on the beach, with product message at bottom, 13" X 28", excellent, **$250.00 (C).**

Acme Quality Paints, porcelain sign featuring artwork of paint can on front, 14½" X 20", good, **$75.00 (C).**

Adam Forepaugh & Sells Bros., Big United Shows, poster featuring circus activity on front, 17½" X 13", excellent, **$55.00 (C).**

Adams Gum Sweet Rubber Tolo Chewing Gum, tin with lift-off lid, made to hold 200 pieces of gum, colors still strong on cover, stork in lower right, 4½" X 4⅝" X 1", excellent, **$1,100.00 (B).**

Adams Pepsin Gum, tin store bin with hinge top, graphics of product messages on all sides and lid, 7" X 6" X 5", excellent, **$330.00 (B).**

Adams Sweet Fern Chewing Gum, two piece cardboard box with artwork of small girl, 4¾" X 8⅝" X 1⅜", excellent, **$130.00 (B).**

Advo Peanut Butter, tin litho container with pry lid, to be used as a measuring cup when empty, 12 oz., excellent, **$120.00 (B).**

Alka-Seltzer...effervescent analgesic alkalizing tablets, paper linen display box, 25¼" X 6¼" X 6¼", excellent, **$20.00 (D).**

Alka-Seltzer, metal store display, 12" X 9½", good, **$55.00 (D).**

American Can Company..., gift to 1907 National Canner's Convention, tin litho paperweight thermometer shaped like canning tin, near-mint, **$350.00 (B).**

American Line...Philadelphia, Liverpool, Queenstown, advertising pocket mirror with graphics of steamship, 1¾" dia., near-mint, **$25.00 (B).**

American Seal Paint, calendar with graphics depicting Uncle Sam and Spanish-American War heroes, 1899, 13" X 21", near-mint, **$334.00 (B).**

American Standard...Heating-Air Conditioning, plastic light-up clock, 15" dia., excellent, **$135.00 (C).**

American Telephone and Telegraph and Associated Companies, Public Telephone porcelain flange sign with Bell System bell in center, 20" X 20", excellent, **$255.00 (C).**

Amrhein's Bread...Ask for...It's fresher, painted metal door push, 26" X 3", red, white on blue, excellent, **$65.00 (D).**

Angelus Marshmallows, die cut easel back cardboard sign in likeness of small angel holding box of product, 5½" X 11¾", excellent, **$875.00 (B).**

Antikamnia Tablets...two every three hours...insomnia & nervousness, metal tip tray with graphics of woman seated in chair in tray center, 4¾", excellent, **$100.00 (B).**

Antisepticon Gum, sign, cardboard litho advertising sign featuring artwork of woman on cover, 6⅜" X 10⅝", excellent, **$1,150.00 (B).**

Atlantic, Pure White Lead Paint, framed poster featuring artwork of Dutch boy with paint bucket and brush sitting on shelf, 20¾" X 35", excellent, **$165.00 (C).**

Aunt Jemima Cooking and Salad Oil, paper panel from 5-gal. tin, Quaker Oats Co., framed, 8" X 13", excellent, **$58.00 (B).**

Automatic Electric Washer Co., Newton, IA, paperweight with artwork of pretty girl inside, excellent, **$55.00 (B).**

B.P.O. Elks, 45th Annual Reunion Grand Lodge, July 1909, Los Angeles, California, round metal tip tray with artwork of large moose in tray center, 4⅛" dia., good, **$25.00 (B).**

B-B Dairy Feeds, Poultry Feeds, metal ad sign from Buffalo, N.Y., 24" X 12", excellent, **$40.00 (B).**

Baby Ruth...Curtiss...Candy and Gum, tape dispenser, porcelain with paper labels, 10½" X 2", excellent, **$50.00 (D).**

Ball Brand Shoes, easel back cardboard sign with graphics of young boy and shoe with message, 1949, 29" X 20", excellent, **$50.00 (B).**

Barber Greene, metal toy grain loader, 6½" X 12", green, excellent, **$225.00 (C).**

Beacon Shoes, There Are None Better, reverse painted glass advertising with lighthouse logo in center, 14½" X 20½", excellent, **$125.00 (D).**

Bell System, die cut porcelain flange sign with message part of sign in die cut circle, 16¼" X 14", excellent, **$155.00 (C).**

Bell System, Public Telephone, flange porcelain sign featuring the bell in the center, 18" X 18", excellent, **$95.00 (C).**

Berry Brothers Toy Wagon, advertising pocket mirror, graphics depicting youngsters with wagon and dog, 2" dia., excellent, **$126.00 (B).**

Betsy's Best Flour, Bake and See Why, paper litho on cardboard with graphics of product bag to left of message, 38½" X 21½", excellent, **$150.00 (B).**

Bettendorf Steel Gear Wagon, metal tip tray with graphics of wagon in center of tray, additional product info below wagon image, 4⅞", excellent, **$275.00 (B).**

Betty Rose, Coats and Suits, painted wood sign, with cut out lettering, 24" X 5¼", excellent, **$65.00 (D).**

Bing Crosby Ice Cream, wax cardboard container featuring artwork of Bing Crosby on front, NOS, pint, near-mint, **$25.00 (C).**

Black Cat Stove and Shoe Polish, celluloid and metal bill hook, celluloid button has graphics of black cat in center, 2¼" dia., near-mint, **$138.00 (B).**

Bob White Baking Powder, paper litho over tin can, never opened, with artwork of bobwhite quail on front, 2⅛" X 3¼", near-mint, **$200.00 (B).**

Borden's Ice Cream, painted metal advertising sign with artwork of Elsie at left of message, 24" X 15", excellent, **$350.00 (C).**

Borden's...The Malted Milk In The Square Package, round metal tip tray with artwork of woman with product package, 4½" dia., excellent, **$230.00 (B).**

Bowey's...Hot Chocolate Powder, tin litho container with small canister lid, graphics of hot chocolate being served, 7" X 10", near-mint, **$70.00 (B).**

Brach's Swing, Swing's the thing, two-part candy box with graphics of majorette twirling baton, 1930s, 9" X 9" X 1½", excellent, **$31.00 (B).**

Bright Globe Range, round metal tip tray with graphics of product on tray center, 4⅛" dia., excellent, **$160.00 (B).**

Bromo-Seltzer for Headaches, embossed tin advertising sign, 20" X 9", near-mint, **$65.00 (B).**

Buddhsa Talcum, Lingering Oriental Fragrance, tin litho container with artwork of Buddha image on front, 16-oz., near-mint, **$30.00 (B).**

BullBrand Feeds...Maritime Milling Co., Inc., Buffalo, NY..., metal tip tray with artwork of bull on tray center, 6⅝" L, excellent, **$75.00 (B).**

Bunte Rabida Dark Caramels, two piece cardboard candy box with factory scenes on both sides, 7½" X 11" X 3½", excellent, **$25.00 (B).**

Buster Brown Shoe Company, calendar with image of Buster and Tige in center of monthly pages and underwater scene at top, 8½" X 19", near-mint, **$40.00 (B).**

Buster Brown Shoes, advertising plate, 5½" dia., near-mint, **$150.00 (C).**

Buster Brown Shoes, bandana, 1940s, excellent, **$75.00 (C).**

Buster Brown Shoes, bas-relief plaster advertising sign with Buster Brown and Tige, 1940s, 17" round, near-mint, **$320.00 (B).**

Campbell's Soup, potholder, with Campbell's kids on surface, good, **$15.00 (D).**

Campfire Marshmallows..., the original food, round tin container with lid, good, **$15.00 (D).**

Candee Rubbers, hanging cardboard sign with graphics of puppy being chased by young girl, 10½" X 12½", near-mint, **$85.00 (B).**

Candee Shoes, hanging cardboard advertising sign from McCord Rubber Co., Chicago, Ill., graphics of kids playing with kittens, 1910s, 10" X 12½", excellent, **$165.00 (B).**

Candy Bros., Fruit Juice Tablets, Always Fresh, tin litho advertising serving tray with artwork of bottles of product, 13¾" X 16¾", excellent, **$925.00 (B).**

Cardui, advertising fan, with graphics of woman on couch on front side, product messages on reverse side, wooden handle, excellent, **$7.00 (D).**

Carmen Condom, early tin litho with great graphic of pin-up girl with fan and shawl, good strong colors, 1⅝" X ⅝", excellent, **$170.00 (B).**

Carnation Gum...Chew Dorne's, "Taste the Smell," tin litho tip tray with artwork of carnations, 4⅜" dia., excellent, **$475.00 (B).**

Carter's Alma Infants Underwear, die cut cardboard easel back store advertising sign with image of young child over message, 14" X 15½", excellent, **$423.00 (B).**

Carter's Infants Underwear, cardboard easel back die cut advertising sign with artwork of infant over message, 14" X 16", excellent, **$220.00 (B).**

Carter's Infants Underwear, cardboard easel back store advertising sign with young child playing with tin climbing monkey, 14½" X 18¾", excellent, **$400.00 (B).**

Carter's Union Suits for Boys, cardboard die cut easel back store advertising sign featuring young boy with scooter, 14" X 15½", near-mint, **$341.00 (B).**

Carter's Union Suits for Girls, easel back die cut cardboard sign with graphics of young girl writing on blackboard, 1910, 15" X 14", near-mint, **$645.00 (B).**

Caterpillar, metal watch fob, picture of dozer on one side and earth scraper on reverse, excellent, **$25.00 (C).**

Celloloid Starch...Mail Trade Marks to...Premium Dept. Philadelphia, cardboard advertising sign with graphics of young girl ironing, 14" X 12½", excellent, **$100.00 (B).**

Ceresota Flour, match holder, bread box style, image of young boy sitting on stool on top of product, 3" X 6", near-mint, **$230.00 (B).**

Chappell's Milk, metal and plastic light-up clock, 16" X 16", gold, red and yellow, excellent, **$165.00 (C).**

Chariots, condom tin with artwork of racing chariot on cover, 2⅛" X 1⅝" X ¼", excellent, **$180.00 (B).**

Chattanooga & St. Louis, spittoon with raised lettering, made of cast iron and porcelain, excellent, **$225.00 (C).**

Cinderella Ice Cream, Tickles Your Tummy, Henderson Creamery Co. Inc., cardboard sign with artwork of young child sitting on steps with bowl of product, 14" X 10½", good, **$95.00 (D).**

Citizen's Coal Company...Our Modern Coal Pocket Insures Clean Coal, round metal tip tray with artwork of head shot of deer with large rack in center, 4¼" dia., excellent, **$30.00 (B).**

Clark Bar...4pm Clark Bar, wooden thermometer with image of product at top of scale, 1920s, 5¼" X 19", excellent, **$125.00 (B).**

Clark's Honest Square, two piece candy box with artwork of elves making candy, 110" X 11" X 2½", excellent, **$28.00 (B).**

Clark's Zagnut...A Real Treat, display case decal featuring product bar both wrapped and unwrapped, 9" X 5", excellent, **$30.00 (B).**

Clinton and Damascus Steel Safety Pins, Oakville Company, Waterbury, Ct., tip tray, graphics of hand holding product, 4½" X 6", excellent, **$85.00 (B).**

Cloverleaf Milk...Famous for Purity, metal frame with bubble glass front, 16½" dia., excellent, **$55.00 (B).**

Cochran, paint products painted metal sign, featuring artwork of paint can man running & spilling paint with message-Made better last longer, 36" X 24", good, **$45.00 (D).**

Colgate's Baby Talc, sample tin litho with graphics of young child on front with screw-on lid, near-mint, **$137.00 (B).**

Colgate's Dactylis Talc Powder, sample tin litho with artwork of young girl on front, near-mint, **$88.00 (B).**

Collins Axe, hanging cardboard sign with graphics of axe and globe, "The Best is the Cheapest," 1915, 10" X 20", near-mint, **$51.00 (B).**

Collins Baking Co., calendar in diamond configuration with tear sheets at bottom of picture, with message of Collins Celebrated Bread, 1909, 8" X 8", excellent, **$55.00 (D).**

Colonial Bread...is good, painted metal door push, adjustable, 36" X 3½", excellent, **$65.00 (D).**

Comfort Talc Powder, tin litho can with artwork of nurse in early uniform, 2" X 3⅜", excellent, **$600.00 (B).**

Consolidated Biscuit Co., biscuit box, shaped like two-story house, with product message on chimney, cardboard, 1932, 9" X 8½" X 5", excellent, **$85.00 (B).**

Consolidated Ice Company, dresser mirror with winter scene on back, excellent, **$80.00 (B).**

Continental Life Insurance Company, metal tip tray, with picture of skyscraper on face, excellent, **$75.00 (C).**

Continental Life Insurance Company...Saint Louis, round metal tip tray with artwork of insurance building in tray center, 4¼" dia., excellent, **$25.00 (B).**

Continental Trailways Bus Depot, porcelain one sided sign, 36" X 18", white & black on red, excellent, **$135.00 (C).**

Corylopsis Talcum Powder Page, tin litho container, with artwork of geisha girl kneeling on front side of container, near-mint, **$193.00 (B).**

Crescent Macaroni, tin lunch pail with wire handles, good, **$65.00 (D).**

Cresota Flour...Prize bread of the world, tin die cut litho match holder with unusual vertical match pocket, 5½" X 2⅜", near-mint, **$575.00 (B).**

Crispo Lily Sodas...Lily Biscuit Co., Chicago, cracker tin with lid, red and white striped, good, **$35.00 (D).**

Crosley Radios and Home Appliances, neon advertising sign, metal back with glass front, good, **$525.00 (D).**

Cunningham's Ice Cream, The Factory Behind The Products, metal serving tray with graphics of manufacturing factory in center, oval-shaped, 1917, 18½" X 15", excellent, **$110.00 (B).**

D. Agostini...Confectionary-Home Made-Ice Cream, paper calendar with metal top and bottom strips, images of American and Italian Lady Liberty, 15½" X 22", excellent, **$55.00 (B).**

Dairy Brand...Ice Cream...New York vanilla, half-gallon round tin, excellent, **$20.00 (C).**

Dairy Brand, Milk-Ice Cream, light-up sign, metal back with reverse painted glass front, 1950s, 25¾" X 6¾", good, **$250.00 (C).**

Dandro Solvent...for dandruff and beautifying the hair, beveled edge tin over cardboard easel back, featuring product bottle in hand at right of message, 13" X 9", near-mint, **$175.00 (B).**

De-Luxe Blue-Ribbon, tin litho condom container with artwork of German shepherd on front cover, 1¾" X 2⅛" X ¼", excellent, **$725.00 (B).**

Decker Bros. Pianos, heavy paper advertising sign featuring graphics of young girl surrounded by a floral wreath, 1882, excellent, **$96.00 (B).**

DeLaval Cream Separator, Jacob Bender, Sutton, Nebr., calendar top with great artwork of young boy with black dog in wagon, 1922, 12" X 19", excellent, **$85.00 (B).**

DeLaval Cream Separators...The World's Standard, round metal tip tray with graphics of woman and child at product, 4¼" dia., excellent, **$140.00 (B).**

DeLaval, die cut tin separator match holder, in shape of product, 4" X 6½", excellent, **$275.00 (B).**

DeLaval Milker, decal on metal, lacquered double sided sign, 1940s, 4¼" X 20", excellent, **$120.00 (B).**

DeLaval...We use...better farm living, better farm income, painted metal sign, good, **$75.00 (D).**

DeWitt's Tonic Pills, easel back cardboard store advertising sign with graphics of fish and yellow-slickered fisherman, 13" X 21", good, **$235.00 (B).**

Diamond Dyes...Fast Colors...Domestic & Fancy Dyeing, wooden dye cabinet, front door cover has tin litho evolution theme, excellent, **$850.00 (C).**

Dixon's Stove Polish, Lime Kiln Club, trade card with graphics of sales pitch for product, 1886, 5" X 6¼", near-mint, **$50.00 (B).**

Doe-Wah-Jack, Round Oak Stove, calendar with full pad of monthly tear sheets, featuring embossed artwork of Indian with peace pipe, 1924, 10½" X 21", excellent, **$330.00 (B).**

Domestic Sewing Machine, paper litho advertising sign, "This is the machine that I'll have..." 1890s, 14" X 20", excellent, **$121.00 (B).**

Donald Duck Florida Orange Juice, can with paper label with likeness of Donald Duck looking around juice glass, 1-qt., excellent, **$25.00 (B).**

Double Tip, Distributed By Department Sales, Co., New York, NY, condom tin with litho of woman sitting at water's edge, 2¼" X 1⅝", excellent, **$750.00 (B).**

Dr. A.C. Daniels, heavy cardboard sign with artwork of horses in center inset with the message surrounding the artwork, 13⅞" X 19⅝", excellent, **$650.00 (B).**

Dr. A.C. Daniels Veterinary Medicine, wooden advertising thermometer, 5⅝" X 24" X ¾", good, **$300.00 (B).**

Dr. Palmers Almomeal Compound, tin litho container in original box with great art of pretty red-haired woman on front, near-mint, **$25.00 (B).**

Dr. Shoop's Health Coffee, tin litho match safe with great graphics of product package, never used, 3½" X 4⅞", near-mint, **$375.00 (B).**

Dr. White's Cough Drops...extremely pleasant, tin litho with hinged top container for product, hard-to-find item, 3½" X 2¼" X ¾", excellent, **$600.00 (B).**

Dreibus Juanette Chocolates, die cut easel back cardboard store advertising sign with woman in bonnet, 8" X 14", excellent, **$47.00 (B).**

Dunham's Cocoanut, die cut paper advertising with graphics of lady with cake, 1915, 13" X 11", near-mint, **$84.00 (B).**

E.F. Young Jr. Pressing Oil, hair dressing oil to be used when pressing hair to keep hair from catching fire, graphics of young black woman, 152 oz., excellent, **$55.00 (D).**

Edison Mazda, calendar advertising light bulbs, 1926, 18" X 30", excellent, **$1,300.00 (C).**

Edison Mazda Lamps, cardboard calendar with Parrish-style litho of young girl in chair reading with full calendar pad, 1917, 4" X 9", excellent, **$175.00 (C).**

Edison-Mazda...Name your car...I'll light it, service station counter display box with great artwork of woman holding box of bulbs, excellent, **$695.00 (D).**

Edison Phonograph, advertising sign featuring litho of woman listening to product, 20¾" X 28", excellent, **$3,100.00 (B).**

Elgin Watches...Arthur J. Nyman and Sons Jewelers, round light-up advertising clock with message in center, number positions occupied by silver points, red, white, and cream, excellent, **$350.00 (D).**

Empire Cream Separator Company...Fisher Building, Chicago, ILL, paper calendar top with artwork of mother and daughter, 1902, 12" X 20", excellent, **$137.00 (B).**

Empress Toilet Powder...Empress Powder Co., New York, NY, tin litho sample size can, 1⅝" X 2⅜" X ⅞", excellent, **$450.00 (B).**

Eveready and Mazda Lamps, product cabinet with graphics of batteries being placed in flashlight, 11" X 9" X 11½", excellent, **$195.00 (B).**

Ex-Lax...the chocolate laxative...millions prefer..., porcelain thermometer with vertical scale in center, excellent, **$135.00 (D).**

Eye-Fix...The Great Eye Remedy, round metal tip tray with artwork of woman being attended by angel image, 4⅛" dia., excellent, **$250.00 (B).**

Fairy..."Have You a Little Fairy in Your Home," die cut cardboard easel back ad sign with fairy on bar of soap, 19" X 23½", near-mint, **$1,850.00 (B).**

Fairy Soap...Have You a Little Fairy In Your Home?, round metal tip tray with artwork of little girl sitting on bar of product, 4⅛" dia., excellent, **$65.00 (B).**

Fanny Farmer, candy container, tin litho in cylinder shape, graphics of Uncle Sam, 1944, 3" X 10", excellent, **$120.00 (B).**

Feen-a-mint...for constipation, porcelain sign with artwork of product blocks tumbling out of package, 29¼" X 7", fair, **$65.00 (C).**

Feen-a-Mint...The Chewing Laxative, Chew It Like Gum, advertising store display holder with artwork of woman on front holding product, excellent, **$395.00 (C).**

Flexo chocolate and vanilla flavored confection, National Licorice Co., two piece box with art of men in row boat off tropical beach, 12" X 8" X 3½", excellent, **$55.00 (B).**

Florist Telegraph Delivery...Interflora-worldwide, with FTD runner in center of message, light-up advertising clock, metal back with curved glass front, 16" X 16", excellent, **$125.00 (D).**

Foley Kidney Pills, porcelain oval door push plate, excellent, **$330.00 (B).**

Fort Bedford P-Nuts 5¢...Does the party on the other side want..., advertising pocket mirror with artwork of box of product on cover, 1¾" dia., excellent, **$300.00 (B).**

Franklin Baker Company (Inc.), Snowdrift Coconut..., sweetened fancy shred, round tin container with paper label, 12" x 14½", excellent, **$35.00 (D).**

Franklin Glass & Mirror, advertising pocket mirror, 3½" dia., excellent, **$25.00 (C).**

Fun-To-Wash Washing Powder, in unopened box with "Mammy" on front, excellent, **$82.00 (B).**

G-E Mazda Lamps...Avoid Bulbsnatching, three-dimensional cardboard store display with original real bulb, 8½" X 12¾", good, **$35.00 (D).**

Garland Stoves and Ranges, cardboard litho advertising sign featuring artwork of boy and dog, 10¼" X 14", excellent, **$925.00 (B).**

Geo. E. Sawyer's Electric Cough Drops, tin litho display box which originally held 5¢ packages, 8½" X 7¼" X 4¼", excellent, **$375.00 (B).**

German Fire Insurance Company...Pittsburgh, Pa., cardboard calendar with patriotic theme, 1905, 10½" X 13½", excellent, **$45.00 (B).**

Gillette Blue Blades 10 for 50¢, metal coin operated dispenser, works only with solid 50¢ pieces, 1950s, near-mint, **$125.00 (D).**

Gillette Safety Razor, celluloid advertising pocket mirror with artwork of baby using razor, with 1909 calendar around outside of artwork, 2¼" dia., excellent, **$160.00 (B).**

Gillette Safety Razor...No Stropping! No Honing!, advertising pocket mirror with 1913 mirror, 2⅛" dia., excellent, **$140.00 (B).**

Gold Cross Talc, tin litho foot powder container, 4½" X 2½", excellent, **$180.00 (B).**

Gold Dust...For Spring House Cleaning, trolley car sign with artwork of house cleaning in progress, 26" X 10½", near-mint, **$1,200.00 (B).**

Gold Dust, sheet music for "Twins Rag," graphics of twins at piano and dancing, excellent, **$25.00 (B).**

Gold Dust Washing Powder, cardboard trade cards with images of twins in wash tub, 3" X 3¾", near-mint, **$71.00 (B).**

Gold Tip Gum...Peppermint, Sterling Mint Co., Inc., New York, cardboard gum package, excellent, **$20.00 (D).**

Gold-Pak, Crown Rubber Co., Akron, OH, litho condom tin...3 for $1.00, 1½" X 2", excellent, **$400.00 (B).**

Gordon's Fresh Foods, Truck Serving The Best, clear glass store jar with original metal lid, 7½" dia., excellent, **$130.00 (C).**

Gordon's Fresh Potato Chips, round metal potato chip can with artwork of old panel delivery truck over message, 11¼" tall, excellent, **$65.00 (C).**

Gorton's Codfish...Eat...in cans ready to use, porcelain door push, 6" X 3½", excellent, **$525.00 (B).**

Grains of Gold, Scientifically Prepared Breakfast Cereal, cardboard box with graphics of wheat grains on box, 1929, 20-oz., excellent, **$10.00 (D).**

Greyhound, light-up wall advertising clock, excellent, **$145.00 (D).**

Greyhound Lines, porcelain station sign with artwork of running dog in center, 36" X 20½", excellent, **$250.00 (D).**

Griffon Safety Razor, tin litho container, 1⅜" X 2¼", excellent, **$220.00 (B).**

Griffon Safety Razor, tin with artwork of man shaving with product, 1¾" X 2¼" X 1⅛", excellent, **$600.00 (B).**

Gruen Watch Time...Post's Jewelry Store, light-up advertising clock, with local message on bottom, ad on plate, excellent, **$425.00 (C).**

Hamilton Brown Shoe Co...Agency, Keep the quality up, painted metal die cut flange sign, 19½" X 14", fair, **$45.00 (D).**

Hamilton Brown Shoe Co...American Lady Show, American Gentleman Shoe, paper poster with couple in period dress, 29¾" X 39¾", excellent, **$250.00 (C).**

Hanson's Drug Store, advertising cardboard die cut calendar for Hanson's Headache Powders, with artwork of young woman in straw Panama hat, 1903, 7¼" X 13", near-mint, **$75.00 (B).**

Harding Cream Co...Cash For Cream, double sided die cut porcelain flange sign shaped like old milk can, 15" X 27", excellent, **$1,700.00 (B).**

Hart Brand Canned Foods, beveled tin litho over cardboard, string hung advertising sign with artwork of product cans, 13" X 9", excellent, **$850.00 (B).**

Hatchway Union Suits, cardboard box with graphics of man walking in product with robe over arm, 1915, 10" X 15" X 1½", excellent, **$30.00 (B).**

Have Some Junket, round metal tip tray with small girl with a bowl of product, 4¼" dia., excellent, **$90.00 (B).**

Heath & Milligan...Sunshine Finishes, tip tray with graphics of two children and dog on floor, 4¼" dia., good, **$55.00 (B).**

Heinsohn Bros. Dairy, calendar, paper calendar with full month pad and original metal strips on top and bottom, artwork of baby in highchair, 1927, 15" X 19½", excellent, **$30.00 (B).**

Hendlers Ice Cream, die cut window display with graphics of ice cream cones with message inside, 1950s, 36" X 23", near-mint, **$45.00 (B).**

Henkel's, pot scraper, tin litho scraper advertising Henkel's Flour, 3¼" X 3", red, blue and white, excellent, **$300.00 (B).**

Heptol Splits...For Health's Sake...Laxative, round metal tip tray with graphics of cowboy riding bucking bronc, 4⅛" dia., good, **$170.00 (B).**

Hershey's Gum, 6 sticks for 5¢ cents, cardboard blotter, 5⅝" X 2⅞", excellent, **$475.00 (B).**

Hickman's Silver Birch Chewing Gum, cardboard store display complete with unopened gum packs, artwork of bird on birch limb, 6¼" X 5¼" X 4¼", excellent, **$1,200.00 (B).**

Hicks Capudine...Its Liquid-effects immediately...10¢, 25¢, and 50¢ cents a bottle, round metal tip tray with graphics of product in tray center, 6" dia., excellent, **$160.00 (B).**

Highland Evaporated Cream, metal tip tray with graphics of cream can in center of tray, 3⅝" dia., excellent, **$120.00 (B).**

Hoffman's Ice Cream...First Choice...Sealtest Approved, die cut porcelain outdoor advertising sign on original metal hanging arm, 25¾" X 22", good, **$175.00 (D).**

Holman's Trailing Arbutus Face Powder, tin litho container designed to be used as trinket box after product is used, 1915, excellent, **$50.00 (D).**

Home Lighting and Cooking Plant...The Incandescent Light and Stove Co., Cincinnati, OH, round metal tip tray with graphics of early kitchen scene, 4⅛" dia., excellent, **$260.00 (B).**

Honey-Fruit Gum...Nothing Like It...Delightful Flavor, tin litho over cardboard, American artworks, 9⅛" X 6¼", excellent, **$2,500.00 (B).**

Horlick's Malted Milk, advertising pocket mirror with graphics of young girl with calf, 2" dia., excellent, **$85.00 (B).**

Horlick's Malted Milk, tin litho with small canister top lid, graphics of cow on front, #10 can, excellent, **$45.00 (B).**

Hoyt & Co., Buffalo Peanut Butter, tin litho pail with wire bail handle, 3¾" X 3¼", excellent, **$325.00 (B).**

Hygienic Kalsomine...Germ proof your walls, cardboard hanging store sign featuring images of housewife and painter, 1909, 11" X 15", excellent, **$47.00 (B).**

Illinois Bell Telephone Company...American Telephone & Telegraph Co., double sided porcelain flange, 12" X 11", near-mint, **$159.00 (B).**

Illinois Watch Company, framed print showing factory scene, 24½" X 16½", excellent, **$75.00 (D).**

Independent Radio and TV Service, round light-up clock with message in center of clock face, 16" dia., excellent, **$75.00 (D).**

Independent Stove Co., Owosso, Mich., cast iron enameled advertising paperweight in shape of alligator, 5½" L, near-mint, **$118.00 (B).**

Interwoven Socks, paper-linen advertising featuring artwork of woman in overstuffed chair knitting, by Norman Rockwell, 28" X 38", excellent, **$95.00 (C).**

J & P Coats...Spool Cotton...Best Six Cord...For hand & machine, painted hardboard, framed, 18" X 30", fair, **$325.00 (D).**

Jack Sanitary Barber Shop, litho on paper with image of a bare-breasted woman who is scantily dressed, great strong colors, 1890s, 14" X 20", near-mint, **$325.00 (B).**

Jackie Coogan salted nut Meal, tin litho container from Dixie Peanut Products with graphics of Coogan on elephant, 8" X 10", excellent, **$210.00 (B).**

Jap Rose Talcum Powder, sample size tin litho with graphics of Japanese girl on front, excellent, **$59.00 (B).**

Jap Rose Soap...Kirk's...Toilet, Bath, Shampoo, cobalt porcelain advertising thermometer, scarce, 1915, excellent, **$260.00 (B).**

Jaw Teasers Bubble Gum, tin litho pail with handle and graphics of gum ball on sides, 5" X 7½", excellent, **$54.00 (B).**

Jaxon Soap, cast iron advertising item in shape of rendering kettle with hole in bottom used for string holder, with embossed product lettering, 4½" X 4½", excellent, **$75.00 (B).**

Jayne's Hair Tonic, paper on cardboard store sign with graphics of women admiring their hair and product message, 1880s, 12" X 15", excellent, **$147.00 (B).**

Jergens Crushed Violet Talcum Powder, tin litho container, with graphics of flower on front, excellent, **$40.00 (B).**

Jersey Creme, die cut string hung cardboard ad sign of two girls in swing reading product ad, excellent, **$43.00 (B).**

Jersey Ice Cream, double sided porcelain advertising sign with graphics of product sandwich on saucer, 20" X 28", excellent, **$120.00 (B).**

John D. Jr. hand soap, tin container, 3-lb., good, **$20.00 (D).**

Johnson and Melaa's Dry Goods, Stoughton, WI, tip tray with graphics of young black child eating watermelon, 2½" X 3¼", excellent, **$165.00 (B).**

Johnson Bros. Funeral Directors...Call Our Ambulance Phone 45, Boaz, Ky., painted metal thermometer with vertical scale between messages, 1910 – 1920s, 8½" X 38½", white on blue, fair, **$85.00 (C).**

Johnson Halter Store, advertising sign, papier-maché horse head equipped with product message embossed in halter, 23" X 21" X 10", excellent, **$425.00 (B).**

Johnson & Johnson...Baby Needs..., molded pressboard with message stenciled and decal of J & J baby in center, 32" X 6", excellent, **$50.00 (B).**

Johnson & Johnson...For Babies, cardboard advertising sign, featuring graphics of baby in diaper under moonlit sky with product box, 14½" X 22", good, **$95.00 (D).**

Johnston Milwaukee, Charm Soda Crackers, cardboard box, 1-lb., excellent, **$15.00 (D).**

Jolly Pops, Those Good Suckers 1¢, metal dispenser with artwork of sunburst on front, 9½" X 20", green panel on red background, excellent, **$105.00 (D).**

Jones Dairy Farm Sausage, tin over cardboard advertising sign with graphics of product farm building and snow-covered tree, 12" X 8", excellent, **$86.00 (B).**

Keen Kutter...E.C Simmons...Cutlery, Tools, die cut cardboard ad in shape of Keen Kutter logo, 10¼" X 13", excellent, **$35.00 (C).**

Keen Kutter Tools...Hank Bros., Paducah, Ky., painted embossed metal sign with logo at left of message, 27" X 10", excellent, **$125.00 (C).**

Kellogg's Corn Flakes, cardboard war-time box with small identification of three fighter planes, "let's go USA keep 'em flying," 1940s, 11-oz., excellent, **$95.00 (D).**

Kellogg's, paper doll cut out of "Daddy Bear" holding cereal box, uncut, 1925, near-mint, **$82.00 (B).**

Kellogg's Rice Crispies...Snap Crackle Pop, cardboard box with graphics of three Krispie creatures, 1948, 5½-oz., excellent, **$50.00 (B).**

Kentucky Cardinal 1¢, match dispenser, with paper label of two birds, in working order, 6" X 13" X 5"", excellent, **$375.00 (D).**

Keystone Ice Cream, outdoor hanging porcelain advertising sign with original extension arm, 28" X 20", excellent, **$155.00 (C).**

King Arthur Flour...Minnesota, double sided heavy porcelain sign with artwork of the king on his horse, 17⅞" X 17⅞", excellent, **$1,050.00 (B).**

Kingan's Butterine, tin litho sign with man being served product with meal, 1920s, excellent, **$33.00 (B).**

Kings Peanut Butter, tin litho pail with graphics of king with product in hand, 1-lb., excellent, **$786.00 (B).**

Kirkman's Floating Soap, heavy paper trolley car sign with great graphics of bar of soap to left of message, 21" X 11", excellent, **$145.00 (C).**

Kis-Me, Yellow Kid, chewing gum die cut cardboard advertising sign of the yellow kid walking while holding a leather satchel with product name on side of case, 3" X 6½", excellent, **$925.00 (B).**

Kleinert's Dress Shield Guimpe, pocket advertising pocket mirror with artwork of product on back side, 2" dia., excellent, **$44.00 (B).**

Knapsack Matches, tin box one cent, wood, metal and glass dispenser, 10" X 10½", excellent, **$675.00 (C).**

Knox Gelatin, litho with great detail, images of older black woman with young girl working on dessert at table, double matted and framed, 1901, 26" X 20", near-mint, **$1,250.00 (B).**

Kodak...Verichrome, safety film, heavy porcelain sign in shape of box of film, 24½" X 12½", excellent, **$250.00 (C).**

Kreger's Bakery and Ice Cream Parlor, calendar with artwork of two young girls on burro being led by young boy, paper litho, 1907, 15" X 20", excellent, **$75.00 (C).**

L.E. Graybill, paper three-dimensional calendar with die cut scene of animals in background with tear sheets at bottom, 1923, 15" X 15", excellent, **$25.00 (D).**

L.S. DuBois, Son & Co., Wholesale Druggist, Paducah, Ky., crock jug with block advertising on front, brown top with cream bottom, excellent, **$135.00 (C).**

Ladies' Home Journal...for spring fashion read..., framed cloth banner with artwork of Irene Bordoni at left of message, 46" X 34", excellent, **$325.00 (D).**

Lance...From the House of Lance, clear glass store jar, Lance embossed on both sides of handle on top and on bottom of jar, 7" X 8½", excellent, **$85.00 (C).**

Lance, our 75th anniversary, store jar with original glass lid, excellent, **$100.00 (D).**

Land O'Lakes, tin litho thermometer, graphics of Indian maid at bottom of vertical scale, 1960s, near-mint, **$90.00 (B).**

Lane Cedar Chest, die cut easel back cardboard store sign, with graphics of moth in clothes drawer, 19" X 29¾", excellent, **$47.00 (B).**

Lava Soap, cardboard fan pull, double sided with artwork of product in center, 11" sq., excellent, **$60.00 (B).**

Lax-ets...candy bowel laxative, celluloid sign, 17" X 14", excellent, **$400.00 (B).**

Laxol...Castor Oil...Like Honey, round metal tip tray with artwork of product bottle, 4¼" dia., excellent, **$65.00 (B).**

Lee Overalls, die cut cardboard store advertising sign, with graphics of young boy in overalls holding hammer, 10" T, excellent, **$90.00 (B).**

Lee Riders, double sided sign with man riding on bucking bronc, 17½" dia., excellent, **$200.00 (B).**

Leopold: The Clothier, Miffinburg, PA, round metal tip tray with scolloped edges and artwork of three white horses in tray center, 4¼" dia., excellent, **$175.00 (D).**

Levenson Hair Shop, celluloid pocket advertising mirror with artwork of red-haired woman on front, 1¾" X 2¾", excellent, **$250.00 (B).**

Liberty Ice Cream...superior Improved, rectangular hard plastic serving tray, excellent, **$18.00 (D).**

Life Savers, tin litho three-tier store display rack would display 9 different flavors, 1920s, 15½" X 14" X 10", excellent, **$600.00 (B).**

Lily White...Bias Fold Tape...Extra Fine Quality, metal store counter display, 15" X 8¼" X 8", good, **$35.00 (D).**

Lions International, porcelain sign with lions' heads on both sides of message, 30" dia., excellent, **$150.00 (D).**

Litchfield Ice Cream, metal-framed plastic front advertising sign, good, **$145.00 (D).**

Little Giant Elevators, farm equipment, painted metal sign with artwork of giant holding ball with farm equipment, excellent, **$85.00 (C).**

Loft Brand Midget Candy Sticks, tin litho with artwork of children feeding candy stick to squirrel, 6" X 4¾", excellent, **$300.00 (B).**

Log Cabin Frontier Inn, with graphics of people on front porch with horse tied to rail, 5-lb., near-mint, **$207.00 (B).**

Log Cabin Syrup, quart-size syrup container with boy at door in blue and hat, tin litho, 1914, excellent, **$75.00 (B).**

Log Cabin Syrup, table-sized tin litho container with graphics of boy in black at door, 1914, excellent, **$75.00 (B).**

Log Cabin Syrup, tin litho container with graphics of boy in blue with hat, table size, 1914, excellent, **$70.00 (B).**

Log Cabin Syrup, tin litho table-sized container, frontier house bank, excellent, **$88.00 (B).**

Log Cabin–Frontier Jail, tin litho syrup container, near-mint, **$141.00 (B).**

Log Cabin–Stockade School, tin litho syrup container with graphics of children playing in front of school, near-mint, **$187.00 (B).**

Lowney's Cocoa, sample tin litho can with graphics of Victorian woman on front, 1⅝" X 1⅜" X 1", excellent, **$250.00 (B).**

Luden's Cough Drops...Give Instant Relief, Reading, Penna., round metal tip tray with graphics of early cough drop box, 3½" dia., excellent, **$900.00 (B).**

Ludwig Pianos...New York, round, metal tip tray with artwork of pretty woman, 4¼" dia., excellent, **$45.00 (B).**

Magic Leather Belt...No Binding-No Pressure, die cut tin litho on wood store bin, with graphics of man with belt, 1915, 15" X 14¼" X 4", excellent, **$200.00 (B).**

Magnolia Brand Condensed Milk, Bordon's Condensed Milk Co., N.Y., wooden box with embossed block painted letters, 19" X 7" X 13", excellent, **$35.00 (C).**

Maine Sardine Council, 4th Boy Scout Jamboree Special, tin litho container, 1957, 4-oz., excellent, **$130.00 (B).**

Manuel Silvia, die cut calendar from Newport, RI, Boot, Shoe and Rubbers retailer with great artwork of woman and two young girls, 1905, 12½" X 18", near-mint, **$325.00 (B).**

Mason & Stout, city bill posters reverse painted glass in wood frame, 23½" X 19½", excellent, **$135.00 (C).**

Master is Good Bread, embossed tin double sided door push bar, 3" X 29½", excellent, **$80.00 (B).**

Masury Paints-Varnishes...Masury is Good Paint, artwork of English-style soldier in spotlight at lower left of message, painted metal, 36" X 24", good, **$35.00 (D).**

McCormick Bee Brand...teas, spices, extracts, drugs..., celluloid pocket advertising mirror, 1¾" X 2⅞", excellent, **$800.00 (B).**

McCormick-Deering Farm Machines, painted tin sign, 27½" X 10", excellent, **$95.00 (C).**

McCulloch Chain Saws, dial-type thermometer, reverse on bubble glass, 1950s, 14" dia., near-mint, **$100.00 (B).**

Meadow Gold...Vanilla Ice Cream, round half-gallon ice cream tin, excellent, **$15.00 (D).**

Melox Dog Food...The Foods that Nourish, porcelain sign with artwork of dog on Melox ball, 18" X 26", excellent, **$525.00 (C).**

Merion, Hair Net, metal store display box of bobbed hair woman with mirror on lid, good, **$95.00 (D).**

MH & M shoes, embossed tin sign die cut in the shape of an arm and hand, 28" X 6½", black on yellow, excellent, **$225.00 (C).**

Michigan Stove Co., "Michigan Stove Co. Stoves are the best," cast iron match holder, 4" X 7", excellent, **$215.00 (B).**

Mickey Mouse Cookies from Nabisco, cardboard box with string carrier, graphics of Mickey Mouse on side, 1940s, 6" X 3" X 2", excellent, **$165.00 (B).**

Millers Falls...The safest name in tools, metal framed plastic front light-up sign, 25" X 8", good, **$55.00 (C).**

Miss Minneapolis, Highest Quality Flour, die cut menu board shows girl holding blackboard, 1918, 19" X 28", excellent, **$45.00 (B).**

Missouri Pacific Lines, paper railroad calendar with tear sheets at bottom, featuring artwork of steam engine moving on tracks, no year, only daily sheets, good, **$135.00 (C).**

Missouri Smoking Pipes, blister pack from country store with full sheet of pipes, NOS, excellent, **$50.00 (D).**

Modern Girl...Beautiful Stockings, box with artwork of woman pulling on stockings, 7½" X 9¾" X 1½", excellent, **$20.00 (D).**

Modern Home Series...Peaslee-Gaulbert Co...Louisville, Ky., oval metal tip tray with graphics of room setting in tray center, 6¼", good, **$40.00 (B).**

Mojud...Thigh-Mold, stretch top garter belt store display, 11" X 11½", excellent, **$100.00 (D).**

Monadnock Peanut Butter, tin litho pail with wire handles on side, graphics of lake scene in center, 1-lb., excellent, **$236.00 (B).**

Monarch...green tea, tin with lid, artwork of tea pot on front, excellent, **$12.00 (D).**

Morrell's Boiled Ham, string hung double sided litho with image of ham being lifted out of cauldron being watched by sad pig, 1900s, 10¼" X 11¼", near-mint, **$333.00 (B).**

Morrell's Pride Meats, pocket advertising mirror, 2" dia., excellent, **$40.00 (B).**

Morris Supreme Peanut Butter, tin litho pail with scene of children at beach, 12-oz., excellent, **$75.00 (B).**

Motorola Service...Car Radio, painted metal sign, good, **$135.00 (D).**

Mr. Peanut, ashtray with image of Mr. Peanut standing behind ashtray shell, bisque composition, 4½" X 3", near-mint, **$40.00 (B).**

Mr. Peanut, plastic figural peanut butter maker, complete with box, 12½" tall, excellent, **$45.00 (C).**

Mr. Peanut, plastic head display store jar, 7½" X 12", excellent, **$65.00 (D).**

Munsing Union Suits, cardboard easel back of youngster with chalkboard, Northwest Knitting Co., 1907, excellent, **$220.00 (B).**

Munsing Wear...Ask for...Fashion Books Take One, store counter display container, with artwork of woman and child, 12" X 14", excellent, **$800.00 (B).**

Munsing Wear...Ask For...Fashion Books Take One, wood frame base tin litho store bin, 12" X 15" X 15", excellent, **$350.00 (B).**

Munsing Wear, cardboard easel back store advertising sign with image of woman at table with flowers, 20" X 30", excellent, **$82.00 (B).**

Munyon's Homeopathic Home Remedy, tin litho store cabinet with 10 drawers, artwork of product salesman on top, excellent, **$506.00 (B).**

My Baby's Talc...Sears Roebuck and Co., tin litho powder container with good strong colors with artwork of cherub on both sides, 2¼" X 6" X 1¼", excellent, **$400.00 (B).**

Nabisco Shredded Wheat, biscuit box with presidential offer on front, cardboard, 1949, 12-oz., 12-biscuit, excellent, **$25.00 (B).**

Naples Velvet Finish...Adams & Elting Co., paper on cardboard advertising sign, artwork of rabbit with pointer showing off different colors, 1920s, 16" X 9", excellent, **$110.00 (B).**

Napoleon's, litho condom tin with artwork of crossed swords, complete with original products, 1⅞" X 1⅝" X ⅜", excellent, **$300.00 (B).**

National Brand Cocoa, Geo. Rashmussen Co., tin litho container with artwork of Capitol building and kids at table, 2½" X 2½" X 4⅞", excellent, **$275.00 (B).**

New Era Dairy...Velvet Rich...Ice Cream, light-up ad clock with metal body, plastic face with message panel to right of clock face, 1960s, 24¾" X 11¾", good, **$225.00 (C).**

New Era Potato Chip, round tin container, 1-lb., excellent, **$50.00 (D).**

Newly Wed...Sugar Stick Candy, pennant with image of young man and woman eating candy, while a young child watches, 25" L, near-mint, **$122.00 (B).**

Noonan's Hair Petrole for falling hair, double sided porcelain flange sign, Zepp's Hair Dressing advertised on other side, 16" X 12", excellent, **$400.00 (B).**

Northwestern National Bank...Portland Trust Co. of Oregon, oval tip tray with artwork of bank building in center of tray, 6⅛" L, excellent, **$95.00 (B).**

Nugget, shoe polish store advertising sign, porcelain, 1920 – 1930s, 42" X 17", good, **$900.00 (C).**

Nylotis Baby Powder, tin litho container with artwork of three babies on front, unopened, near-mint, **$169.00 (B).**

O Cedar Mops...cleans as it polishes, die cut tin litho store display, 20¼" X 18½" X 4¼", excellent, **$375.00 (B).**

Oceanic Oysters...in Season, tin over cardboard advertising sign, 9¼" X 13¼", yellow lettering on green, excellent, **$75.00 (B).**

Old Dutch Cleanser, tin over cardboard ad sign with hands shown scrubbing pan and product container in lower right, excellent, **$450.00 (B).**

Old Reliable Peanut Butter, tin litho pail with wire side-mounted bail, 1-lb., excellent, **$75.00 (C).**

Old Virginia Catsup, cardboard give-away Halloween mask of Mammy with products information on reverse, 9" X 10¼", excellent, **$225.00 (B).**

Oliver Implements...plowmakers for the world, painted die cut tin flange sign, with artwork of the earth in center, 18" X 18", excellent, **$225.00 (C).**

On Time Gum, stenciled chewing gum tin with top mounted wire handle, 7¾" X 5¼" X 2", excellent, **$900.00 (B).**

Opex Lacquers...enamels, porcelain flange sign with the Sherman Williams Paint logo at top left and right, 22" X 16", excellent, **$225.00 (D).**

Overland Co. Garage, painted tin service sign, 23½" X 12", excellent, **$175.00 (D).**

Pacific Coast Steamship Co., round metal tip tray with company flag in tray center, 3⅝" dia., excellent, **$75.00 (B).**

Pan American Airlines, advertising table lighter, excellent, **$100.00 (C).**

Parke Davis Wormwood Drug, tin with turn-of-the-century drug house graphics on all four sides, 1900s, 4½" X 4" X 9", excellent, **$77.00 (B).**

Parker Brothers, Inc., Touring...Improved Edition, automobile card game, in original package, complete, good, **$15.00 (D).**

Pastum...J. Sarubi, hair dressing, double sided tin litho flange sign, 18½" X 7", excellent, **$83.00 (B).**

Peacock, condom tin litho container with artwork of peacock in full feathers, 1⅝" X ⅝", excellent, **$250.00 (B).**

Pennsylvania Railroad...Conway Yard, paper calendar with 3-month tear sheets at bottom with artwork of railyards at top, 1958, good, **$55.00 (C).**

Pennsylvania Railroad...Dynamic Progress, paper calendar, no pad, artwork at top of modern train passing piggy-back freight traffic, 1956, good, **$25.00 (C).**

Pennsylvania Railroad...Mass Transportation, paper calendar with 3-month tear sheets at bottom of artwork, 1955, excellent, **$55.00 (C).**

Pennsylvania Railroad...Vital Lines To The World..., paper calendar with 3-month tear sheets at bottom, artwork of ship/rail loading facility, 1957, good, **$45.00 (C).**

Pepto-Bismol, die cut cardboard bottle sign, 10⅞" X 27¼", excellent, **$65.00 (D).**

Perfection Dyes...For Silk, Woolen, Cotton and Feathers, embossed tin dye cabinet front door sign, 10" X 14", excellent, **$115.00 (B).**

Peter Pan Bread, broom holder, tin front is stenciled with product message, wooden top has holes for brooms, excellent, **$350.00 (B).**

Peter Pan Cottage, cardboard item that came with variety of products, all products listed on reverse side, 10½" X 12" X 9", excellent, **$70.00 (B).**

Peter Rabbit Peanut Butter, tin litho pail with wire side-mounted handles, 1-lb., excellent, **$484.00 (B).**

Peterson Restaurant and Meat Market, die cut embossed calendar with artwork of young girl on cover, partial monthly tear sheets, 1917, 9" X 11", near-mint, **$40.00 (B).**

Petter, Use the Petter blue book, double bubble electric clock, great graphics, 1950s, 15" dia., fair, **$100.00 (C).**

PEZ, tin litho clicker advertising candies with moveable die cut boy and girl, 2½" X 3½", excellent, **$250.00 (B).**

Phinney-Walker...Clocks for automobiles..."On Time," Models for every type of car, with great graphics of clock in front of city scene, cardboard, 15" X 20", excellent, **$395.00 (C).**

Pickaninny Peanut Butter, tin litho pail with graphics of black girl sitting on front with slip lid and side-mounted pail handles, 1-lb., excellent, **$214.00 (B).**

Pioneer Glass & Paint Co., calendar with artwork of Indian maiden in canoe, partial months pad, 1923, 10" X 14", excellent, **$30.00 (B).**

Pittsburgh Paint...Satisfaction in service since 1855, tin self- framed ad sign with graphics of product container, 38" X 27", near-mint, **$390.00 (B).**

Plano Harvesting Machines, calendar with artwork of Indian and full calendar pad, 1905, 13" X 19", near-mint, **$165.00 (B).**

Planters Novola Peanut Oil, with litho image and message on sides, metal container, 5-gal., excellent, **$175.00 (D).**

Planters Peanut Butter, pail with litho of Mr. Peanut, 3½" X 3⅞", excellent, **$900.00 (B).**

Planters Peanut, clear embossed leap year jar with tin litho lid and two paper labels on sides with artwork of woman holding a bag, 1940s, 5¾" X 5" X 7½", excellent, **$800.00 (B).**

Planters Peanut Oil...Hi-Hat, one-pint tin container with original spoon lid, near-mint, **$85.00 (B).**

Planters Peanut, promotional item, mail-in for papier-maché peanut-shaped give-away, 1948, 6" X 11", excellent, **$80.00 (B).**

Planters Peanuts, barrel store jar with etched lid and embossed Mr. Peanut running around jar, 1935, near-mint, **$286.00 (B).**

Planters Peanuts Canadian Clipper, glass store jar with good strong graphics on lid of Mr. Peanuts, 1938, near-mint, **$175.00 (B).**

Planters Peanuts, coloring book, Seeing the USA with Mr. Peanut, mint, **$75.00 (C).**

Planters Peanuts, die cut cardboard sign of Mr. Peanut and small child in cowboy attire, easel back, 6½" X 14", near-mint, **$215.00 (B).**

Planters Peanuts, fish bowl store jar with decal of fish, product message on fish body, hard-to-find item, 1929, near-mint, **$220.00 (B).**

Planters Peanuts, football glass store jar, embossed "Planters Salted Peanuts" on both sides, 1930, near-mint, **$302.00 (B).**

Planters Peanuts, glass "fish bowl" store jar with Planters embossed on base, horizontal paper label, 1929, excellent, **$190.00 (B).**

Planters Peanuts, glass store jar for 5¢ peanut bags with decal on jar front, excellent, **$185.00 (B).**

Planters Peanuts, glass store jar with frosted label featuring image of Mr. Peanut along with advertising for four products, 1963, excellent, **$80.00 (B).**

Planters Peanuts, leap year glass store jar with paper label, 1940, near-mint, **$150.00 (B).**

Planters Peanuts...My! these Planters Peanuts are delicious, waxy cardboard store display box with die cut likeness of woman aviator, 9½" X 9¼" X 7", excellent, **$425.00 (B).**

Planters Peanuts, seven-sided embossed store jar with paper label, 1926, excellent, **$225.00 (B).**

Planters Peanuts, six-sided store jar with Mr. Peanut decals on all sides, etched glass lid, 1936, near-mint, **$160.00 (B).**

Planters Peanuts, streamlined glass store jar with yellow metal lid, 1937, near-mint, **$155.00 (B).**

Planters, plastic clip on earrings, in original gift box, ⅞" X 1¼", excellent, **$70.00 (B).**

Planters Salted Peanuts, round container tin with artwork of Mr. Peanut pennant on front, 8½" X 9¾", excellent, **$25.00 (D).**

Playboy, cuff links, excellent, **$20.00 (D).**

Poll Parrot, neon advertising store sign, excellent, **$1,250.00 (C).**

Poll Parrot Shoes, Happy Shoes for Happy Feet, cardboard ad sign with boy and bird graphics in wooden frame, 13" X 21", excellent, **$78.00 (B).**

Poll Parrot, store advertising sign, cardboard, good, **$75.00 (C).**

Poll Parrott, advertising shoe bank, excellent, **$75.00 (C).**

Poll Parrot, neon over porcelain sign with die cut bird sitting on perch at top of sign, excellent, **$1350.00 (D).**

Poll Parrot Shoes...for Boys, for Girls, die cut metal advertising sign with cut out of parrot at top, rare and hard to find, double sided, excellent, **$1250.00 (D).**

Popsicle...everybody likes...refreshing, easy to eat, painted tin advertising sign, 28" X 10", excellent, **$400.00 (D).**

Post Toasties...with peaches and cream, paper advertising showing milk being poured on bowl of cereal, framed, 15¼" X 12¼", excellent, **$135.00 (D).**

Postum Cereal, tin litho sample container with slip lid, good, **$15.00 (B).**

Postum...Drink...There's a Reason...Health First, round tin string holder with message in center, excellent, **$280.00 (B).**

Power House...Bigger, two piece 24-count candy box with artwork of product bar on front, 9" X 5" X 2", excellent, **$5.00 (B).**

Prairie Farms...Milk...Ice Cream, round plastic body and cover light-up advertising clock, 16" dia., good, **$135.00 (D).**

President Suspenders...Absolute Comfort...J.H. Beamer, round metal tip tray with artwork of pretty woman in tray center, 4⅛" dia., excellent, **$25.00 (B).**

Primley's California Fruit Chewing Gum...sweeter than honey, cardboard die cut easel back standup advertising sign with bear holding product package, 13⅞" X 10½", excellent, **$4,000.00 (B).**

Priscilla Crayons...High Quality Brilliant Colors, tin litho container with brilliant colors on artwork of crayons in hand, 1937, near-mint, **$70.00 (B).**

Public Telephone, die cut porcelain flange sign with older model 202 phone in center of message, 16" X 16", excellent, **$375.00 (C).**

Pulver Chewing Gum... One Cent Delivers a tasty chew, metal dispenser, 8½" X 20", white on green, excellent, **$650.00 (C).**

Purity Butter Pretzels, die cut cardboard litho advertising sign with easel back and artwork of boy holding giant pretzel, 13" X 22", near-mint, **$120.00 (B).**

Putnam Fadeless Dyes...Monroe Drug Co., with artwork of Gen. Putnam on horse, store display tin with original wooden dye package dividers, 16¼" X 8" X 11¼", excellent, **$150.00 (C).**

Putnam Fadeless Dyes, tin store display box with artwork of woman admiring clothing, 16½" X 8" X 11¼", excellent, **$135.00 (D).**

Quadriga Cloth...The girl who sews has better clothes, wooden die cut advertising sign with logo at left of message, 20" X 6½", excellent, **$75.00 (D).**

Quaker Crackels, cardboard store sample dispenser with artwork of Quaker on front, would dispense sample by moving lever on side, 21" X 22" X 5½", excellent, **$225.00 (B).**

Quasar...Pete's Discount...Whirlpool, painted metal thermometer with dealer information in bottom panel, good, **$25.00 (C).**

Quick Meal, oval porcelain sign with artwork of egg and chick chasing insect, 44¾" X 33½", excellent, **$215.00 (C).**

Quick Meal Steel Ranges, ten-page booklet, featuring Buster Brown and Tige on front and back with product information inside, 1910, near-mint, **$100.00 (B).**

R.M. Weaver, Stocks and Bonds, Woolworth Bldg., Lancaster, PA, round tip tray with graphics of man about to receive working end of horned goat, 4¼" dia., excellent, **$95.00 (B).**

Rainbow Dyes, wooden cabinet with tin insert on door, "One Dye for All Fabrics," 11½" X 5" X 19", good, **$225.00 (B).**

Ramer's Chocolates, self-framing tin ad sign with graphics of products on table, 19" X 13", good, **$61.00 (B).**

Ramon's Brownie Pills, painted wood thermometer with the little doctor at right of the scale, 9" X 21", excellent, **$425.00 (B).**

Ramon's Brownie Pills...The Little Doctor Brings Happy Days, with artwork of the doctor at right of scale, tin litho in cream color, 9" X 21", near-mint, **$332.00 (B).**

Rat Bis-Kit, die cut easel back display for rat bait, NOS, artwork of rat eating product, 8¾" X 12", excellent, **$300.00 (B).**

Rawleigh's Good Health Cocoa...packed by The W.T. Rawleigh Co., Freeport, Ill., USA, sample tin with great litho of Mr. Rawleigh and outdoor scene, 1¼" X 1¾" X ⅝", excellent, **$180.00 (B).**

Ray Cotton Company, Franklin, Mass., Agents Cotton Mills Waste Association, cast iron inkwell with heavily embossed lettering, 8" X 3¾" X 3", excellent, **$95.00 (C).**

RCA Nipper, bank made of pot metal, covered by felt, marked Radio Corporation of American, 6", near-mint, **$185.00 (B).**

RCA, placemat, with Donald Duck and Nipper dog logo, good, **$15.00 (C).**

Red Cap, At Your Service Everywhere 5¢, 24-count two piece cardboard candy box with graphics of red-capped man carrying vendor box of product, 7" X 10" X 2½", excellent, **$36.00 (B).**

Red Goose...Ask for a Golden Egg, egg machine made of papier-maché and cardboard, eggs contain prizes, excellent, **$325.00 (B).**

Red Goose Shoes, round metal body glass front light-up advertising clock with Red Goose in center with message over goose, excellent, **$575.00 (D).**

Red Head Bottle Caps, resealable bottle caps on blister pack from country store NOS, 1940s, excellent, **$40.00 (D).**

Red & White Corn Flakes, cardboard box with #2 Davy Crockett edition, graphics of bowl of cereal on front, 13-oz., excellent, **$60.00 (B).**

Red Seal Battery...A battery for every use, flange painted metal sign in likeness of dry seal battery, good, **$135.00 (D).**

Red Seal Peanut Butter, tin litho container with artwork of three fiddlers, 12-oz., excellent, **$196.00 (B).**

Red Wing, pot scraper, advertising Red Wing Flour, with artwork of flour bag on front, tin litho, 3" X 2½", excellent, **$1,050.00 (B).**

Reddi-Kilowatt, mechanical pencil, excellent, **$10.00 (C).**

Redmen Archery...Shoot, painted wooden advertising sign with artwork of Indian head in center of message, 24" X 34", excellent, **$250.00 (C).**

Resinol Soap & Ointment...For All Skin Diseases...At All Drug Stores, round metal tip tray with artwork of red-haired woman in center of tray, 4¼" dia., excellent, **$170.00 (B).**

Rexall...Compare the price and save on..., light-up clock with message to left of clock face, excellent, **$85.00 (C).**

Rexall...From the ...store, clear glass store bowl with heavily embossed lettering, 4¼" X 4¾", excellent, **$35.00 (D).**

Rockford High Grade Watches Oscar Holmes, Cambridge, Minn., metal tip tray with artwork of woman sitting beside tree, 4⅞" L, good, **$45.00 (B).**

Rosemary Foods...the highest standard of purity and excellence, metal wagon with rubber tires, 15" X 14" X 34", good, **$75.00 (C).**

Rough Riders Baking Powder, paper lith on cardboard container with artwork of "Teddy Roosevelt" look-alike on horse, excellent, **$100.00 (B).**

Round Oak Stoves, Ranges & Furnaces, metal pocket match safe, with celluloid advertising on sides, 1½" X 3" X ⅜", excellent, **$325.00 (B).**

Royal Baking Powder...Full Weight...Full Strength, wooden box with product name on paper label on box ends and debossed painted on sides, 14¾" X 8½" X 7¾", good, **$30.00 (D).**

Royal Insurance Company...Agency of the leading fire Co. of the world, painted wooden sign with artwork of shield in center of message, 22¼" x 31¼", good, **$95.00 (D).**

Ruff-Stuff...The Sandpaper That Satisfies, painted metal store display box with dividers for different grit pages, 12" X 23" X 14", excellent, **$100.00 (B).**

S & H Green Stamps...We Give, light-up advertising clock with clock face at top of message panel, 15¼" X 22¾", excellent, **$100.00 (D).**

S.J. Tuft...Corsets A Specialty, die cut cardboard dust pan with girl with broom artwork, good, **$25.00 (D).**

S&H Green Stamps, porcelain, double sided hanging sign, excellent, **$210.00 (D).**

Satin Luminall...one coat, painted metal thermometer with vertical scale in center with product messages at top and bottom, 8½" X 38½", excellent, **$55.00 (D).**

Satin Skin Cream, by Albert F. Wood Mfr., poster featuring artwork of pretty girl with fan, 1903, 28" X 42½", excellent, **$55.00 (C).**

Schmauss Garden Cafe...Milwaukee, Wis., round metal tip tray with very colorful graphics of restaurant interior scene, 6" dia., excellent, **$65.00 (B).**

School Boy Peanut Butter, tin litho pail with side-mounted wire bail, 2-lb., excellent, **$88.00 (B).**

Sea Gull Baking Powder, tin container with paper litho of sea gull in flight, unopened, 2⅛" X 3¼", excellent, **$275.00 (B).**

Seal of Kentucky Mustard, Covington, Ky., paper litho on cardboard, with graphics of seal of Kentucky on front, 1½-oz., near-mint, **$223.00 (B).**

Sealtest...Dairy Products, square plastic light-up advertising clock, 15¼" sq., good, **$1,115.00 (C).**

Sealy Mattress, scene of cotton being picked in southern field, with product name at bottom of frame, cardboard self-framing, 61" X 41", fair, **$95.00 (D).**

Search Light Match Box Holder, with litho of instruction on front and original box, mint, **$150.00 (B).**

Sears, Roebuck and Co., Chicago, oval metal tip tray with factory scene and Lady Justice, 6", excellent, **$75.00 (B).**

Seneca Red Top Socks, cardboard box with artwork of Indian in center of arrowhead with kids ice skating, 5" X 14" X 2", near-mint, **$58.00 (B).**

Sergeant's Dog Care Products, cardboard display with die cut dog at top with moveable back leg, 14½" X 25¼", excellent, **$135.00 (D).**

Shaker and New Tariff Ranges, trade card with graphics of Lt. Greenley with Eskimos at North Pole, 10" X 6", near-mint, **$130.00 (B).**

Sharples, The Pet of the Dairy, match holder, with image of mother and daughter, great graphics, 2" X 7", excellent, **$150.00 (B).**

Sheboygan Natural Mineral Water, Better Than Imported, tin litho of graphics of Indian being served by black waiters, 1910, 10" X 14", excellent, **$660.00 (B).**

Silver Star, condom litho tin with artwork of streaking star, Silver Star Rubber Co., New York, NY USA, 2¼" X 1⅝" X ¼", good, **$825.00 (B).**

Simoniz...Gives Lasting Beauty and Saves Finish, too!, cardboard store display with metal can in center with artwork of man and woman polishing table and car, excellent, **$135.00 (D).**

Singer Mfg. Co...Sewing Machine Makers for the World, heavily embossed calendar with artwork of young girl, 1898, 9" X 12", excellent, **$53.00 (B).**

Singer Sewing Machine, litho on cardboard with graphics of woman with costume,"Costume made on the...," framed, 1880s, 25½" X 35", excellent, **$166.00 (B).**

Slicker Pipe & Tool Company, oil and gas well supplies with great litho at top of tear sheets of fishing scene, 1927, excellent, **$45.00 (D).**

Slicker Pipe & Tool Co., paper calendar with tear sheets at bottom with great litho scene of boys at swimming hole, partial pad, 1926, excellent, **$35.00 (C).**

Smith Bros., cough drop advertising paperboard sign with both brothers asking the public to be kind and not cough in public by buying their product, 24" X 16", excellent, **$98.00 (B).**

Smith Brothers Black Cough Drops, sample product box, cardboard with graphics of Smith Bros. on front, near-mint, **$30.00 (B).**

Smooth Sailin', two-part candy box with sailboats on both sides, Hollywood Brands, Centralia, ILL, 10" X 8" X 2", near-mint, **$28.00 (B).**

Snag Proof Boots from Lambertville Rubber Co., calendar, artwork of "L" girl in cameo surrounded by brownies with products, 1910s, 8" X 12", excellent, **$116.00 (B).**

Sno-King...peanuts caramel nougat, candy bar store box with great graphics of snow scenes on front, 10" X 7¾" X 2", excellent, **$35.00 (D).**

South Bend Watches...Sold By W.F. Sellers & Co., tin litho retailers sign, 19" X 13", excellent, **$192.00 (B).**

Squirrel Brand Peanut Butter, tin litho with pry lid, graphics of squirrel on front, 3-lb., excellent, **$225.00 (B).**

Squirrel Brand Salted Peanuts, tin litho 10-lb. pail with side-mounted wire handles, has artwork of squirrel on front, 8¼" X 9¼", excellent, **$850.00 (B).**

Squirrel Peanut Butter, Canadian Nut Co., Vancouver, MN, tin litho with graphics of squirrel eating a peanut, 3¾" X 3", excellent, **$625.00 (B).**

St. Johnsbury Crackers, C.H. & Geo. H. Cross, Inc., cracker box, 10" X 7" X 8", excellent, **$40.00 (B).**

Standard Mixed Paint of America...Goes Farthest...Locks Best...Wears Longest, round metal tip tray with artwork of product can in center of tray, 4⅛" dia., excellent, **$15.00 (B).**

State Fair Rolled Oats, Sedalia, Mo., container with slip lid, graphics of fair building on front, 1-lb., 4-oz., excellent, **$130.00 (B).**

Steamer City of Erie...Record 22⁹³⁄₁₀₀ miles per hour...Daily Between Cleveland & Buffalo, rectangular metal tip tray with graphics of ship at sea, 6⅝" L, excellent, **$250.00 (B).**

Stillwell Ham, A.J. Stillwell Meat Co., Hannibal, Mo., paper on cardboard with graphics of ham in center, 11" X 14", near-mint, **$60.00 (B).**

Stollwerck...gold brand chocolate & cocoa, round metal tip tray, 5⅛" dia., excellent, **$20.00 (D).**

Stratford Regency, The Dependable Pen, three-dimensional cardboard store display with original pen, 1945, good, **$33.00 (D).**

Success Manure Spreader, metal tip tray with graphics of man working with product, 4¾" L, excellent, **$130.00 (B).**

Summit Shirt, pennant with graphics of young man in the process of putting on French cuffs, 25" L, excellent, **$99.00 (B).**

Sunbeam...White Stroehmann, door push bar with die cut likeness of loaf of bread, with Sunbeam girl, excellent, **$165.00 (D).**

Sunshine Peanut Butter, tin litho metal pail with wire handles, 1-lb., excellent, **$91.00 (B).**

Super-Superb, typewriter ribbon tin with graphics of beaver gnawing on tree, excellent, **$35.00 (B).**

Superman Orange Juice, Producers Dairy, waxed cardboard container, unused, graphics of Superman on all sides, 64-oz., near-mint, **$25.00 (D).**

Sweatheart Pure Peanut Butter, tin litho pail with wire handles with slip lid, 9¼" X 10½", excellent, **$82.00 (B).**

Sweet-Orr...pants, shirts, overalls, porcelain sign with union made label in center of message, 24" X 10", excellent, **$225.00 (C).**

Sweet-Orr Trousers Union Made, double sided porcelain flange sign, 18" X 8", excellent, **$350.00 (B).**

Swell Magic Colors Bubble Gum, cardboard store display with original bubble gum cigarette packages, priced per package, 1960s, excellent, **$3.00 (D).**

Swift's Arrow Borax American's Best, die cut cardboard double sided arrow sign with product box in center, excellent, **$75.00 (B).**

Swift's Ice Cream, light-up advertising clock, metal body with message at top of clock face, excellent, **$235.00 (C).**

Swift's Pride Soap and Washing Powder, cardboard fan with wood handle featuring artwork of woman with wash basket, 1910s, 9½" dia., excellent, **$165.00 (B).**

SWP/Cover the earth, die cut porcelain sign in likeness of paint can pouring paint on earth, 48" X 36", excellent, **$125.00 (D).**

Sylcraft...Undergarments of Quality, cardboard box with artwork of pretty woman on box top, 11¼" X 11½" X 1½", excellent, **$30.00 (D).**

Sylvania HaloLight, neon window sign, 20" X 19", excellent, **$250.00 (D).**

T T Bitters...Stulz Bros., Kansas City, Mo., Sole Owners, wall hung tin litho match holder, 3⅜" X 4⅞", excellent, **$425.00 (B).**

Taft Oil Burners...authorized dealer for cook stoves...for room heaters, heavy porcelain enamel sign, 22" X 13¾", excellent, **$350.00 (B).**

Taystee Bread...Enjoy...Famous for its freshness...today and everyday, paper advertising sign with artwork of chef holding bread, 1950s, 12" X 18", excellent, **$40.00 (B).**

Teddie Peanuts, John W. Leavitt Co., Boston, Mass., tin litho peanut container with center artwork of large peanut, 10-lb., 8¼" X 9⅝", excellent, **$300.00 (B).**

The Aristocrat Gums, 5¢ Cigarette Form, gum box with original contents, excellent, **$20.00 (D).**

The Badger Mutual Fire Insurance Co., cast metal badger paperweight, excellent, **$65.00 (C).**

The Fair's Millinery/Opening Fall Season 1905, metal tip tray, featuring artwork of sitter hunting dog "on point", 1900s, excellent, **$25.00 (C).**

The "Flower" of the Family...It's William Tell Flour, round metal tip tray with artwork of red-haired woman, 4¼" dia., excellent, **$120.00 (B).**

The Franklin Life Insurance Company...Springfield, Illinois, round metal tip tray with artwork of Ben Franklin on tray, 4¼" dia., excellent, **$20.00 (B).**

The Home Insurance Co., collapsible drinking cup in leather case, excellent, **$30.00 (C).**

The Kuntz Remmler Co., rectangular tip tray, with graphics of street scene and Kuntz building on tray front, 6" tall, excellent, **$100.00 (B).**

The May Company...Ohio's Largest Department Store, round metal tip tray with artwork of woman with flower in hair, 4¼" dia., excellent, **$90.00 (B).**

The Source of Cottolene...Best for Shortening, Best for Frying, round metal tip tray with artwork of black woman and child picking cotton, 4¼" dia., excellent, **$60.00 (B).**

The Turkish Dyes, wood store dye cabinet with inside dividers, sliding door has heavy waxed litho, 16½" X 11" X 28½", excellent, **$375.00 (B).**

The Wichita Construction Co., litho on canvas type paper with artwork of Indian girl on front with full calendar pad, near-mint, **$465.00 (B).**

Thomas & Clarke, Peoria, Ill., Crackers...Biscuits...Cakes, tin store box with product message painted on front, 7½" X 7½" X 9", excellent, **$150.00 (C).**

Thompson's Ice Cream, round metal serving tray, fair, **$30.00 (D).**

Three Knights, Goodyear Rubber Co., NY, condom tin with litho of three knights on horseback, 2⅛" X 1⅝", excellent, **$150.00 (B).**

Timely Clothes, plastic and metal advertising clock with figure of Minute Man in center of face ringing bell, 18" X 18¼", excellent, **$65.00 (D).**

Tiny-tot Toilet Powder, tin litho container with graphics of baby in soft bed, excellent, **$40.00 (B).**

Tom Sawyer Apparel for Real Boys, die cut cardboard ad sign with artwork of young boy painting sign, 1940s, 21" X 6", near-mint, **$125.00 (C).**

Towle's Log Cabin, silverplate spoon with log cabin facsimile at top of spoon, stem is shaped like tree trunk, 1910, **$63.00 (B).**

Trojan-Enz Condom, tin litho container with artwork of Roman helmeted man in center, 2⅛" X 1⅝" X ¼", excellent, **$300.00 (B).**

Tums...Bring on your hot mince pie–all foods agree with me now, I use Tums for my Tummy, die cut easel back cardboard store sign, 9¼" X 15¼", excellent, **$60.00 (B).**

Tums...for the tummy...for acid indigestion, heartburn, painted metal vertical scale thermometer with messages at top and bottom of scale, 4" X 9", near-mint, **$75.00 (C).**

Tums, tin litho display cabinet with drawers in back that holds product, with product message on back and front sides, 12" X 6" X 7", excellent, **$83.00 (B).**

TWA, metal airplane ashtray, 10" X 6", excellent, **$150.00 (C).**

U.S. Army, I Want You, framed poster of Uncle Sam by famous artist James Montgomery Flagg, framed, 33" X 43", excellent, **$250.00 (C).**

U.S. School Garden...Raised 'em myself in my..., cardboard poster with artwork of young boy with large basket full of vegetables, framed, excellent, **$175.00 (D).**

UMWA, miner's hat, salesman sample hat on wood display complete with helmet light, 15" X 17½", good, **$75.00 (C).**

Uncle John's Syrup, five piece paper store window display, with original envelope, measurement of Uncle John is 40" X 24", near-mint, **$600.00 (B).**

Uneeda Biscuit...Don't Forget, string hung cardboard sign with kid in slicker, never used, 21" X 16½", excellent, **$275.00 (B).**

United Van Lines...W. Jeff Hammond Moving & Storage, light-up advertising clock with metal body and glass face, excellent, **$150.00 (D).**

UTH stockings, tin container with great artwork of woman on cushion, 2" X 6¼", excellent, **$210.00 (B).**

Velvet... Ice Cream and Dairy Products, plastic light-up clock, 15½" sq., excellent, **$175.00 (C).**

Velvet Ice Cream, light-up advertising clock with clock under message panel, which is reverse painted glass, good, **$235.00 (C).**

Velvet... the Best Milk & Ice Cream, light-up clock with message panel to right of clock face, excellent, **$95.00 (C).**

Voigt Cream Flakes, cardboard cereal box with graphics of woman and cow on front, excellent, **$215.00 (B).**

W.J. Guy Implement dealer, embossed tin sign with farm implements in row between message lines, 28" X 10", excellent, **$242.00 (B).**

Walter A. Wood Implements calendar 1892, double sided cardboard calendar with young girls in front of rake, implements on reverse, 1892, 6" X 7", near-mint, **$50.00 (B).**

Walter A. Wood, Hoosick Falls, NY, USA, cardboard calendar for mowing and reaping machines with great graphics of horsedrawn reaping machine, 7½" X 8¾", near-mint, **$140.00 (B).**

Welch Juniors...Drink a bunch of grapes, horizontal painted tin sign with artwork of product to left of message, 40" X 18", excellent, **$375.00 (C).**

Wells Richardson Lactated Food for Infants and Invalids, tin litho container with slip lid, 1879, near-mint, **$77.00 (B).**

Welsbach Assures Dependable Lighting Service, round metal tip tray with graphics of woman in chair with small girl in floor, 4⅛", excellent, **$220.00 (B).**

Western Auto, light-up advertising clock, 12" dia., good, **$135.00 (C).**

Western Union, bell page with product name on front, 3½" X 5¾", excellent, **$65.00 (C).**

Western Union...Telegraph Here, double sided porcelain flange sign, 25" X 17", near-mint, **$220.00 (B).**

Western Union...Telephone your telegrams from here, flanged porcelain sign with artwork of candlestick phone at lower left of message, 18" X 19½", excellent, **$195.00 (C).**

White King...Washes Everything, tin litho with additional reverse on glass light-up clock face showing image of king in center, 1927, 24" X 17" X 6", excellent, **$1,275.00 (B).**

White Rose Flour...Bakes Better Bread, painted wooden sign, self-framing, 74" X 26", good, **$325.00 (D).**

White Squadron Spice, store bin with slant front, litho contains graphics of ships and other patriotic items, 7" X 9" X 10", excellent, **$223.00 (B).**

Wilson's Certified Smoked Ham, die cut cardboard easel back ad sign with art of Uncle Sam slicing product, 29½" X 40", excellent, **$180.00 (B).**

Wood's Mowers, Walter A. Wood Mowing and Reaping Machine, cardboard ad sign depicting mowers and reapers in use, 1895, 27" X 19", good, **$350.00 (B).**

Woodward Candy Co., metal tip tray with artwork of man and woman in early dress with product, 6¾" L, excellent, **$190.00 (B).**

Woodward's Fine Chocolates, round metal tip tray with graphics of product box in tray center, 4¼"L, excellent, **$110.00 (B).**

Wrigley Pepsin Chewing Gum, box, 1900s, excellent, **$325.00 (C).**

Wrigley's Chewing Sweet peppermint flavor...after every meal, felt sign complete with trademark, 7¾" X 5⅜", near-mint, **$160.00 (B).**

Wrigley's...happy to serve you...after every meal, metal litho serving tray for Spearmint tray, 13¼" X 10½", excellent, **$1,450.00 (B).**

Wrigley's...make sure it's Wrigley's, cardboard store counter display, 13" X 13", excellent, **$375.00 (C).**

Wrigley's Soap, metal tip tray with graphics of cat sitting on product bars, 3⅝" dia., excellent, **$170.00 (B).**

Wrigley's Spearmint, gum box, 1910s, excellent, **$135.00 (C).**

Zuane's LaParot Talc, tin litho with great graphics of colorful bird on front, excellent, **$185.00 (B).**

Courtesy of Muddy River Trading Co./Gary Metz

B-1 Lemon-Lime Soda, poster in its original wood frame with B-1 logo at top center, excellent, **$240.00 (B).**

Courtesy of Muddy River Trading Co./Gary Metz

Barq's, tin over cardboard sign, "Drink Barq's it's good," featuring artwork of sandwich and bottle of Barq's, 11" X 14", excellent, **$150.00 (B).**

Courtesy of Patrick's Antiques

Binder's Beverages...they're better, painted metal sign with bottle in center of message, 20" X 28", orange & black on white, fair, **$50.00 (D).**

Courtesy of Muddy River Trading Co./Gary Metz

Canada Dry, The best of them all, with artwork of bottle in hand, embossed door push, excellent, **$100.00 (B).**

Courtesy of Muddy River Trading Co./Gary Metz

Cherry-Cheer, Drink...It's Good, hanging cardboard sign, great graphics, 1920s, 7" X 11", excellent, **$210.00 (B).**

Courtesy of Muddy River Trading Co./Gary Metz

Cheer Up, Drink..., glass with message in spotlight, excellent, **$30.00 (B).**

Courtesy of Muddy River Trading Co./Gary Metz

Cheerio, It's Lewie's Refreshing Beverages I Want, tin over cardboard sign, featuring artwork of man holding bottles of Cheerio, 11" X 8", good, **$35.00 (B).**

Courtesy of Muddy River Trading Co./Gary Metz

Cherry Smash, Our Nation's Beverage, cardboard bottle topper, 1920s, excellent, **$70.00 (B).**

Courtesy of Pleasant Hill Antique Mall & Tea Room/Bob Johnson

Chero-Cola, Drink...There's none so good, painted metal sign, with sunburst and bottle to left side of sign, good, **$70.00 (D).**

Courtesy of Wildflower Antique Mall

Coca-Cola, aluminum 12-bottle carrier, with embossed lettering on each side, 1940s, excellent, **$225.00 (D).**

Coca-Cola, double bottle thermometer of embossed tin 1941, 7" X 16", excellent, BEWARE: this thermometer has been reproduced, **$475.00 (B).**

Courtesy of Muddy River Trading Co./Gary Metz

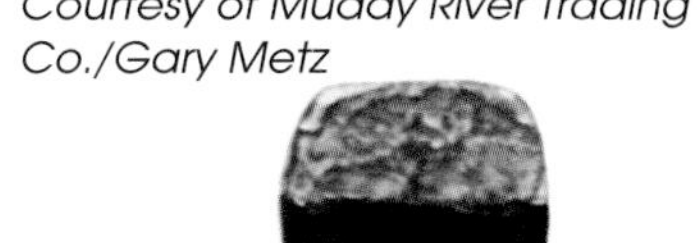

Coca-Cola...Drink Bottled...So Easily Served, leather boudoir clock, bottle-shaped with clock face in center of body, 1910, 3" X 8", good, **$1,300.00 (B).**

Courtesy of Affordable Antiques/Oliver Johnson

Coca-Cola bicycle, manufactured by Huffy in 1986 to commemorate the 100th anniversary of Coca-Cola, 26", mint, **$895.00 (D).**

Coca-Cola, Drink, button with curved sides, metal, 12" dia., white lettering on red, excellent, **$300.00 (C).**

Courtesy of Affordable Antiques/Oliver Johnson

Coca-Cola, Drink..., Cavalier 6-case master, wet box, red with white lettering, good, **$695.00 (D).**

Courtesy of Muddy River Trading Co./Gary Metz

Coca-Cola...Drink Coca-Cola In Bottles, mirror with thermometer at upper left, with silhouette girl panel at bottom, 1939, 10" X 14", excellent, **$850.00 (B).**

Courtesy of Affordable Antiques

Coca-Cola drink dispenser, Vendo # 23, restored, 1940s – 1950s, near-mint, **$1,295.00 (D).**

Courtesy of Patrick's Collectibles

Coca-Cola...Drink...ice cold, fountain dispenser, white on red, excellent, **$725.00 (D).**

Courtesy of Patrick's Collectibles

Coca-Cola...Drink... Ice Cold, Westinghouse 10-case master dry box with a hinged lid that opens side to side instead of front to back, embossed, restored, 1950s, 45⅛" X 36" H X 30½" D, white on red, excellent, **$1,850.00 (D).**

Courtesy of Patrick's Collectibles

Coca-Cola...Drink, In Bottles, small dual chute machine with four bottle stacks inside that alternately dispense the product, will only use 6½-oz. bottle, 1950s, 25" W X 58" H X 15" D, white logo on front on red, good, **$1,500.00 (D).**

Courtesy of Patrick's Collectibles

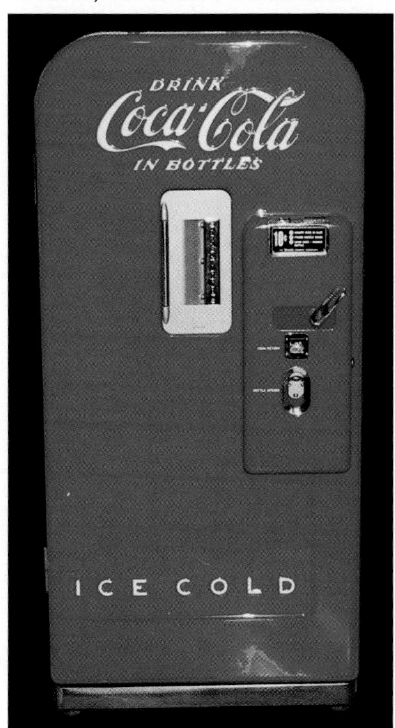

Coca-Cola...Drink, In Bottles, successor to the table top 27, much sought after for home use because of their compact size, restored, 1950s, 25½" W X 52" H X 17½" D, white on red, near-mint, **$2,195.00 (D).**

Courtesy of Al & Earlene Mitchell

Coca-Cola...Drink in bottles, wood framed clock with message spotlighted in center of face, 1940s, 16" X 16", good, **$195.00 (C).**

Courtesy of Muddy River Trading Co./Gary Metz

Coca-Cola, Drink...Delicious and Refreshing, cowboy cardboard, in original wood frame, good graphics, excellent, **$1,150.00 (B).**

Coca-Cola, Drink..., iron frame is 24" dia. with a 16" metal button on one side and a 10" button on reverse side, excellent, **$875.00 (C).**

Courtesy of Affordable Antiques

Coca-Cola, Drink..., masonite with bottle in spotlight at bottom of diamond, made by Evans-Glenn Co., Marietta, GA, Made In USA, 12-46, 1946, 48" X 48", good, **$695.00 (D).**

Coca-Cola...Drink..., take enough home, adjustable wire carton rack, with message sign at top, excellent, **$165.00 (D).**

Courtesy of Patrick's Collectibles

Courtesy of Patrick's Collectibles

Coca-Cola...Drink, painted metal self-framing sign with couple at right of message, 1940s, 33½" X 12", excellent, **$500.00 (D).**

Courtesy of Affordable Antiques–Oliver Johnson

Coca-Cola...Drink, Refreshment right out of the bottle, cardboard poster, 1940s, good, **$700.00 (D).**

Courtesy of Patrick's Collectibles

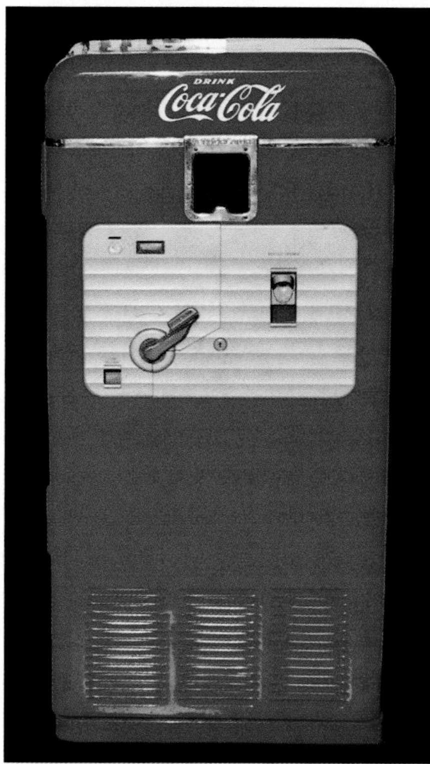

Coca-Cola...Drink, Vendo 39 with bottle drop at center of door, approx. 80,000 made, restored, 40s – 50s, 27" W X 58" H X 16" W, white on red, near-mint, **$2,995.00 (D).**

Courtesy of Patrick's Collectibles

Coca-Cola...Have a Coke, metal self-framing sign with spotlight bottle in center, 18" X 54", white and yellow on red, excellent, **$325.00 (D).**

Courtesy of Patrick's Collectibles

Coca-Cola...Enjoy big king size...ice cold here, metal self-framing painted metal sign with fishtail in center and bottle at right, 27¾" X 19¾", red, white, and green, good, **$225.00 (D).**

Courtesy of Patrick's Collectibles

Coca-Cola...It's the real thing, with dynamic wave contour logo, metal picnic cooler with side handles and metal latching top, 18" X 13" X 16½", white on red, good, **$150.00 (D).**

Coca-Cola, Join the friendly circle, horizontal poster with artwork of friends swimming around float with cooler of Cokes, 1955, 36" X 20", excellent, **$450.00 (C).**

Courtesy of Wildflower Antique Mall

Coca-Cola, Sprite Boy advertising decal featuring Sprite Boy in bottle cap hat beside Coke bottle, 4½" X 8", near-mint, $**15.00 (D).**

Courtesy of Creatures of Habit

Coca-Cola, Serve...Taste treat for the year, paper double sided store advertising, framed, 1956, excellent, **$125.00 (D).**

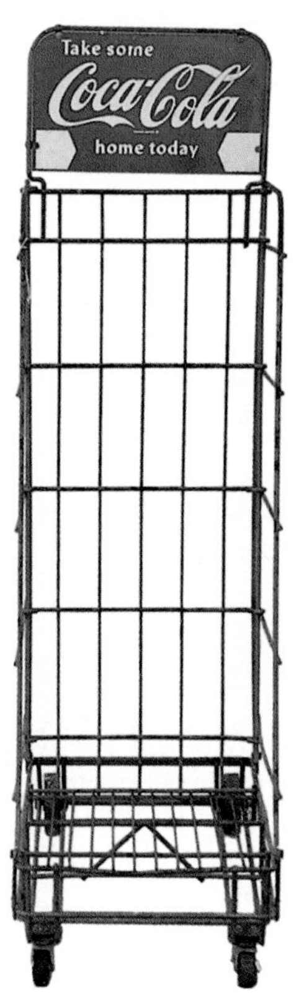

Coca-Cola, Take Some Home Today, wire bottle rack, with metal rack sign at top, good, **$45.00 (D).**

Courtesy of Affordable Antiques

Coca-Cola...things go better with..., painted metal self framing sign, with message to left of bottle, 35¼" sq., red, white, and green, good, **$275.00 (D).**

Courtesy of Patrick's Collectibles

Courtesy of Wildflower Antique Mall

Coca-Cola, wax cardboard carton case, red on yellow, excellent, **$75.00 (D).**

Coca-Cola... Wherever Ginger Ale, Seltzer or Soda is Good...Coca-Cola is Better–Try It, metal lithographed serving tray of topless woman, 1908, excellent, **$4,600.00 (C).**

Dad's Old Fashioned Root Beer, painted tin sign, 26¾" X 19", good, **$225.00 (C).**

Crystal Club Pale Dry Ginger Ale, painted metal advertising sign with dial-type thermometer located in neck of bottle, 7" X 27", excellent, **$100.00 (C).**

Courtesy of Patrick's Collectibles

Diet-Rite Cola...sugar free, self-framing painted metal sign with bottle to left of message, 33" X 12", excellent, **$95.00 (D).**

Dodger Beverage, die cut steel sign in shape of bottle, 16" X 65", excellent, **$450.00 (C).**

Courtesy of Patrick's Collectibles

Double Cola...Drink, Double measure, Double pleasure, metal door push bar, 34" X 4½", red on aluminum, excellent, **$135.00 (D).**

Courtesy of Patrick's Collectibles

Double Cola...Drink, Ideal "slider", a great box because of its large capacity and small room, this particular version is painted in the 1940s scheme, restored, 1950s, 37" W X 42" H X 19½" D, yellow and black on red, near-mint, **$1,895.00 (D).**

Courtesy of Patrick's Collectibles

Double Cola...Drink, menu board with message at top center, 19¾" X 27½", green, white, yellow,and black, excellent, **$160.00 (D).**

Double Cola, Drink, painted metal flange sign, copyright 1947, The Double Cola Co., Chattanooga, Tenn., 18" X 15", near-mint, **$325.00 (C).**

Courtesy of Patrick's Collectibles

Double Cola...Enjoy, metal self-framing menu board with message at top center, with burst coming from behind oval logo, 19½" X 28", white lettering on red oval, black, excellent, **$125.00 (D).**

Courtesy of Muddy River Trading Co./Gary Metz

Double-Orange, Truly Delightful, round cardboard sign, artwork by Rolf Armstrong, 1920s, 18" dia., excellent, **$190.00 (B).**

Courtesy of Muddy River Trading Co./Gary Metz

Dr. Pepper, A lift for life, double sided cardboard sign in original wood frame, with 10, 2, and 4 clock at top, 1950s, 31½" X 19", near-mint, **$400.00 (B).**

Courtesy of Muddy River Trading Co./Gary Metz

Dr. Pepper, clock in the Art Deco style with reverse painted glass front, electric, rare, 1930s, 22" X 17", excellent, **$3,700.00 (B).**

Courtesy of Patrick's Collectibles

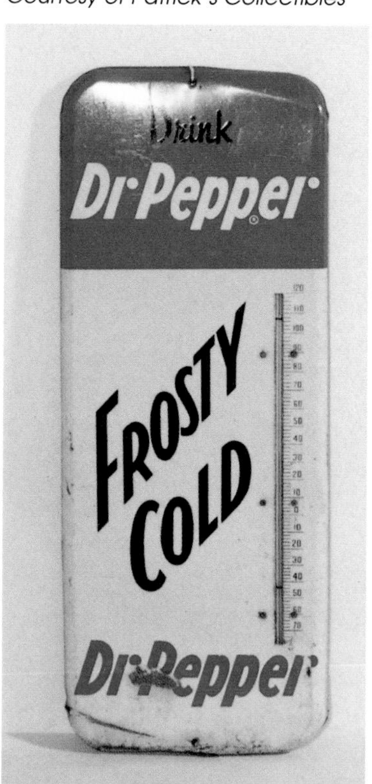

Dr. Pepper...Drink, Frosty Cold, metal thermometer, 10" X 25½", white, red, and black, good, **$250.00 (D).**

Courtesy of Patrick's Collectibles

Dr. Pepper...Drink, metal picnic cooler with top wire bail handle, 18" X 12" X 9", white on green, good, **$75.00 (D).**

Courtesy of Muddy River Trading Co./Gary Metz

Dr. Pepper, glo glass brand glass sign, "Energy-up Drink Dr. Pepper, Good For Life, Ice Cold", 1930s, 14" X 11", excellent, **$2,500.00 (B).**

Dr. Pepper...Good For Life!, wooden bottle carrier with "Loaned Not Sold Deposit Returnable" message on handle, rare and hard to find, 12-package, 15¼" X 5¼" X 9¼", excellent, **$275.00 (D).**

Courtesy of Rare Bird Antique Mall–Jon & Joan Wright

Courtesy of Muddy River Trading Co./Gary Metz

Dr. Pepper, telechron electric clock with message under hands stem, 1930s near-mint, **$350.00 (B).**

Courtesy of Muddy River Trading Co./Gary Metz

Dr. Swett's, The Original Root Beer, embossed tin sign, 24" X 9", good, **$425.00 (B).**

Courtesy of Muddy River Trading Co./Gary Metz

Dr. Pepper, cardboard hanging sign with artwork of clock face 10, 2, & 4 hands, 13" x 13", circa 1920s, very good, **$3,100.00 (B).**

Courtesy of Muddy River Trading Co./Gary Metz

Evervess Sparkling Water...for your table at every meal, celluloid sign, a Pepsi-Cola product, 9" dia., excellent, **$250.00 (B).**

Gin Seng, The Beverage of Purity, rectangular metal serving tray, excellent, **$125.00 (C).**

Courtesy of Muddy River Trading Co./Gary Metz

Grape Dee-Light, Gee but it's good, Jacob Onuschak, Northampton, PA., with great graphics, cardboard hang up sign, 1920s, 10½" X 14", excellent, **$45.00 (B).**

Courtesy of Muddy River Trading Co./Gary Metz

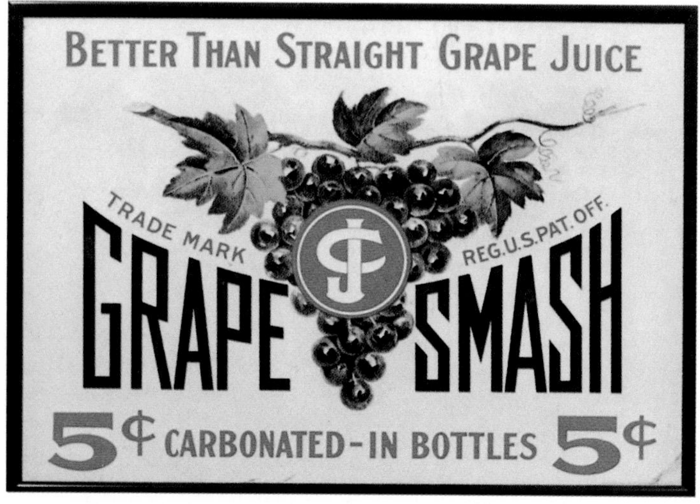

Grape Smash, Better Than Straight Grape Juice, tin sign, 13½" X 9½", excellent, **$325.00 (B).**

Harrison's Heart O' Orange sold here, round embossed tin sign, 14¼" dia., excellent, **$250.00 (C).**

Courtesy of Muddy River Trading Co./Gary Metz

Hazle Club...Finer Flavor Drink, embossed tin door push, excellent, **$90.00 (B).**

Hazle Club Tru-Orange, painted metal flange sign, 14" X 20", excellent, **$130.00 (C).**

Courtesy of Muddy River Trading Co./Gary Metz

Hires Root Beer, die cut bottle thermometer, 1950s, 28" tall, excellent, **$165.00 (B).**

Hires Root Beer, reverse painted glass, chain-hanging sign, 7¼" X 8¼", excellent, **$1,700.00 (C).**

Hires, Drink in Bottles, cardboard ad sign featuring the artwork of Haskell Coffin on the girl and flare glass, 1910s, 15" X 21", excellent, **$575.00 (B).**

Courtesy of Muddy River Trading Co./Gary Metz

Courtesy of Muddy River Trading Co./Gary Metz

Hires... Drink, It hits the spot, Try a bottle and you'll buy a case, embossed tin sign with artwork of man holding bottle, 15¾" X 9¾", excellent, **$225.00 (B).**

Courtesy of Muddy River Trading Co./Gary Metz

Hires R-J Root Beer, with real root juices, round tin embossed sign, 12" dia., excellent, **$150.00 (B).**

Courtesy of Muddy River Trading Co./Gary Metz

Hires Root Beer, Finer Flavor because of Real Root Juices, tin door push with beveled edges, excellent, **$150.00 (B).**

Hires Root Beer German-made mug, 5" tall, excellent, **$210.00 (B).**

Courtesy of Muddy River Trading Co./Gary Metz

Courtesy of Muddy River Trading Co./Gary Metz

Hires Root Beer with Roots, Barks, Herbs, stainless steel drugstore dispenser sign, excellent, **$95.00 (B).**

Courtesy of Muddy River Trading Co./Gary Metz

Hires....Say, oval sign, framed, with artwork of Hires child holding early Hires mug, 1900s, 20" X 24", excellent, **$600.00 (B).**

Courtesy of Patrick's Collectibles

Hires...So refreshing, made with roots, barks, herbs, painted metal sign, AAA Sign Co., Cottsville, Ohio, 13½" X 11½", excellent, **$95.00 (D).**

Courtesy of Buffalo Bay Auction Co.

Hood's Sarsaparilla, die cut calendar with graphics of pretty girl and roses with full calendar pad, 1904, excellent, **$75.00 (B).**

Courtesy of Muddy River Trading Co./Gary Metz

Hires...So Refreshing, double sided tin flange sign, excellent, **$200.00 (B).**

Hood's Sarsaparilla, calendar featuring girl wearing a flowery bonnet, 1886, 7¼" X 14¾", excellent, **$50.00 (C).**

Hood's Sarsaparilla, calendar, die cut with artwork of pretty girl in bonnet, 1894, 5½" X 8¾", excellent, **$55.00 (C).**

Courtesy of Muddy River Trading Co./Gary Metz

Howel's Orange Julep, pedestal glass, 1920s, excellent, **$120.00 (B).**

Courtesy of Morford Auctions

Indian Rock Ginger Ale 5¢, syrup dispenser with Indian scenes on both sides, complete with ball pump,12" tall, excellent, **$2,250.00 (B).**

Courtesy of Muddy River Trading Co./Gary Metz

Lakeside Grape Juice, from selected grapes, The Beverage of Quality, metal serving tray, with great graphics of grapes and bottle, 13½" dia., excellent, **$110.00 (B).**

Courtesy of Riverview Antique Mall

Husemann's Soda, Clear and Sparkling, embossed painted tin sign, from Red Bud, Ill., 19½" X 13½", good, **$65.00 (D).**

Courtesy of Muddy River Trading Co./Gary Metz

Lunch Ice Cream Soda, die cut porcelain sign, excellent, **$280.00 (C).**

Lemon-Kola, tin over cardboard sign, featuring artwork of girl with flared glass with straw, rare, 6¼" X 9¼", excellent, **$400.00 (B).**

Courtesy of Muddy River Trading Co./Gary Metz

Lime Cola...Drink, round celluloid sign, 1950s, 9" dia,, excellent, **$130.00 (B).**

Lift Beverage...Drink, It's Good For You, painted tin sign, 12" X 24", excellent, **$175.00 (C).**

Courtesy of Muddy River Trading Co./Gary Metz

Majestic Bottling Company, seltzer bottle, Lynchburg, VA, excellent, **$15.00 (B).**

Courtesy of Rare Bird Antique Mall–Jon & Joan Wright

Mil-Kay...Drink...The Vitamin Drink...Large Bottle 5¢, metal advertising sign with artwork of black man with serving tray with product, scarce, 1941, 55" X 31½", good, **$825.00 (D).**

Courtesy of Muddy River Trading Co./Gary Metz

Mason's Old Fashioned Root Beer...Everybody's Favorite, cardboard bottle rack sign with beach scene, 10" X 10", excellent, **$95.00 (C).**

Marquette Club Ginger Ale, die cut easel back sign, man has attached glass eyes, 1940s, 8" X 11", excellent, **$140.00 (B).**

Courtesy of Patrick's Collectibles

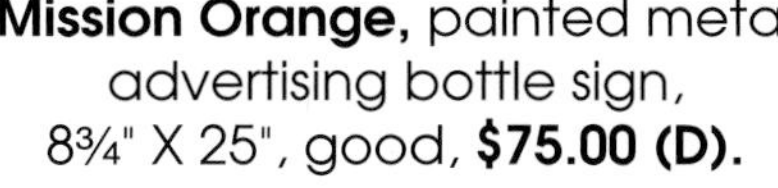

Mission Orange, painted metal advertising bottle sign, 8¾" X 25", good, **$75.00 (D).**

Courtesy of Wm. Morford Investment Grade Collectibles

Moxie, die cut tin advertising sign, graphics of, girl with glass of Moxie, "I like it" message at bottom, 6" dia., excellent, **$725.00 (B).**

Modox Indian Herb, tin litho die cut tip tray with strong colors, 5⅝" X 5", excellent, **$500.00 (B).**

Courtesy of Richard Opfer Auctioneering, Inc.

Courtesy of Richard Opfer Auctioneering, Inc.

Moxie, die cut tin litho match holder, resembling Moxie drink bottle, 7" H, excellent, **$500.00 (B).**

Moxie...I just love...don't you, round metal tip tray with litho of woman with glass of product and leaf border, 6" dia., excellent, **$235.00 (B).**

Moxie, fan with young cowboy on rocking horse and Frank Archer on reverse side, excellent, **$200.00 (B).**

Courtesy of Wm. Morford Investment Grade Collectibles

Moxie, tin litho over cardboard advertising string hanger sign, also has easel back for counter top applications, 10" X 2⅝", near-mint, **$150.00 (B).**

Courtesy of Muddy River Trading Co./Gary Metz

Moxie, tin litho thermometer, great graphics on this piece, 1920s, 12" X 9½", excellent, **$1,500.00 (B).**

Courtesy of Patrick's Collectibles

Nehi...Drink Beverages, metal self-framing painted sign with bottle to right of message, Robertson 1504, 17¾" X 53½", red, white, and gray, excellent, **$325.00 (D).**

Courtesy of Muddy River Trading Co./Gary Metz

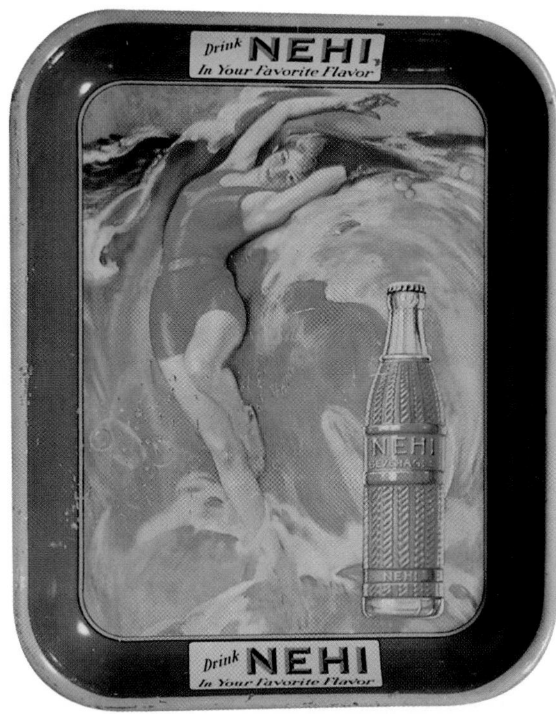

Nehi, Drink... In Your Favorite Flavor, serving tray featuring girl on wave with bottle of Nehi in foreground, good, **$160.00 (B).**

Courtesy of Patrick's Collectibles

Nesbitt's...a soft drink made from real oranges, metal thermometer displaying spotlighted bottle under message and at top of scale, not an easy piece to find, 7" X 23", yellow and orange on blue, good, **$160.00 (D).**

Courtesy of Patrick's Collectibles

Nichol Kola...America's taste sensation 5¢, painted metal sign, The Parker Metal Dec. Co., Baltimore, Ohio, 27½" X 11¼", white, orange, and black, excellent, **$95.00 (D).**

Nichol Kola...America's taste sensation, painted metal sign, 18½" X 11½", orange, black, and white, good, **$95.00 (D).**

Courtesy of Patrick's Collectibles

Courtesy of Patrick's Collectibles

Nichol Kola...Drink...America's taste sensation, with embossed bottle in center of sign, 8" X 24", excellent, **$95.00 (D).**

Courtesy of Patrick's Collectibles

Nichol Kola...Drink...Vitamin B1 added...America's taste sensation, with marching soldier at lower left, painted metal sign, 20" X 28", excellent, **$95.00 (D).**

Courtesy of Muddy River Trading Co./Gary Metz

NuGrape, A Flavor You Can't Forget, rectangular metal serving tray, featuring artwork of girl with bottle, excellent, **$120.00 (B).**

Courtesy of Muddy River Trading Co./Gary Metz

NuGrape, Drink...A Flavor You Can't Forget, serving tray with great graphics of woman and child in front of fountain and pool, good, **$250.00 (B).**

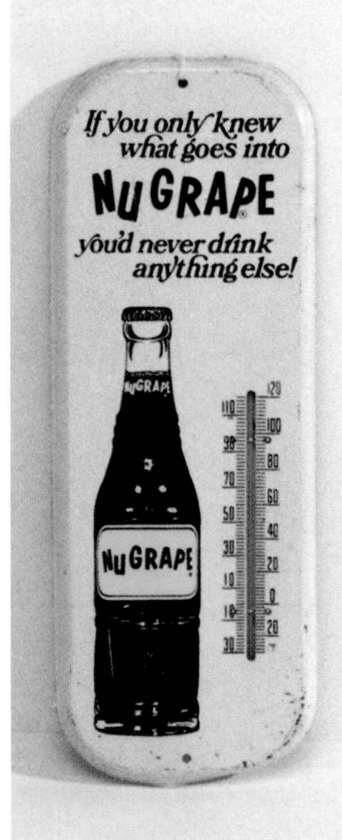

NuGrape, metal thermometer with artwork of bottle at left of scale, 6" X 16¼", yellow, grape, and white, excellent, **$100.00 (D).**

Courtesy of Muddy River Trading Co./Gary Metz

Orange Crush, counter dispenser, stainless steel with porcelain sign sides, 11" X 17" X 20", excellent, **$2,100.00 (B).**

Courtesy of Patrick's Collectibles

Orange Crush...Drink, with bottle in snow at outer edge of sign, 17½" X 11½", near-mint, **$75.00 (D).**

Courtesy of Patrick's Collectibles

Orange Crush, painted metal menu board with message and bottle at top, 19" X 27¼", good, **$125.00 (D).**

Courtesy of Riverview Antique Mall

Orange Crush, embossed metal sign, self-framing with bottle in center, 17" X 53¼", excellent, **$460.00 (D).**

Courtesy of Muddy River Trading Co./Gary Metz

Orange Crush, tin flange sign with Crushy at the bottom of the diamond, 1930s, 18" X 18", excellent, **$450.00 (B).**

Courtesy of Muddy River Trading Co./Gary Metz

Orange-Julep... Drink, It's JULEP Time, bottle topper, excellent, **$65.00 (B).**

Courtesy of Muddy River Trading Co./Gary Metz

Orange Julius A Devilish Good Drink, with artwork of devil figure in center, rare, 1920s, 24" X 35", good, **$800.00 (B).**

Courtesy of Muddy River Trading Co./Gary Metz

Orange-Crush...Drink, The National Fountain Drink, Color Added, tin over cardboard sign with artwork of girl with glass of Orange Crush, 1920s, 6¼" X 9¼", good, **$500.00 (B).**

Courtesy of Patrick's Collectibles

Orange-Crush, PELCO 510-E, electric drink box, other versions of this box were made for other drinks, most were embossed, 1940 – 1950s, 10-case, orange, near-mint, **$2,995.00 (D).**

Courtesy of Muddy River Trading Co./Gary Metz

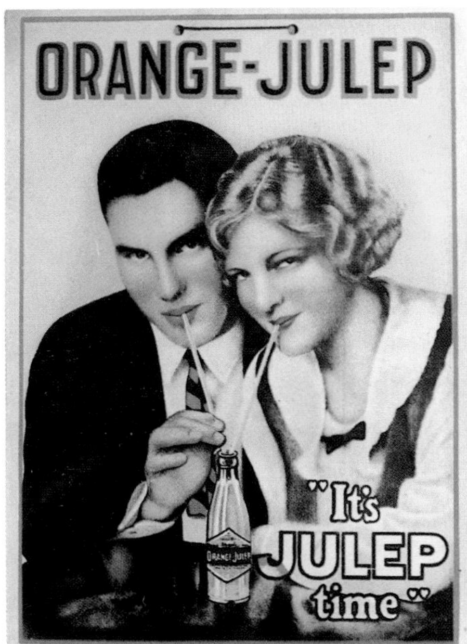

Orange-Julep, cardboard hang up sign, featuring artwork of man and woman drinking from a single bottle with two straws, 1930s, 7¾" X 11", excellent, **$140.00 (B).**

Courtesy of Muddy River Trading Co./Gary Metz

Orange-Julep, Drink, metal serving tray, featuring girl at beach with umbrella, and holding a glass of Orange-Julep, good, **$130.00 (B).**

Courtesy of Muddy River Trading Co./Gary Metz

Pal Ade, tin door push, excellent, **$75.00 (B).**

Palmer's Root Beer, barrel sign, NOS, 19" X 14", near-mint, **$375.00 (C).**

Courtesy of Affordable Antiques

Pepsi...Be sociable...Serve, cardboard poster with woman in hat holding six-pack in palm with bottle cap logo at left, double sided, 36" X 24¾", good, **$125.00 (D).**

Pepsi, cardboard ad in wood frame, hard-to-find piece even in less than perfect condition, 25" X 32", poor, **$250.00 (C).**

Courtesy of Muddy River Trading Co./Gary Metz

Pepsi, "The light refreshment," light-up plastic clock, 1950s, near-mint, **$600.00 (B).**

Courtesy of Muddy River Trading Co./Gary Metz

Pepsi-Cola...A nickel drink worth a dime, featuring artwork of early Pepsi bottle, fiberboard sign, 1930s, 12¾" X 14¾", good, **$140.00 (B).**

Courtesy of Antiques Cards & Collectibles/Ray Pelly

Pepsi-Cola, advertising 45 rpm record in original paper cover, with original mailing package, "Your Man In Service," excellent, **$55.00 (D).**

Courtesy of Muddy River Trading Co./Gary Metz

Pepsi-Cola, base for patrol boy, cast iron, 1950s, 24" dia., good, **$150.00 (B).**

Courtesy of Muddy River Trading Co./Gary Metz

Pepsi-Cola...Bigger, Better, tin thermometer, 6¼" X 15¾", excellent, **$525.00 (B).**

Pepsi-Cola...Buy Here round cardboard sign, 21" dia., good, **$95.00 (C).**

Courtesy of Muddy River Trading Co./Gary Metz

Pepsi-Cola, chain-hung reverse glass mirror with cap logo, 1950s, 9½" dia., good, **$130.00 (B).**

Courtesy of Muddy River Trading Co./Gary Metz

Pepsi-Cola, Coast to Coast, Bigger and Better, metal serving tray with artwork of United States map with Pepsi bottle, excellent, **$410.00 (B).**

Courtesy of Muddy River Trading Co./Gary Metz

Pepsi-Cola, die cut bottle sign, 1930s, 12" X 45", excellent, **$625.00 (B).**

Courtesy of Muddy River Trading Co./Gary Metz

Pepsi-Cola door pull handle, 2¾" X 12", excellent, **$210.00 (B).**

Courtesy of Muddy River Trading Co./Gary Metz

Pepsi-Cola, Drink, countertop light-up sign, 1950s, 14" dia., excellent, **$175.00 (B).**

Courtesy of Muddy River Trading Co./Gary Metz

Pepsi-Cola, die cut cardboard sign, 1930s, 21" X 15", excellent, **$375.00 (B).**

Courtesy of Muddy River Trading Co./Gary Metz

Pepsi-Cola, Drink...Delicious Delightful, embossed tin sign, 1910s, 3½" X 9¾", excellent, **$275.00 (B).**

Courtesy of Antiques Cards & Collectibles/Ray Pelly

Pepsi-Cola, Drink...Delicious Heathful, script hat pin on emblem for employee, excellent, **$50.00 (D).**

Courtesy of Muddy River Trading Co./Gary Metz

Pepsi-Cola...Drink, Double Size 5¢, double sided hand stenciled canvas banner, rare piece, 1930s, good, **$275.00 (B).**

Courtesy of Muddy River Trading Co./Gary Metz

Pepsi-Cola...Drink, fan, 1912, 8" X 9", good, **$1,000.00 (B).**

Courtesy of Muddy River Trading Co./Gary Metz

Pepsi-Cola, Drink...Ice-Cold, plastic bottle cap light-up sign, 1950s, 16" dia., excellent, **$500.00 (B).**

Pepsi-Cola...Drink Iced, self-framed painted tin sign, 55" X 17½", excellent, **$750.00 (C).**

Courtesy of Muddy River Trading Co./Gary Metz

Pepsi-Cola, hits the spot, calendar, complete with full pad, featuring girl with bottle, 1941, 15" X 23", near-mint, **$340.00 (B).**

Courtesy of Muddy River Trading Co./Gary Metz

Pepsi-Cola, Drink...The Light Refreshment, glass light-up sign with convex glass, 1950S, 16" dia., excellent, **$1,250.00 (B).**

Courtesy of Muddy River Trading Co./Gary Metz

Pepsi-Cola, embossed tin sign, 1950s, 3½" X 4", excellent, **$100.00 (B).**

Pepsi-Cola, Hot Dogs Hamburgers Ice Cold Bigger Better, 5¢, embossed tin sidewalk sign, 1930s, 20" X 28", good, **$325.00 (B).**

Courtesy of Muddy River Trading Co./Gary Metz

Courtesy of Muddy River Trading Co./Gary Metz

Pepsi-Cola Hot Popcorn, foil-backed sign, good, **$95.00 (B).**

Courtesy of Muddy River Trading Co./Gary Metz

Pepsi-Cola Ice Cold, Sold Here, celluloid sign, 9" dia., excellent, **$250.00 (B).**

Courtesy of Rare Bird Antique Mall–Jon & Joan Wright

Pepsi-Cola...Ice Cold...Hits The Spot, metal salesman sample box cooler with embossed bottle caps on lid & sides, logo on front, rare item, excellent, **$2,500.00 (D).**

Courtesy of Muddy River Trading Co./Gary Metz

Pepsi-Cola, Ice Cold, salesman sample cooler, rare and hard to find, good, **$3,200.00 (B).**

Pepsi-Cola, light-up clock with bottle cap in the center and yellow face, 1970s, excellent, **$325.00 (B).**

Courtesy of Muddy River Trading Co./Gary Metz

Courtesy of Patrick's Collectibles

Pepsi-Cola, metal and glass light-up clock, with bottle cap in center, good strong colors, 9¼" X 12½", red, white, blue cap on yellow, excellent, **$160.00 (D).**

Courtesy of B.J. Summers

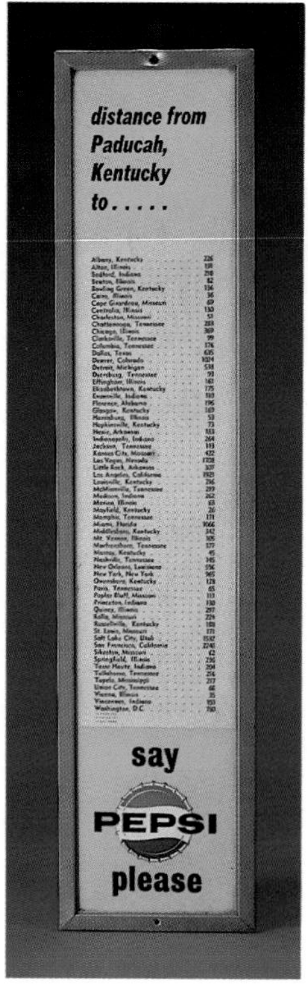

Pepsi-Cola, mileage chart, measuring mileage from Paducah, Ky., to various parts of the country, metal and plastic, 1950s, 7" X 31", yellow, white, and black, excellent, **$35.00 (C).**

Courtesy of Muddy River Trading Co./Gary Metz

Pepsi-Cola, More Bounce to the Ounce, celluloid sign, 9" dia., excellent, **$225.00 (B).**

Courtesy of Muddy River Trading Co./Gary Metz

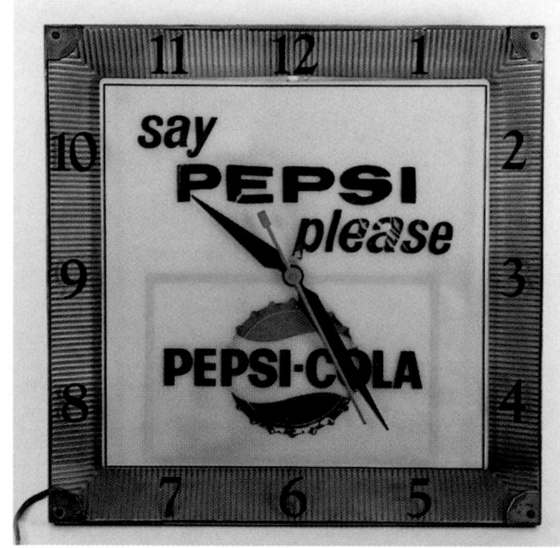

Pepsi-Cola... say Pepsi please, plastic and metal light-up clock, 16" X 16", good, **$125.00 (C).**

Courtesy of Muddy River Trading Co./Gary Metz

Pepsi-Cola...say please, with facsimile of glass of Pepsi in snow, 1970s, excellent, **$65.00 (B).**

Courtesy of Muddy River Trading Co./Gary Metz

Pepsi-Cola, self-framed cardboard sign featuring girl with lace hat and an early bottle of Pepsi-Cola, 1930s, 30" X 20", excellent, **$800.00 (B).**

Courtesy of Muddy River Trading Co./Gary Metz

Pepsi-Cola serving tray, 12" dia., good, **$150.00 (C).**

Courtesy of Muddy River Trading Co./Gary Metz

Pepsi-Cola, small milk glass tray, about the correct size for a tip tray, 4¼" X 3¼", excellent, **$200.00 (B).**

Courtesy of Muddy River Trading Co./Gary Metz

Pepsi-Cola, single case countertop store rack, 1930s, excellent, **$500.00 (B).**

Courtesy of Muddy River Trading Co./Gary Metz

Pepsi-Cola, syrup dispenser, rare, and hard to find, 1900s, excellent, **$3,700.00 (B).**

Courtesy of Muddy River Trading Co./Gary Metz

Pepsi-Cola ...think young, Say Pepsi please, glass under glass light-up clock, 1955, excellent, **$800.00 (B).**

Courtesy of Muddy River Trading Co./Gary Metz

Pepsi-Cola trolley car sign, featuring boy and girl with early bottles of Pepsi, 28" X 11", excellent, **$240.00 (B).**

Courtesy of Morford Auctions

Popeye, Drink, I Yam what I yam and I yam tops, cardboard stand-up display sign advertising Popeye Brand soda, rare, 1929, 22" tall, excellent, **$550.00 (B).**

Courtesy of Muddy River Trading Co./Gary Metz

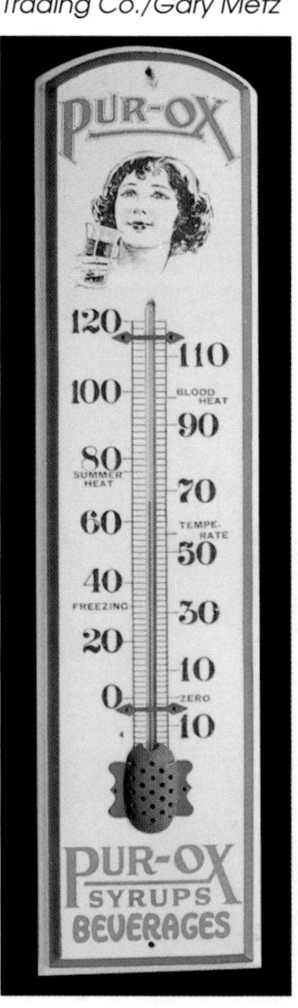

Pur-ox, Syrups, Beverages, wooden thermometer, 5" X 21", excellent, **$400.00 (B).**

Courtesy of Muddy River Trading Co./Gary Metz

Perry's Quality Beverages, triple filtered, nothing finer, tin door push, excellent, **$55.00 (B).**

Courtesy of Patrick's Collectibles

Royal Crown Cola, aluminum picnic cooler, with bail handles at each end, hinged lid, fair, **$60.00 (D).**

Courtesy of Affordable Antiques

Royal Crown Cola, die cut painted metal bottle sign of 1936 bottle, 15¾", X 59¾", excellent, **$395.00 (D).**

Courtesy of Patrick's Collectibles

Royal Crown Cola...Drink...Best by taste test, metal picnic cooler with swing top handle and front drain spout, red on yellow, fair, **$85.00 (D).**

Royal Crown Cola...Drink, metal menu board with message and logo at top, 19¾" X 28", red, blue, black, and white, excellent, **$95.00 (D).**

Courtesy of Patrick's Collectibles

Courtesy of Patrick's Collectibles

Royal Crown Cola...Drink...Better taste calls for RC, painted metal sign, NOS, 23" X 15", white lettering on red, near-mint, **$110.00 (D).**

Courtesy of Riverview Antique Mall

Royal Crown Cola, heavily embossed bottle sign, 15½" X 58½", excellent, **$165.00 (D).**

Courtesy of Antiques Cards & Collectibles/Ray Pelly

Royal Crown Cola, miniature bottle, 1936, 3" tall, good, **$50.00 (D).**

Courtesy of B.J. Summers

Royal Crown Cola, painted metal convex sign featuring artwork of bottle, 19" X 36", fair, **$25.00 (C).**

Courtesy of Muddy River Trading Co./Gary Metz

Royal Crown Cola, "RC tastes best!" says Barbara Stanwyck, with artwork of Barbara Stanwyck holding a bottle of RC, trolley car sign, 28" X 11", good, **$140.00 (B).**

Royal Crown Cola, self-framed tin sign with bottle embossed in center, AM 11-39, 16" X 36", good, **$175.00 (C).**

Courtesy of Muddy River Trading Co./Gary Metz

Royal Crown, Drink... Cola Best By Taste Test, mirrored thermometer and barometer, rare piece, 12" X 24", good, **$250.00 (B).**

Courtesy of Muddy River Trading Co./Gary Metz

Royal Crown, Drink...twice as good – twice as much, with the Good Housekeeping seal, embossed tin sign, 1930s, 27½"X 15", good, **$350.00 (B).**

Courtesy of Muddy River Trading Co./Gary Metz

Royal Crown Cola, Take home RC for your family!, artwork of mother and children shopping for RC, trolley car sign, 1950s, 28" X 11", good, **$110.00 (B).**

Courtesy of Patrick's Collectibles

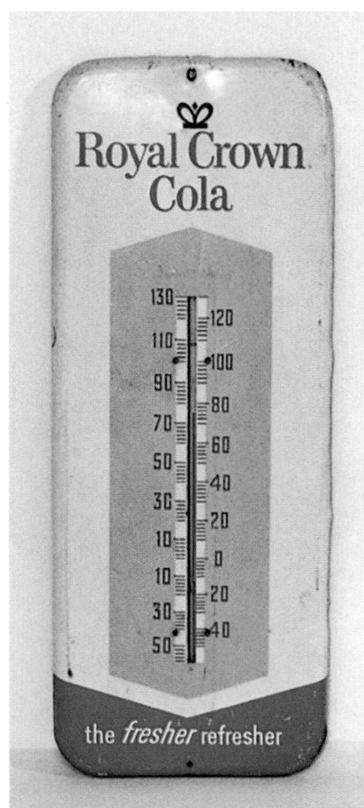

Royal Crown Cola...the fresher refresher, metal thermometer, 10" X 26", white, red, and blue, good, **$120.00 (D).**

Courtesy of Riverview Antique Mall

7UP, chest cooler with outside bottle opener, 34" X 19" X 38", good, **$275.00 (D).**

Courtesy of Rare Bird Antique Mall–Jon & Joan Wright

7UP...Fresh Up with a ...Float, paper ad with graphics of product bottle and glass floating in ice field, 1950s, excellent, **$13.00 (D).**

Courtesy of Muddy River Trading Co./Gary Metz

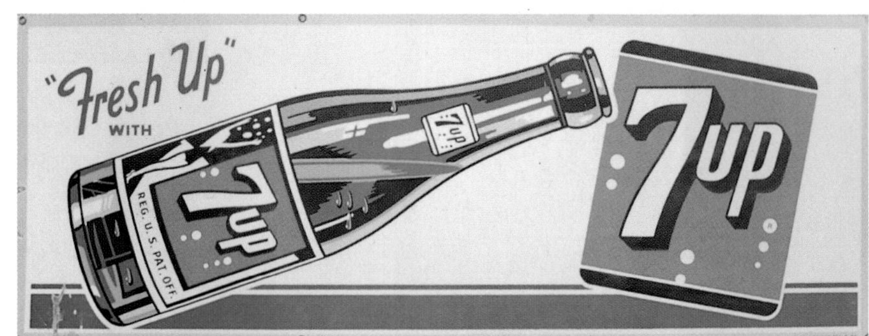

7UP, Fresh up with..., artwork of tilted bottle, porcelain sign, 40" X 15½", excellent, **$210.00 (B).**

7UP, Fresh Up with...embossed painted tin sign "31-10-51 Made In U.S.A. Stout Sign Co., St. Louis, Mo.," 30¼" X 12", excellent, **$95.00 (C).**

Courtesy of Muddy River Trading Co./Gary Metz

7UP, Some Mixer, tin over cardboard sign, 6" X 6¼", excellent, **$110.00 (B).**

7UP, fresh up! with...it likes you, embossed painted metal sign with raised edge, rare sign, 30" X 39½", excellent, **$1,000.00 (C).**

Courtesy of Muddy River Trading Co./Gary Metz

7UP, Fresh up with...the all-family drink, artwork of six-pack of 7up, metal sign, Canadian, 1950s, 3" X 5", good, **$500.00 (B).**

Courtesy of Muddy River Trading Co./Gary Metz

7UP, Go steady with this cool clean taste, artwork of boy and girl next to jukebox, cardboard sign in original wooden sign, 33" X 21", excellent, **$300.00 (B).**

Courtesy of B.J. Summers

7UP, lighted advertising clock, metal body with glass face cover, Pam Clock Company, Rochelle, NY, 1960s, 14¾" dia., white, green, black, and red, excellent, **$550.00 (C).**

Courtesy of Muddy River Trading Co./Gary Metz

7UP, Look for this sign, calendar with woman in swimsuit, 1942, 7" X 12", excellent, **$160.00 (B).**

Courtesy of Antiques Cards & Collectibles/Ray Pelly

7UP the uncola, plastic toy dispenser, with advertising decals of soda, green and white, good, **$15.00 (D).**

7UP, We Proudly Serve, die cut painted flange sign, excellent, **$425.00 (C).**

Courtesy of Patrick's Collectibles

7UP...your taste away, metal self-framing menu board, with message at top, 19½" X 30", good, **$65.00 (D).**

Courtesy of Muddy River Trading Co./Gary Metz

Smile, easel back tripod tin sign with Smile man serving at counter, 1920s, 27" X 41", good, **$1,000.00 (B).**

Sun Crest, self-framed embossed painted tin sign, 41" X 23", excellent, **$325.00 (B).**

Solo, Drink...High in Quality, 6 fruity flavors, painted tin litho, 15" X 30", good, **$50.00 (C).**

Spiffy, A Swell Cola Drink, painted metal flange sign, 12½" X 10", fair, **$75.00 (C).**

Courtesy of Patrick's Collectibles

Squirt...Enjoy, never an after-thirst, metal menu board with message at top, 19¾" X 28", white, yellow, red, and black, fair, **$70.00 (D).**

Spur, Drink Canada Dry... Ice Cold, It's A Finer Cola, embossed tin sign, 13½" X 30", good, **$75.00 (B).**

Courtesy of Muddy River Trading Co./Gary Metz

Courtesy of Muddy River Trading Co./Gary Metz

Squirt, thirsty drink, featuring Squirt Boy with bottle, 1959, 26" X 19", excellent, **$70.00 (B).**

Courtesy of Patrick's Collectibles

Sun Crest...Drink, refreshes you best, metal thermometer with artwork of bottle to right of scale, 6" X 16½", blue, orange, and white, good, **$135.00 (D).**

Courtesy of Patrick's Collectibles

Sun Drop...Have you had your lemonade today, made with pure lemon juice, sold only in bottles, self-framing metal sign, scarce, 40" X 22¼", orange, blue, and white, good, **$325.00 (D).**

Courtesy of Muddy River Trading Co./Gary Metz

Sun Spot, Drink America's Favorite...made with real orange juice, embossed tin sign, 1940s, 11½" X 14½", **$70.00 (B).**

Courtesy of Affordable Antiques

Sun Crest Beverages, Swihart light-up clock with convex front glass, great graphics, 15" X 18", near-mint, **$285.00 (D).**

Sun Crest, telechron electric light-up clock with bottle in center in green spotlight, good strong graphics, 1940s, excellent, **$350.00 (B).**

Courtesy of Muddy River Trading Co./Gary Metz

Courtesy of Muddy River Trading Co./Gary Metz

Sunkist orange juice, I'll tell you a secret...Every day, artwork of girl with a glass, litho by Forbes, 1920s, 28" X 42", excellent, **$600.00 (B).**

Courtesy of Muddy River Trading Co./Gary Metz

True Fruit Soda, delicious, cardboard sign with artwork of grapes and berries, 1905, 9" X 16", excellent, **$90.00 (B).**

Courtesy of Muddy River Trading Co./Gary Metz

Tru Ade, Drink a better beverage, Not Carbonated, double sided porcelain sign, 1951, 20" X 14", excellent, **$230.00 (B).**

Vernor's Ginger Ale, deliciously different!, with artwork of woman with bottle, cardboard sign with wood frame, 21" X 11¾", excellent, **$250.00 (C).**

Courtesy of Muddy River Trading Co./Gary Metz

Vernor's Ginger Ale, Ice Cold, chrome topper sign from fountain dispenser, excellent, **$60.00 (B).**

Courtesy of Muddy River Trading Co./Gary Metz

Ward's Orange-Crush...Sold Here, double sided tin flange sign, 1920s, 11" X 9", excellent, **$650.00 (B).**

Courtesy of Muddy River Trading Co./Gary Metz

Welch Juniors, Drink A Bunch Of Grapes, tin over cardboard easel back sign, 9" X 6", good, **$450.00 (B).**

Courtesy of Muddy River Trading Co./Gary Metz

Welch Juniors Grape Juice, embossed tin sign, 1930s, 19½" X 13½", good, **$400.00 (B).**

Courtesy of Muddy River Trading Co./Gary Metz

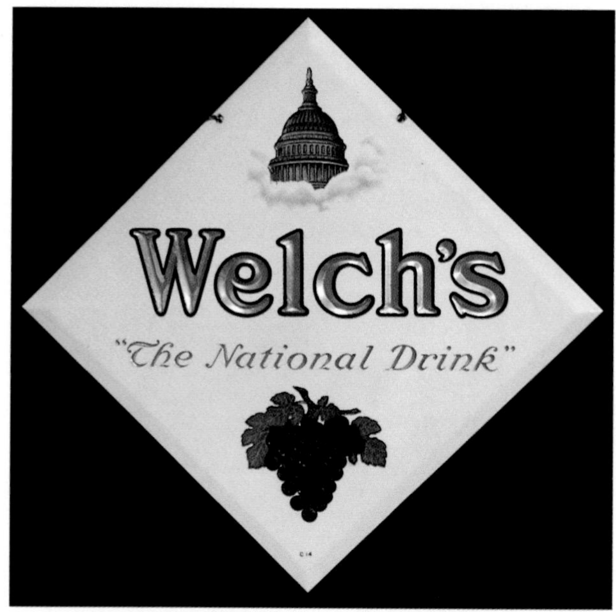

Welch's, "The National Drink," celluloid over tin made by Whitehead and Hoag, 10" X 10", excellent, **$625.00 (B).**

Whistle, die cut cardboard store advertising sign, with graphics of small elf next to product bottle, 1951, excellent, **$82.00 (B).**

Courtesy of Buffalo Bay Auction Co.

Courtesy of Rare Bird Antique Mall–Jon & Joan Wright

Whistle, paper ad, NOS with graphics of boy and product bottle, 1950s, near-mint, **$25.00 (D).**

Courtesy of Buffalo Bay Auction Co.

Whistle soda, cardboard vertical advertising sign, 1948, 2¾" X 23", near-mint, **$95.00 (B).**

Courtesy of Eric Reinfeld

Whistle, cardboard die cut bottle sign, 1936, excellent, **$140.00 (C).**

Courtesy of Richard Opfer Auctioneering, Inc.

White Rock…The World's Best Table Water, rectangular tip tray with fairy on rock over water, 6" tall, excellent, **$130.00 (B).**

Zipp's Cherri-o, syrup dispenser, 1920s, excellent, **$1,500.00 (B).**

NOT PICTURED:

Apollinaris, "The Queen of Table Waters," paper sign in frame and mat, "Pretty Polly...The Queen of the Turf," art of horse and handler, 22½" X 27½", good, **$34.00 (B).**

Apollinaris..."The Queen of Table Waters," rectangular metal tip tray with artwork of woman with glass of product, 6" tall, excellent, **$60.00 (B).**

Armour's...Drink...Veribest Root Beer, milk glass dispenser, near-mint, **$1,210.00 (B).**

Big Boy..., Pale Dry in green bottles only 5¢, embossed tin advertising sign, 19" X 9", excellent, **$88.00 (B).**

Cali-Orange Syrup Dispenser, with frosted globe on reverse painted base with product decal on front and reverse side, excellent, **$290.00 (B).**

Cer-ola...A Triumph in Soft Drinks...Made by Kolb at Bay City, Mich., hanging cardboard Prohibition advertising sign, 11" X 17", excellent, **$75.00 (C).**

Coca-Cola, whirly bird eight-sided spinning sign, NOS, 1950s, near-mint, **$775.00 (C).**

Coca-Cola, acid etched green glass seltzer bottle, excellent, **$225.00 (C).**

Coca-Cola..., bell-shaped pewter glass tumbler with Coca-Cola on shoulder, excellent, **$350.00 (C).**

Coca-Cola..., bobbed hair girl with bottle, metal serving tray, 1927, excellent, **$825.00 (C).**

Coca-Cola, calendar, artwork of Victorian girl at table with fern, 1898, good, **$7,500.00 (C).**

Coca-Cola, calendar, Elaine seated with parasol holding glass of Coke, with full pad, framed, 1915, excellent, **$4,000.00 (C).**

Coca-Cola, calendar featuring June Caprice, early star, with glass of Coke and with full pad, although this is an early piece, it is somewhat common, 1918, excellent, **$375.00 (C).**

Coca-Cola, calendar, girl with snow skies, 1947, good, **$295.00 (C).**

Coca-Cola, calendar with artwork of Army nurse holding a bottle of Coke, complete with all pads, 1943, excellent, **$575.00 (C).**

Coca-Cola, calendar with artwork of two women at beach, one with parasol and glass, other sitting with bottle of Coke, no month pad, 1918, excellent, **$1,250.00 (C).**

Coca-Cola, calendar with Betty in bonnet, this is the version with her holding the product, but with message at upper right of picture, 1914, good, **$1,800.00 (C).**

Coca-Cola, calendar with boy at well with dog, enjoying a bottle of Coke, with partial pad, 1932, excellent, **$725.00 (C).**

Coca-Cola, calendar with girl in blue hat with glass of Coke, full calendar pad, framed, 1921, excellent, **$1,275.00 (C).**

Coca-Cola, calendar with woman wearing broad-brimmed hat, partial calendar pads, 1944, good, **$300.00 (C).**

Coca-Cola, ceramic dispenser with base, bowl, spigot and lid, marked The Wheeling Pottery Co., 1896, 18" tall, excellent, **$5,200.00 (C).**

Coca-Cola, clear flare glass with etched syrup line, Coca-Cola in curve section of 5¢, excellent, **$700.00 (C).**

Coca-Cola...Delicious Refreshing, wooden thermometer, Coca-Cola 5¢, 1905, 4" X 15", excellent, **$700.00 (B).**

Coca-Cola, die cut metal bottle thermometer, 1933, excellent, **$300.00 (B).**

Coca-Cola, die cut metal bottle thermometer of Dec. 25th, 1923 bottle, 1931, excellent, **$375.00 (C).**

Coca-Cola...Drink 5¢, glass change receiver with reverse glass lettering, 1904, 6" dia., good, **$320.00 (B).**

Coca-Cola, Drink..., 50th anniversary poster featuring two girls sitting on product banner holding bottles of Coke, 1936, 27" X 47", excellent, **$1,850.00 (C).**

Coca-Cola...Drink...Delicious and Refreshing, oval Betty serving tray, 1914, excellent, **$300.00 (C).**

Coca-Cola...Drink...Delicious and Refreshing, oval metal serving tray with the Hamilton King Coca-Cola Girl holding a glass of Coke, 1913, excellent, **$325.00 (C).**

Coca-Cola...Drink...Delicious and Refreshing, paper bottle topper of woman in yellow scarf with umbrella, 1927, excellent, **$2,000.00 (B).**

Coca-Cola, Drink...die cut porcelain script sign with copyright in tail of first C, excellent, **$750.00 (C).**

Coca-Cola...Drink... Have a Coke, adjustable paper visor, good, **$5.00 (D).**

Coca-Cola...Drink...Have a Coke, cooler radio, 1950s, excellent, **$675.00 (C).**

Coca-Cola...Drink...Ice Cold, green Vernonware bowl, 1930s, excellent, **$450.00 (C).**

Coca-Cola...Drink...Ice Cold, miniature music box shaped as a box cooler, plays "Let me call you sweetheart," 1950s, excellent, **$150.00 (C).**

Coca-Cola...Drink...Ice Cold, small crystal radio in shape of radio cooler, 1950s, excellent, **$250.00 (C).**

Coca-Cola...Drink...in bottles, new moulded plastic cooler in the shape of drink machine, 22½" X 35" X 12", red, excellent, **$275.00 (D).**

Coca-Cola...Drink...in Bottles, waxed cardboard container, used both as popcorn container and ice bucket, 5T3 Lily Nestrite tub, excellent, **$25.00 (D).**

Coca-Cola...Drink, Knowles china sandwich plate with bottle and glass in center, excellent, **$250.00 (C).**

Coca-Cola...Drink, metal cargo truck with working headlights and taillights, 1950s, red, yellow, and white, excellent, **$375.00 (C).**

Coca-Cola...Drink, painted metal "curb service" serving tray, 1927, excellent, **$1,000.00 (C).**

Coca-Cola...Drink, syrup bottle with metal lid, 1920s, excellent, **$1,200.00 (C).**

Coca-Cola, electric light-up clock, aluminum body with glass front, Drink Coca-Cola in red dot center, with original box, Modern Clock Adv. Co., 15" dia., excellent, **$575.00 (B).**

Coca-Cola, embossed tin bottle thermometer on background plate, 1938, excellent, **$275.00 (D).**

Coca-Cola...exposition girl, oval metal serving tray, 1909, 13½" X 16½", excellent, **$2,500.00 (C).**

Coca-Cola...fishing boy with dog, metal serving tray, 1931, excellent, **$850.00 (C).**

Coca-Cola, Flapper Girl calendar, with partial calendar pad, framed, this particular calendar shows both the bottle and glass, 1929, excellent, **$875.00 (C).**

Coca-Cola...foxskin fur girl with glass of Coke, metal serving tray, 1925, excellent, **$375.00 (D).**

Coca-Cola...Francis Dee, metal rectangular serving tray, 1933, excellent, **$950.00 (B).**

Coca-Cola, frosted glass anniversary cigarette case, 1936, excellent, **$500.00 (C).**

Coca-Cola, girl in bathing suit and hat with beach towel, 1930, excellent, **$375.00 (C).**

Coca-Cola...Have a Coke, plastic and metal door pull, handle shaped like a bottle, 1950s, excellent, **$200.00 (D).**

Coca-Cola, Hilda Clark metal serving tray, 1903, 9¼" dia., excellent, **$3,500.00 (C).**

Coca-Cola, Hospitality in your hands, horizontal cardboard poster featuring artwork of woman with serving tray of bottled Coke, 1948, 36" X 20", excellent, **$325.00 (C).**

Coca-Cola...ice skater, rectangular metal serving tray featuring artwork of girl in ice skates sitting on log, 1941, excellent, **$345.00 (C).**

Coca-Cola...Johnny Weissmuller, metal serving tray BEWARE: this tray has been reproduced, 1934, excellent, **$900.00 (B).**

Coca-Cola...Madge Evans, metal serving tray, 1935, excellent, **$325.00 (C).**

Coca-Cola...menu girl, metal serving tray, 1950s, excellent, **$75.00 (D).**

Coca-Cola, metal serving tray, girl in afternoon, 1938, excellent, **$225.00 (C).**

Coca-Cola, metal serving tray, Soda Jerk, 1928, excellent, **$825.00 (C).**

Coca-Cola, metal serving tray with artwork of two girls at early model convertible, 1942, excellent, **$375.00 (C).**

Coca-Cola, miniature red 6-pack, excellent, **$85.00 (C).**

Coca-Cola...Now! 12-oz. cans too!, rack sign with graphics of cans & bottles circling the globe, 10½" X 22", excellent, **$45.00 (D).**

Coca-Cola, oval metal serving tray with "yellow girl," 1920, 13¼" X 16½", excellent, **$775.00 (C).**

Coca-Cola, painted metal tray with artwork of "sailor girl" fishing on dock, Drink...Delicious and Refreshing, 1940, excellent, **$325.00 (C).**

Coca-Cola, red-haired girl with yellow scarf, metal serving tray with solid background, 1950 – 1952, excellent, **$250.00 (C).**

Coca-Cola, running girl on beach in yellow bathing suit, 1937, excellent, **$325.00 (C).**

Coca-Cola, Soda Fountain calendar, 1901, good, **$4,500.00 (C).**

Coca-Cola, Sold Here...Ice Cold, arrow sign with original hanging arm, 1927, 30" X 21½", red, green, and white, excellent, **$725.00 (C).**

Coca-Cola...Sprite Boy...Take some home today, metal toy cargo truck, 1940s, red and yellow, excellent, **$450.00 (C).**

Coca-Cola...swimsuit girl with glass, metal serving tray, fountain sales, 1929, excellent, **$425.00 (C).**

Coca-Cola, Take Some Home Today, vertical cardboard poster in original frame, artwork of girl with bottle of product at party, 16" X 27", excellent, **$675.00 (C).**

Coca-Cola, toy shopping cart, masonite, excellent, **$550.00 (C).**

Coca-Cola, woman in evening wear with glass, full pad, framed, 1928, excellent, **$825.00 (C).**

Crush, thermometer, aluminum and plastic dial-type scale with graphics of half-sliced orange above product name in center of dial, 1950s, 12½" dia., near-mint, **$37.00 (B).**

Crush...Thirsty...Crush that thirst, painted metal thermometer with crush cap at top of vertical scale, excellent, **$45.00 (C).**

Dad's...Root Beer...Diet, bottle cap sign, 29" dia., excellent, **$85.00 (B).**

Dee-Light...Drink, It's Delicious, painted tin sign with artwork of bottle in center, 6" X 17¾", good, **$15.00 (D).**

Delaware Punch...Delicious Anytime, metal advertising clock, 18" X 14", fair, **$145.00 (D).**

Donald Duck Beverages, self-framing metal sign with Donald Duck graphics with product message, 28" X 20", excellent, **$365.00 (B).**

Donald Duck Cola...Tops for Flavour, die cut paper on cardboard with graphics of bottle cap to left of bottle sitting on ice, duck image on bottle, 22" X 26", excellent, **$77.00 (B).**

Double Cola...Make it a Double...or nothing, painted metal thermometer, red & white, good, **$75.00 (C).**

Double Cola...You'll like it better, painted metal thermometer, vertical scale, blue, red, and white, good, **$65.00 (D).**

Dr. Pepper...and Ice Cream, paper ad in original aluminum frame with logo at top, graphics of product in ice, 1950s, 22" X 17", excellent, **$66.00 (B).**

Dr. Pepper, Drink...Good for Life...Drink a bite to eat at 10–2–4, 3" X 3" X 6", near-mint, **$182.00 (B).**

Dr. Pepper...Drink good for life, porcelain sign, 26½" X 10½", excellent, **$185.00 (D).**

Dr. Pepper...Drink...Good For Life, tin litho emergency plate with original paper insert for emergency numbers, 4" X 8", excellent, **$231.00 (B).**

Dr. Pepper...Drink, tin litho advertising sign with chevron under product message, 27¾" X 11¾", near-mint, **$71.00 (B).**

Dr. Pepper... Have a Picnic, New York World's Fair poster with artwork of picnic scene, excellent, **$30.00 (D).**

Dr. Pepper...Hot or Cold, painted metal thermometer with Dr. Pepper logo in oval at bottom center, red & white, good, **$65.00 (D).**

Dr. Pepper, paper calendar with artwork of girl in bowling alley holding a bottle of Dr. Pepper, 1961, 16" X 23½", excellent, **$45.00 (C).**

Dr. Pepper, plastic store window advertising, 13" X 9½", excellent, **$45.00 (C).**

Dr. Pepper...When Hungry, Thirsty or Tired, painted metal thermometer with bottle facsimile at right of scale,10–2–4 dial at bottlom left, good, **$65.00 (C).**

Evervess...Yes, Yes!...Thank You...Evervess Sparkling Water, metal tip tray with artwork of Evervess bird with top hat and cane, excellent, **$50.00 (B).**

Ferro-Phos. Co., Pottstown, PA...Drink Ferro-Phos...The Favorite Beverage, Five cents, non-narcotic, non-alcoholic, round tip tray with artwork of product in tray center, 4⅛", excellent, **$200.00 (B).**

Frostie Root Beer...the smooth one, painted metal thermometer with Frostie at top over the vertical scale, excellent, **$45.00 (D).**

Fruit Bowl...Drink, Nectar for a Nickel, embossed tin sign with tilted bottle under product message, 6¼" X 19½", excellent, **$65.00 (B).**

Googh's Sarsaparilla...Take for all blood diseases, framed paper advertisement showing small girl angel, 11" X 14", excellent, **$125.00 (D).**

Graf's Beverages, "The Best What Gives," with spotlighted Graf man to left of message, tin litho advertising sign, 29½" X 11½", excellent, **$150.00 (B).**

Grapette...Enjoy...Soda, oval painted metal sign, fair, **$125.00 (C).**

Hires Cork Fasteners, cardboard store display for bottle tops, these were used for Hires home-brewed root beer, 11" X 9", good, **$350.00 (B).**

Hires...Drink, menu board with bottle image and message at top of blackboard, 16" X 29", excellent, **$68.00 (B).**

Hires...In Bottles, painted metal sign ,with artwork of tilted bottle at right of message, 27" X 10", excellent, **$95.00 (D).**

Hires R-J Root Beer, glass and metal counter dispenser, 22" tall, excellent, **$225.00 (C).**

Hires Root Beer, pocket advertising mirror featuring the "ugly kid", good, **$275.00 (C).**

Hood's Sarsaparilla, calendar, die cut cardboard with unused calendar pad with artwork of young girls on front, near-mint, **$95.00 (B).**

Hood's Sarsaparilla, round calendar, "The Sewing Circle" with artwork of children sewing, 1892, near-mint, **$121.00 (B).**

Imperial Dry Ginger Ale, rectangular metal tip tray with graphics of product bottle at right of message, 6⅛" L, near-mint, **$45.00 (B).**

Life...Drink, It's good for you, Three Star Bottling Works, porcelain advertising sign with product bottle image, 12" X 24", near-mint, **$200.00 (B).**

M & S Soda, beveled edge tin over cardboard with image of bottle at right of message, 13" X 9", near-mint, **$33.00 (B).**

Mason's Root Beer, chalkboard menu, good, **$50.00 (D).**

Moxie...Drink, ashtray with Frank Archer promoting product, excellent, **$70.00 (B).**

Moxie...Drink, embossed tin sign, 1938, 27" X 19", white on red with yellow outline, excellent, **$125.00 (B).**

Moxie...Drink...Very Healthful, round metal tip tray with product message in center of tray, 6" dia., excellent, **$40.00 (B).**

Moxie, FDR die cut advertising promoting benefits of Moxie as proclaimed by FDR, good full image of FDR, 12" X 4", excellent, **$305.00 (B).**

Moxie...I Just Love...Don't You, round metal tip tray with great graphics of leaf border and woman with glass of product in center, 6" dia., excellent, **$120.00 (B).**

Moxie..."I like it," round tip tray with graphics of woman with glass of product, 6" dia., excellent, **$170.00 (B).**

Moxie...Learn to Drink...Very Healthful, cardboard die cut easel back advertising sign with likeness of Frank Archer promoting product, sitting on product box, 19" X 40", excellent, **$790.00 (B).**

Moxie, Lowell bottle, nerve food, excellent, **$65.00 (C).**

Moxie...makes you eat, sleep, and feel better, round metal tip tray, 6" dia., excellent, **$45.00 (B).**

Moxie Match Holder, die cut litho in shape of bottle of product, 2½" X 7⅛", excellent, **$500.00 (B).**

Moxie...the National Health Beverage, round metal tip tray, 3½" dia., excellent, **$195.00 (B).**

Nehi...Drink, painted tin sign with bottle in spotlight at right of message, 45" X 18", excellent, **$85.00 (D).**

Nehi Orange...Drink...and other Nehi flavors, paper advertising sign, 7¼" X 12", excellent, **$30.00 (B).**

Nesbitt's...a soft drink made from real oranges, in spotlight, painted metal sign, 32" X 32", white orange, black on yellow, poor, **$50.00 (D).**

Nesbitt's, painted metal thermometer with logo at top of vertical scale and bottle to left of scale, rolled sides and corners, orange & white, excellent, **$95.00 (C).**

Nesbitt's...the finest soft drink ever made...Don't say orange say..., painted metal thermometer with vertical scale, excellent, **$55.00 (D).**

Niagara Punch...Drink, painted tin sign with product bottle at left of message, 20" X 9", excellent, **$110.00 (C).**

NuGrape, advertising clock with bottle in center, 1940 – 1950s, 13¼" X 16", excellent, **$175.00 (C).**

NuGrape...If you only knew what goes into...you'd never drink anything else!, light up advertising clock with message panel to right of clock face, excellent, **$275.00 (C).**

NuGrape...More Fun With Soda, round painted metal sign with likeness of bottle cap, excellent, **$110.00 (C).**

NuGrape Soda, painted metal bottle shaped thermometer with vertical scale at bottom center of bottle, excellent, **$95.00 (D).**

Nutmeg...Ice Cold Club Beverages, painted tin advertising sign, with artwork of bottle at left, 28" X 10", excellent, **$100.00 (D).**

Orange Crush, glass, Art Deco style, made of Bakelite and frosted glass, rare, excellent, **$450.00 (C).**

Orange Crush, glass, with flared top and etched syrup line, near-mint, **$195.00 (C).**

Orange Crush...Taste, plastic light-up advertising clock, 15" sq., excellent, **$125.00 (C).**

Pepsi-Cola...Drink...5¢, embossed painted metal sign, self-framing, 58½" X 36", good, **$125.00 (D).**

Pepsi-Cola...More Bounce to the ounce, painted tin sign with bottle breaking through sign beside bottle cap logo to right of message, unusual and hard to find, 36" X 14", good, **$195.00 (C).**

Pepsi...say "Pepsi" please, metal menu board, excellent, **$45.00 (D).**

Pepsi...say...please, vertical scale thermometer with message at top and logo at bottom, painted tin, red, white, yellow, and blue, excellent, **$55.00 (C).**

Pepsi-Cola, animated cardboard boy and girl, excellent, **$675.00 (C).**

Pepsi-Cola, Drink Iced, porcelain store sign, 60" X 36", good, **$475.00 (C).**

Pepsi-Cola, Drink, metal self-framing sign, with the price 5¢, 1950s, 40" X 34", fair, **$330.00 (D).**

Pepsi-Cola...Drink, self-framing painted tin sign with bottle cap graphics in center of sign, good, **$1,150.00 (D).**

Pepsi-Cola, glass with syrup line and double dot, near-mint, **$25.00 (C).**

Pepsi-Cola, glass with syrup line, "Hits The Spot", near-mint, **$55.00 (C).**

Pepsi-Cola...Have a Pepsi, plastic and metal fountain counter dispenser, excellent, **$250.00 (D).**

Pepsi-Cola, light-up bottle cap, 16" dia., excellent, **$575.00 (C).**

Pepsi-Cola, stand-up cardboard advertising of girl with product, easel back, 1940s, 20" X 15", excellent, **$775.00 (C).**

Pepsi-Cola, straws in original unopened box with graphics of 5¢ bottle, near-mint, **$540.00 (B).**

RC...Royal Crown Cola, painted metal thermometer with vertical scale under message, excellent, **$55.00 (C).**

Red Raven, "Ask the Man," round metal tip tray, with graphics of woman with red raven, 4" dia., near-mint, **$376.00 (B).**

Red Raven ...For Headache...For Indigestion, rectangular metal tip tray with graphics of red raven and woman on tray center, 6⅛"L, excellent, **$170.00 (B).**

Richardson Root Beer...Rich in Flavor, tin litho ad sign, 1950s, 14" X 10", red, white, and black, near-mint, **$57.00 (B).**

Rock Spring ...Sparkling water...ginger ale kola, round metal serving tray, 12" dia., excellent, **$15.00 (D).**

Royal Crown Cola...Taste Best, says Barbara Stanwyck, paper poster with star promoting product, 1948, excellent, **$50.00 (D).**

Royal Crown Cola...We Serve...Ice Cream, embossed metal sign, 1936, near-mint, **$121.00 (B).**

Safety First...Compliments of the Atlanta Coca-Cola Bottling Company, school tablet with graphics of crossing guard, 8½" X 11", excellent, **$9.00 (D).**

7UP Enjoy a...Float, 7up with your favorite Ice Cream, cardboard bottle topper, with arrow, 1953, near-mint, **$20.00 (D).**

7UP First Against Thirst, plastic thermometer with vertical scale in center with messages at top & bottom, 6¾" X 17¾", excellent, **$45.00 (C).**

7UP, "Fresh Up," for Thanksgiving, cardboard bottle topper with graphics of turkey, 1948, 6½" X 10", near-mint, **$20.00 (D).**

7UP fresh up, painted metal door push bar, 31½" X 3", excellent, **$65.00 (D).**

7UP Fresh up with, cardboard bottle topper with artwork of little girl sitting at bottom of slide, 5" X 8½", excellent, **$20.00 (C).**

7UP Nothing Does It Like, painted metal open/closed sign with product bottle to right of information strips, good, **$55.00 (C).**

7UP Real...Likes You, square advertising clock with graphics in center on orange background, wood frame and glass front, 1940s, 15½" sq., near-mint, **$225.00 (B).**

7UP Sold Here, round self-framed embossed metal sign, hard item to locate, 1940s, 8½", white on red, excellent, **$70.00 (B).**

7UP the uncola, round metal serving tray, 12" dia., excellent, **$15.00 (D).**

7UP, tin door push plate with product message at top, 3" X 12", white background, near-mint, **$20.00 (B).**

7UP, Top o' the Morning, cardboard bottle topper with Leprechaun graphics, NOS, 1954, near-mint, **$20.00 (D).**

Seven-Up, porcelain thermometer, good, **$70.00 (C).**

Sprite...Enjoy, painted metal thermometer with vertical scale over message, green & white, excellent, **$30.00 (C).**

Squeeze...Drink...that distinctive carbonated beverage, painted metal sign with artwork of young children sitting on bench, 28" X 20", excellent, **$145.00 (D).**

Squirt...enjoy...never an after thirst, painted metal thermometer with artwork of Squirt to right of vertical scale, excellent, **$45.00 (C).**

Stoeckers...It's got the pep...Old-fashioned lemon soda, painted embossed tin sign with artwork of lemon leaf in center of message, good, **$55.00 (C).**

Sun Spot...Drink bottled sunshine, round painted metal flange sign, excellent, **$185.00 (C).**

Sun Spot Orange Drink, "Drink America's favorite," tin store advertising sign, 26" X 8", good, **$125.00 (C).**

Sun-Crest, die cut metal bottle thermometer with vertical scale at bottom of bottle, excellent, **$75.00 (C).**

Sunkist, porcelain sign advertising the growers, fair, **$135.00 (C).**

Taka-Kola...Every Hour...Take No Other, round metal tip tray with woman over clock face on tray center, 4¼" dia., excellent, **$325.00 (B).**

Triple 16 Cola...It's Bigger, It's Better, 16 ounces, embossed tin advertising sign with tilted bottle under message, 11½" X 31½", excellent, **$25.00 (B).**

Tru-Ade, Drink...Naturally Delicious Orange, metal door push, 31" X 2½", orange on yellow, excellent, **$25.00 (B).**

Twin Coladie, cut easel back cardboard store sign with graphics of two young children sampling product, 1930s, 6" X 9", near-mint, **$30.00 (B).**

Vess...Drink, light-up metal clock with metal body, 18" dia., excellent, **$145.00 (D).**

Ward's Orange Juice....Drink, painted tin sign with artwork of bottle to left of message, 28" X 20", excellent, **$125.00 (C).**

Whistle...Thirsty? Just...Refreshing Fruit Flavor, decal unused in shape of bottle cap, near-mint, **$5.00 (D).**

White House Ginger Ale...Standard Bottling & Extract Co. Boston, round metal tip tray with bottle of product in center, 4¼" dia., excellent, **$90.00 (B).**

White Rock...The World's Best Table Water, round metal tip tray with fairy image on rock looking over water, 4¼" dia., excellent, **$300.00 (B).**

SPORTING GOODS

Courtesy of Muddy River Trading Co./Gary Metz

DuPont Smokeless Shotgun Powder, titled The end of a good day, featuring artwork of hunting scene, framed, 1911, 18" X 27", excellent, **$650.00 (B).**

Courtesy of Pleasant Hill Antique Mall & Tea Room/Bob Johnson

Federal Monark Target Load, shotgun shell box, good, **$10.00 (D).**

Courtesy of Pleasant Hill Antique Mall & Tea Room/Bob Johnson

Hiawatha Airway, shot shells box, good, **$8.00 (D).**

Hercules Powder Company, calendar, featuring artwork of boy and dog, 1941, 13" X 29½", excellent, **$85.00 (C).**

Courtesy of Broadway House Antiques

Marlin Blades, in original box, good, **$9.00 (D).**

Courtesy of Old Homeplace Antiques, Jackie Thomas

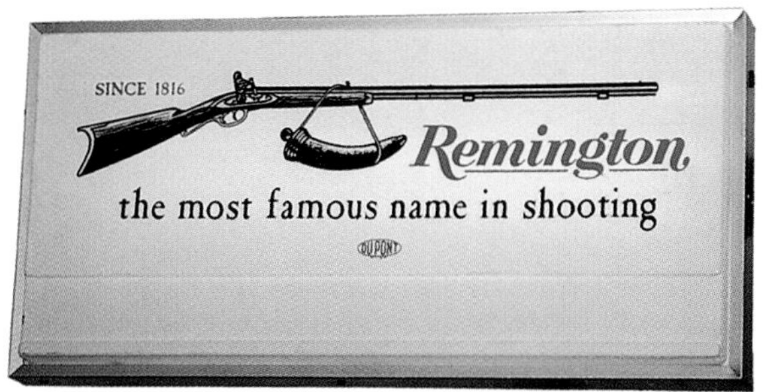

Remington, light-up advertising sign, featuring artwork of muzzle loader with powder horn, "the most famous name in shooting," metal and plastic, 25" X 12", good, **$85.00 (D).**

Courtesy of Riverview Antique Mall

UMC Cartridges, die cut painted tin flange sign, likeness of bull head, good, **$695.00 (D).**

Courtesy of Riverview Antique Mall

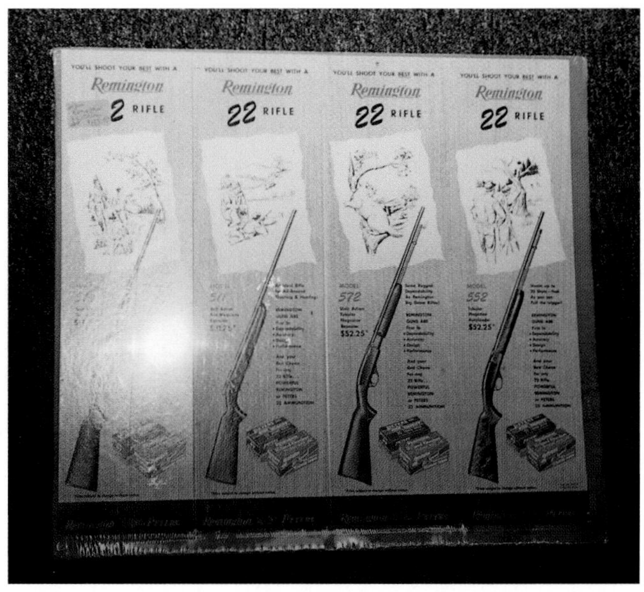

Remington, cardboard window sign, advertising .22 rifle, 20½" X 18½", good, **$135.00 (D).**

Courtesy of Morford Auctions

Remington UMC, Sportsmen's Headquarters, Firearms & Ammunition, double sided die cut flange sign featuring the Remington bears, 7" X 8", excellent, **$2,200.00 (B).**

Courtesy of Pleasant Hill Antique Mall & Tea Room/Bob Johnson

Western Super X shotgun shells, box, good, **$10.00 (D).**

Western Winchester, paper litho poster, featuring scene of men in cabin getting ready for duck hunting, good, **$45.00 (C).**

Western Winchester, paper litho poster, scene of men in camp with deer in background, good, **$45.00 (C).**

Courtesy of Pleasant Hill Antique Mall & Tea Room/Bob Johnson

Western Xpert Super Target Load, shotgun shell box, fair, **$9.00 (D).**

Winchester Double A trap loads, shotgun shell box, fair, **$7.00 (D).**

Courtesy of Pleasant Hill Antique Mall & Tea Room/Bob Johnson

Courtesy of Pleasant Hill Antique Mall & Tea Room/Bob Johnson

Winchester Ranger Mark 5, shotgun shell box, fair, **$9.00 (D).**

Courtesy of Pleasant Hill Antique Mall & Tea Room/Bob Johnson

Winchester Ranger, shotgun shell box, fair, **$8.00 (D).**

Courtesy of Pleasant Hill Antique Mall & Tea Room/Bob Johnson

Winchester Ranger Super Target Load, shotgun shell box, good, **$10.00 (D).**

Courtesy of Pleasant Hill Antique Mall & Tea Room/Bob Johnson

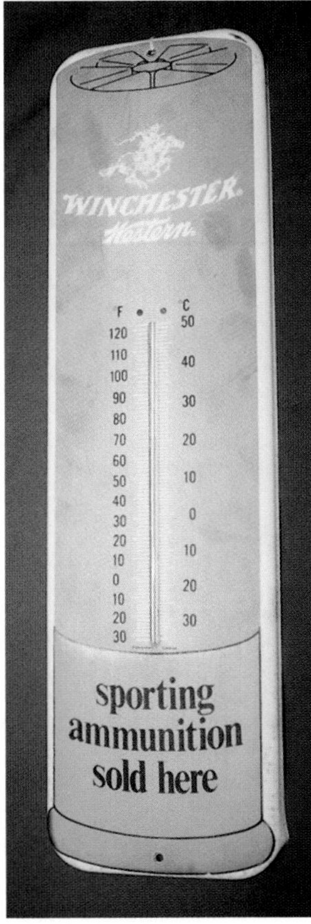

Winchester Western, thermometer, "sporting ammunition sold here," shape of shotgun shell, 12" X 32", fair, **$55.00 (D).**

Winchester, window display, 4-panel fold display, front side displays Winchester products, back side shows Winchester logo of Junior Rifle Corp., 20¼" X 48" each panel, good, **$500.00 (D).**

Winchester, window display, showing target practice scene, 48" tall, good, **$350.00 (C).**

NOT PICTURED:

American Eagle Shot Shells, one piece cardboard box with eagle logo on front, excellent, **$35.00 (B).**

Arrow Loaded Paper Shells, two piece cardboard box, excellent, **$85.00 (B).**

DuPont, paper calendar with original metal strips with artwork of hunters with dogs, for DuPont Powder, partical calendar pad, 1907, 15" X 29¼", excellent, **$633.00 (B).**

Evinrude...rowboat and canoe motors..., round metal tip tray "On The Crest Of The Wave," with graphics of product in action, 4" dia., excellent, **$250.00 (B).**

Fiendoil Tin, "The enemy of corrosion," litho container, cleans and protects firearms, excellent, **$46.00 (B).**

Hercules Powder, Black Sporting, paper litho label on tin container with artwork of Hercules on front cover, 1-lb., excellent, **$60.00 (B).**

Peters Cartridge Co., paper calendar with artwork of hunting dogs in field, 1909, 13¾" X 27", good, **$165.00 (B).**

Peters High Velocity, shotgun shell box for .410 gauge with graphics of duck leaving water, 25 shell size, excellent, **$60.00 (B).**

Peters High Velocity, two piece cardboard box with art of goose in flight, near-mint, **$35.00 (B).**

Peters...Packs the Power, "Know your game," paper ad chart, with top and bottom metal strips, 24" X 35", excellent, **$176.00 (B).**

Remington, Household Knives, "At last I've found a knife that cuts," cardboard ad sign with graphics of woman at kitchen table with product, 12" X 18", good, **$98.00 (B).**

Remington...Let 'er rain, with hunter in boat, 1925, 15" X 28½", excellent, **$560.00 (B).**

Remington Nitro Express...Long Range Game Loads, cardboard shell box with Remington UMC spotlight at top of message, full box, excellent, **$95.00 (B).**

Victor Duck Decoys, papier-maché, hand-painted store advertising piece, 6" X 6" X 4½", excellent, **$575.00 (B).**

Western Field Shotgun Shells, one piece cardboard box with graphics of quail on front of box, 25 count, excellent, **$156.00 (B).**

Winchester, after shave talc, tin container with great litho of hunter and his dog on front, near-mint, **$205.00 (B).**

Winchester Cartridge Shop, World War Two paper motivational shop poster, "reveille for workers...taps for japs," 14" X 22", excellent, **$190.00 (B).**

Winchester Gun Advisor Center, tin litho shield-shaped sign on wood, 1950s, 20" X 20", near-mint, **$100.00 (B).**

Winchester Leader Waterproofed Paper Shot Shells, Winchester Repeating Arms Co., two piece shell box with DuPont label on side, excellent, **$240.00 (B).**

Winchester Nublack Loaded Black Powder Shells, 10-gal., two piece box with graphics of wild fowl in flight, 25 count, excellent, **$140.00 (B).**

TEA & COCOA

Courtesy of Pleasant Hill Antique Mall & Tea Room/Bob Johnson

Cocomalt, chocolate flavor food drink, mfg. by R.B. Davis Co, Hoboken N.J., good, $**18.00 (D).**

Courtesy of Pleasant Hill Antique Mall & Tea Room/Bob Johnson

Live-Well Pure Cocoa, cardboard container, Joyce-Laughlin Co., Peoria, Ill., 2-lb., poor, **$40.00 (D).**

NOT PICTURED:

American Ace Tea, paper litho on cardboard with pry lid, graphics of pilot on one side and airplane on other side, 4-oz., excellent, **$140.00 (B).**

Blake's Tea, blue & white stoneware pot with pouring spout and graphics of Grant cabin, excellent, **$190.00 (B).**

Grand Union Tea Company, trade card, with artwork of Mrs. Cleveland, Lady of the White House, and WI product locations on reverse side, 7" X 13½", excellent, **$60.00 (B).**

Lipton's Teas...Will You Have Some?, paper litho of young lady with tea tray in front, strong colors and great depth, 1899, near-mint, **$1,324.00 (B).**

Remer's Tea Store, cardboard advertising die cut sign featuring cup on edge with cat drinking from saucer, 10" X 6¼", excellent, **$35.00 (D).**

Salada Tea...Delicious Flavor, porcelain door push, 34" X 3½", good, **$65.00 (D).**

Van Houten's Coca, cardboard ad in original oak frame with artwork of woman in hat, frame etched Van Houten's Coca, 24¼" X 30¼", good, **$75.00 (D).**

Courtesy of Richard Opfer Auctioneering, Inc.

Apache Trail Cigars, rare tin litho, with great graphics of Indian on horseback, good strong colors, 5¾" H, excellent, **$875.00 (B).**

Courtesy of Buffalo Bay Auction Co.

Admiral Cigarettes, sign, paper litho of scantily clad woman on board ship at look out, 16" X 22½", excellent, **$150.00 (B).**

Betsy Ross 5¢ Cigar, advertisement, self-framed tin sign, 20" X 24", good, **$500.00 (C).**

Courtesy of Chief Paduke Antique Mall

American Clean Cutter, tobacco cutter, rare design and difficult to find, good, **$295.00 (D).**

Courtesy of Chief Paduke Antique Mall

Big Ben, tobacco tin, featuring artwork of horse on front of tin, Brown Williamson Tobacco Co., rare piece, 1-lb., good, **$65.00 (D).**

Courtesy of Richard Opfer Auctioneering, Inc.

Bob White, tobacco tin, great litho of quail on front and hunting scene on back, 4" L, good, **$160.00 (B).**

Courtesy of Pleasant Hill Antique Mall & Tea Room/Bob Johnson

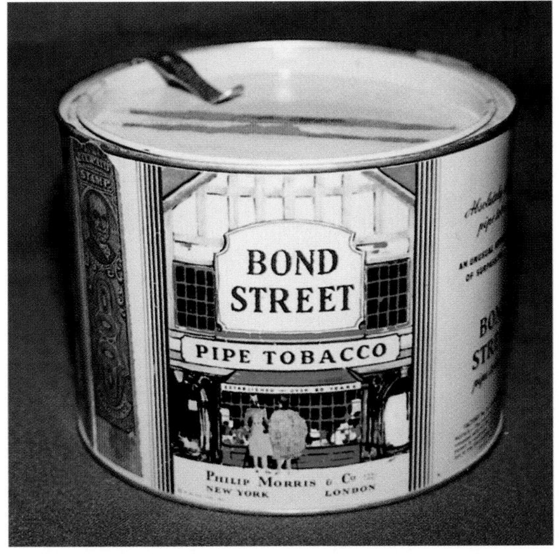

Bond Street Pipe Tobacco, Philip Morris & Co, New York, London, tin, excellent, **$35.00 (D).**

Courtesy of Muddy River Trading Co./Gary Metz

Boot Jack Chewing Tobacco, Costliest Because Best, reverse painted glass sign with beveled edges and original chain, 1900s, 8" X 12", excellent, **$550.00 (B).**

Buchanan & Lyall's Planet Neptune Chewing Tobacco, cloth scroll, pat. June 12, 1877, 11½" X 15½", fair, **$25.00 (C).**

Courtesy of Richard Opfer Auctioneering, Inc.

Bull Dog Cut Plug, die cut tin litho match striker, deluxe straight leaf finest bright burley tobacco, great graphics of dog, "won't bite," 6¾"H, excellent, **$1,800.00 (B).**

Courtesy of Richard Opfer Auctioneering, Inc.

Bull Durham, litho sign on textured paper, framed under glass, 23¼" X 29¼", excellent, **$500.00 (B).**

Bull Durham, Genuine Smoking Tobacco, round tin with original wood frame, rare item, 36" X 38", excellent, **$2,300.00 (C).**

Bull Durham Standard Smoking Tobacco, composition bull with embossed lettering, 22"W X 17¾"H X 7½"D, excellent, **$1,800.00 (C).**

Courtesy of Chief Paduke Antique Mall

Cavalier, cigarette tin, 100 count with key lift lid, 100 count, poor, **$10.00 (D).**

Courtesy of Chief Paduke Antique Mall

Burr-Oak, tobacco cutter, Harry Eeissinger Tobacco Co., Louisville, Ky., excellent, **$225.00 (D).**

Courtesy of Chief Paduke Antique Mall

Central Union, cut plug tin pail with top wire bail handle, The United States Tobacco Company, fair, **$65.00 (D).**

Courtesy of Chief Paduke Antique Mall

Chateau Quebec, a cool mellow pipe tobacco, round tin, fair, **$23.00 (D).**

Courtesy of Pleasant Hill Antique Mall & Tea Room/Bob Johnson

Climax Thin Plug, P. Lorillard Co., tobacco tin, good, **$40.00 (D).**

Top of tobacco tin.

Courtesy of Chief Paduke Antique Mall

Chew STAG Tobacco, cutter, excellent, **$140.00 (D).**

Courtesy of Chief Paduke Antique Mall

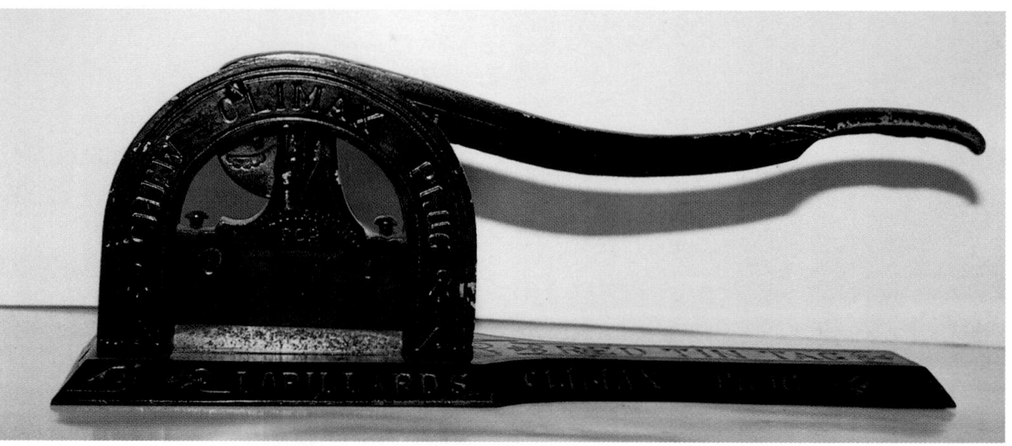

Climax Plug Tobacco, cutter, P. Lorillard Tobacco Co., excellent, **$140.00 (D).**

Courtesy of Chief Paduke Antique Mall

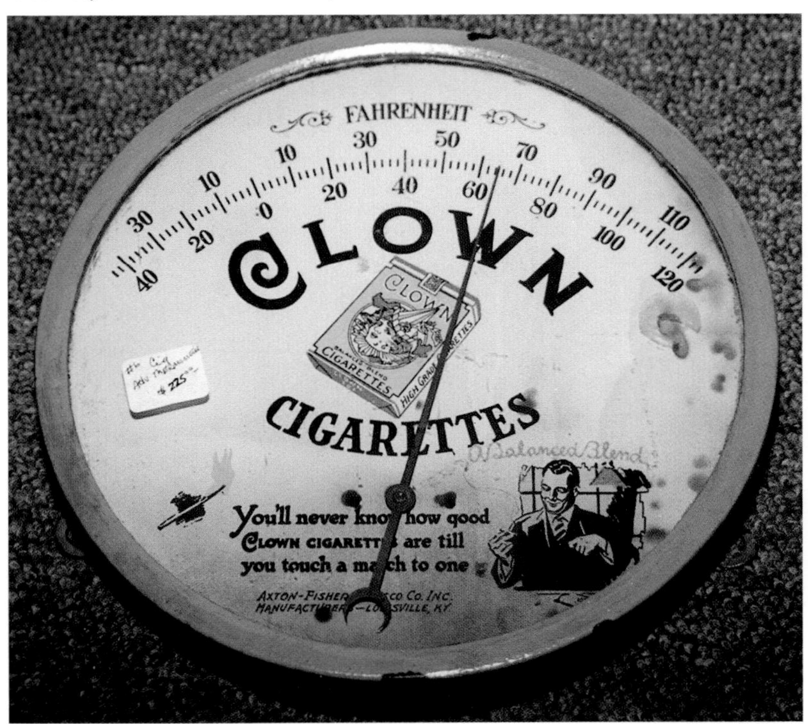

Clown Cigarettes, round dial-type thermometer, "You'll never know how good Clown Cigarettes are till you touch a match to one," good, **$225.00 (D).**

Colonial Club 5¢ Cigar, litho on canvas type paper, featuring artwork of woman in green dress with straw hat, near-mint, **$800.00 (B).**

Courtesy of Richard Opfer Auctioneering, Inc.

Continental Cubes Cigars, litho tin, rare piece, difficult to find, 7½" H, fair, **$200.00 (B).**

Courtesy of Chief Paduke Antique Mall

Cookie Jar DeLuxe Mellow Mild Modern Cigarettes, cigarette package featuring artwork on cookie jar on front, rare, excellent, **$15.00 (D).**

Courtesy of B.J. Summers

Covington Bros. Co. Whole-sale Grocers, Paducah, Ky., tobacco cutter, good, **$135.00 (C).**

Courtesy of Chief Paduke Antique Mall

Cupples Co., arrow tobacco cutter, excellent, **$120.00 (D).**

Courtesy of Pleasant Hill Antique Mall & Tea Room/Bob Johnson

Cuban Seal, For Satisfaction, cigar tin, good, **$35.00 (D).**

Courtesy of Pleasant Hill Antique Mall & Tea Room/Bob Johnson

Dan Patch Cut Plug, Scotten Dillon Co., Detroit, tin, with graphics of horse and sulky, good, **$25.00 (D).**

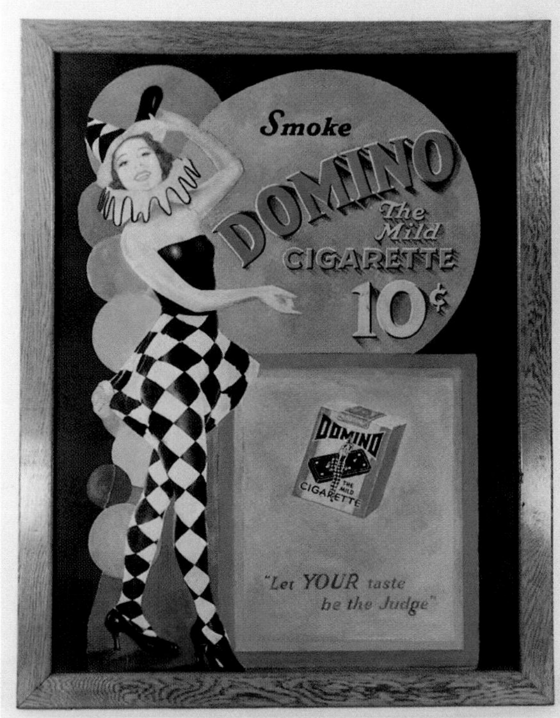

Domino, Smoke..The Mild Cigarette, Let your taste be the judge, framed die cut cardboard advertisement, 34" X 42", excellent, **$450.00 (C).**

Domino, The Mild Cigarette, die cut framed heavy cardboard sign, unusual and hard to find, 28" X 44½", excellent, **$475.00 (C).**

Courtesy of Chief Paduke Antique Mall

Drummond Tobacco Co., Enterprise Mfg. Co., Philadelphia, Pat. April 13, 1875, excellent, **$135.00 (D).**

Courtesy of Muddy River Trading Co./Gary Metz

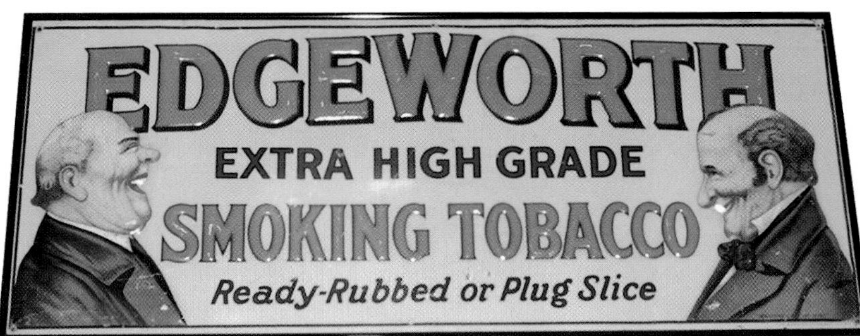

Edgewood Smoking Tobacco, Extra High Grade, heavily embossed tin sign, 27" X 11", excellent, **$475.00 (B).**

Courtesy of Riverview Antique Mall

Eisenlohr's Cinco 5¢ Cigar, painted metal sign, 24" X 12", good, **$65.00 (D).**

El Moriso Guaranteed Hi-Grade Cigar, cardboard advertising sign, 13½" X 10¼", excellent, **$50.00 (C).**

Courtesy of Creatures of Habit

Fatima...Turkish Cigarettes, artwork of veiled woman in center of message, in original frame, 27" X 26½", excellent, **$200.00 (D).**

Courtesy of Chief Paduke Antique Mall

Empire Tobacco, cutter, excellent, **$95.00 (D).**

Courtesy of Muddy River Trading Co./Gary Metz

Favorite Straight Cut Cigarettes, featuring artwork of hunting dog, double sided tin flange side, 18" X 9", excellent, **$2,100.00 (B).**

Courtesy of Buffalo Bay Auction Co.

Game Fine Cut, Jno. J. Bagley & Co., metal store cabinet with great litho images, excellent, **$425.00 (B).**

Courtesy of Wm. Morford Investment Grade Collectibles

Forest & Stream, litho pocket tin, featuring artwork of two men fishing out of a canoe, excellent, **$600.00 (B).**

Courtesy of Richard Opfer Auctioneering, Inc.

Fountain Tobacco, tin, strong colors on litho of fountain, 6¼" H, excellent, **$375.00 (B).**

Courtesy of Morford Auctions

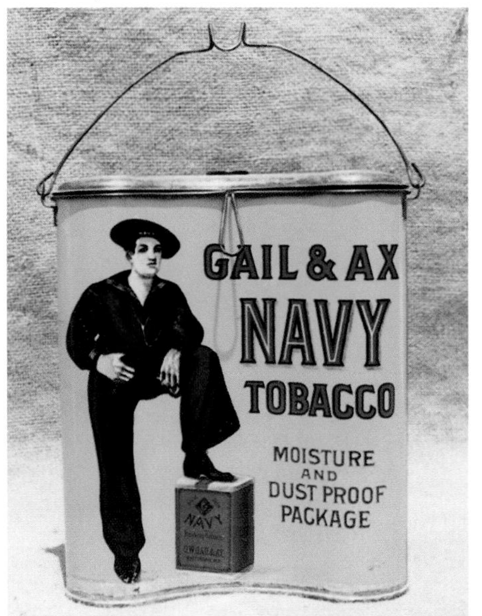

Gail & Ax Navy Tobacco, rare kidney-shaped pail, with bail handle and great graphics, 7" X 8½", excellent, **$2,300.00 (B).**

Garcia Grande Cigars, die cut paper on cardboard easel back store sign, featuring woman with box of product, 30" X 35", excellent, **$247.00 (B).**

Courtesy of Chief Paduke Antique Mall

George Washington Cut Plug, tobacco pail with side wire bail handles, good graphics on front of container, good, **$85.00 (D).**

Courtesy of Morford Auctions

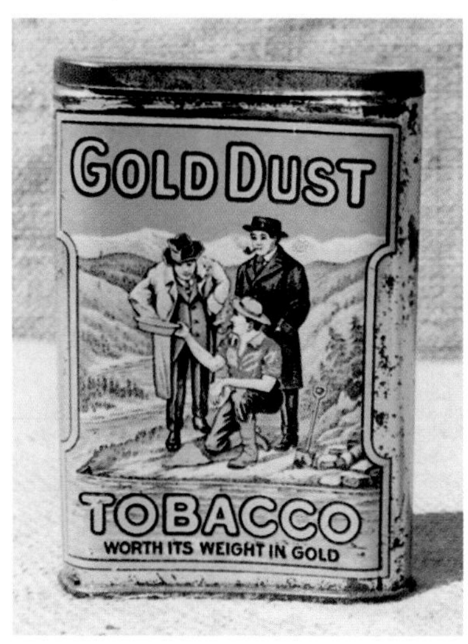

Gold Dust Tobacco, pocket tin, with great graphics, excellent, **$2,650.00 (B).**

Courtesy of Chief Paduke Antique Mall

Golden Grain Smoking Tobacco, bag, Brown & Williamson with Raleigh wrapping papers on back, good, **$25.00 (D).**

Courtesy of Chief Paduke Antique Mall

Granger Pipe Tobacco, round tin, back side has a message explaining why this tobacco is cooler to smoke, good, **$26.00 (D).**

Courtesy of Pleasant Hill Antique Mall & Tea Room/Bob Johnson

H.B Franklin & Co., Chicago, Ill., Each Cigar Is A Perfect Smoke And Extra Value, cigar box, good, **$25.00 (D).**

Harvester, Heart of Havana Cigar, painted tin self-contained framed oval sign, "A.C. Co 71-A" at bottom, 9" X 13", excellent, **$125.00 (C).**

Courtesy of Pleasant Hill Antique Mall & Tea Room/Bob Johnson

Hit Parade Cigarettes, flip top box, good, **$8.00 (D).**

Courtesy of B.J. Summers

HALF and HALF Burley and Bright Pipe Tobacco, glass jar with cardboard lid, 1-lb., excellent, **$35.00 (C).**

Courtesy of Chief Paduke Antique Mall

Herbert Tareyton Cigarettes, 100-piece flat tin, fair, **$42.00 (D).**

Courtesy of Buffalo Bay Auction Co.

Hi-Plane, litho vertical pocket tobacco tin with double prop plane, excellent, **$115.00 (B).**

Hot Ball, chewing and smoking tobacco, embossed tin litho advertising sign with jester holding package, rare piece, good, **$900.00 (B).**

Courtesy of Richard Opfer Auctioneering, Inc.

Courtesy of Richard Opfer Auctioneering, Inc.

Honey Moon Tobacco, one sided tin litho advertising sign from Penn Tobacco Co., featuring couple sitting on quarter moon, 9¾" H, excellent, **$525.00 (B).**

Imperial Club 5¢ Cigar, painted embossed tin sign, Wolf & Co. Selling Agents, 13½" X 10", good, **$75.00 (C).**

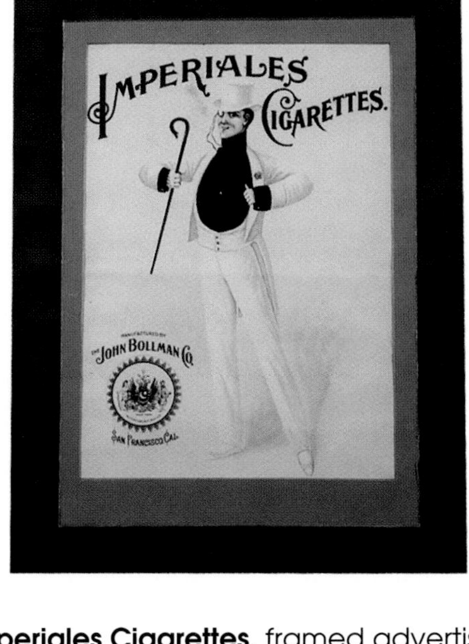

Imperiales Cigarettes, framed advertisement, manufactured by The John Bollman Co., San Francisco, Calif., 16" X 20", excellent, **$225.00 (C).**

J.G. Dill's Best Cut Plug, tobacco tin, good, **$20.00 (C).**

Courtesy of Chief Paduke Antique Mall

John Finzer & Bros., Louisville, Ky., tobacco cutter, excellent, **$160.00 (D).**

Courtesy of Chief Paduke Antique Mall

Just Suits, cut plug metal tobacco pail, Buchanan & Lyall of New York, N.Y., U.S.A., good, **$75.00 (D).**

Courtesy of Pleasant Hill Antique Mall & Tea Room/Bob Johnson

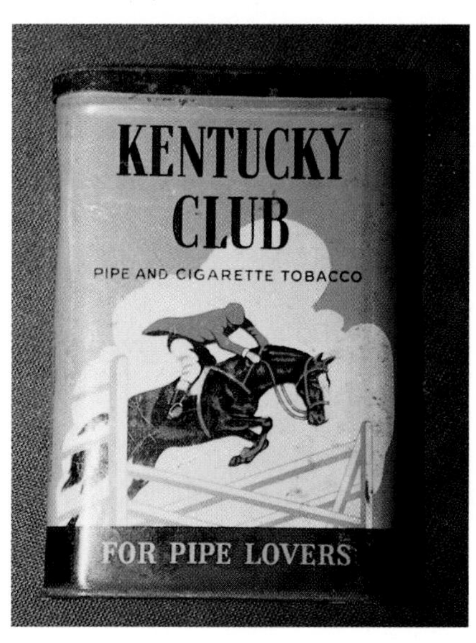

Kentucky Club, pipe and cigarette tobacco tin, good, **$15.00 (D).**

Courtesy of Pleasant Hill Antique Mall & Tea Room/Bob Johnson

Kent Cigarettes, painted tin sign, 30" X 12", excellent, **$15.00 (D).**

Courtesy of Buffalo Bay Auction Co.

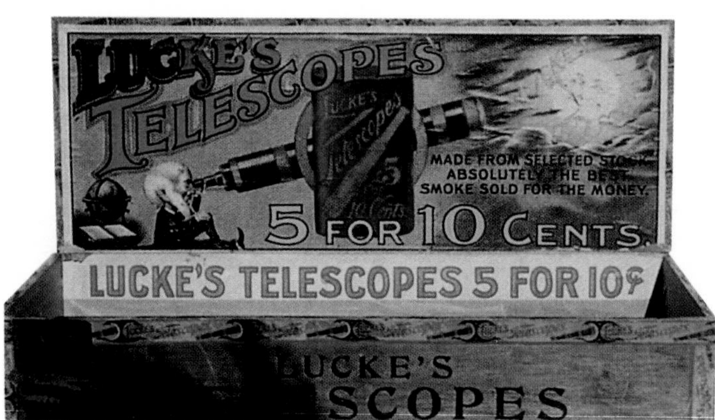

Lucke's Telescopes, wood cigar box, 100-count with litho of man at telescope,1880s, near-mint, **$405.00 (B).**

Courtesy of Riverview Antique Mall

Kool Cigarettes...Mild Menthol Cork tipped, die cut cardboard of girl in scarf holding mask, 32" X 47", excellent, **$175.00 (D).**

La Palina, cigar counter display jar with embossed lettering on jar, 6½" X 8" excellent, **$130.00 (C).**

La Preferencia Seconds, My! This IS a Mild Cigar, 5¢ Straight, framed paper advertisement, 23¼" X 19¼", excellent, **$35.00 (C).**

Courtesy of Chief Paduke Antique Mall

Lucky Strike Filter 100's, green carton, never been opened, excellent, **$45.00 (D).**

Courtesy of Muddy River Trading Co./Gary Metz

Lucky Strike, girl in spotlight, tin sign signed by "Bazz," 1950s, 17" X 24", excellent, **$300.00 (B).**

Lucky Strike, Harry Heilmann, Detroit Tigers...World's Leading Batter, "I smoke Luckies because they are the best," paper trolley car sign, 21" X 11", excellent, **$1,250.00 (C).**

Courtesy of Muddy River Trading Co./Gary Metz

Lucky Strike, pin-up girl, painted tin sign, 15" X 21", excellent, **$250.00 (B).**

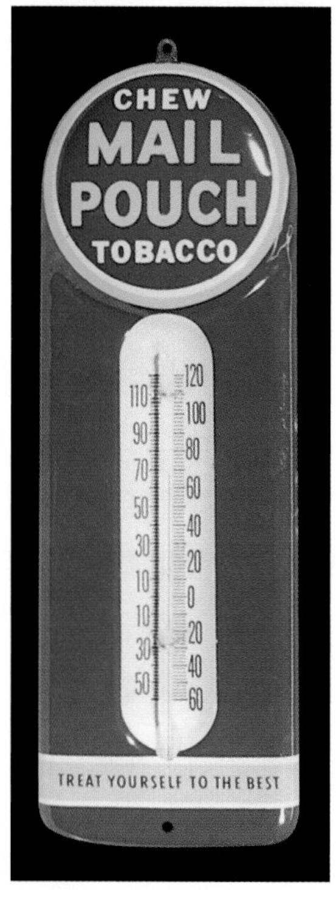

Mail Pouch, chew tobacco, treat yourself to the best, painted embossed metal thermometer, 1950s, 3" X 9", excellent, **$350.00 (B).**

Courtesy of Muddy River Trading Co./Gary Metz

Courtesy of Chief Paduke Antique Mall

Master Mason Plug Smoking Tobacco, tin, It's good tobacco, Quebec, 3-lb., good, **$65.00 (D).**

Marvels Mild Cigarettes, carton, good, **$40.00 (D).**

Courtesy of Chief Paduke Antique Mall

Courtesy of Chief Paduke Antique Mall

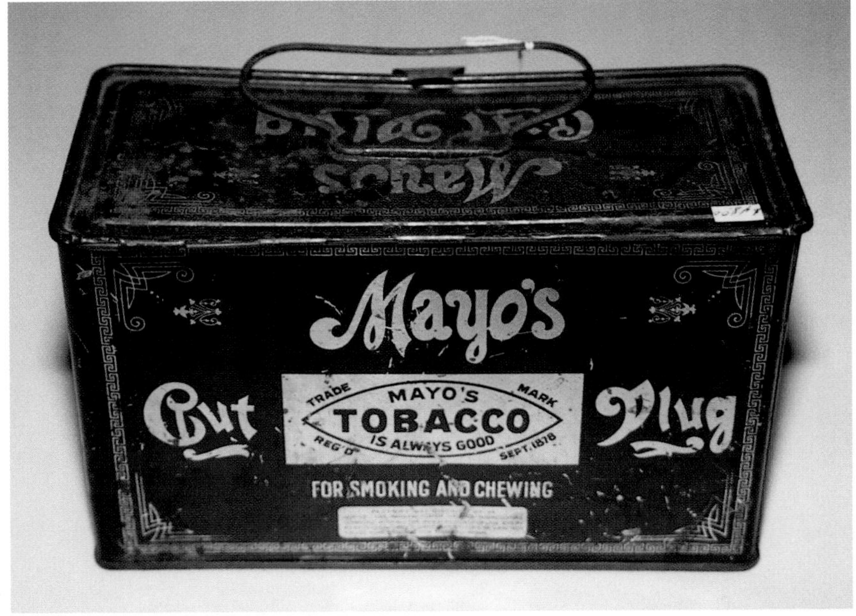

Mayo's Cut Plug, smoking and chewing tobacco, tin pail with wire, good, **$48.00 (D).**

Courtesy of Muddy River Trading Co./Gary Metz

Mayo's Plug, porcelain sign with rooster standing on plugs of tobacco, "Smoking cock o' the walk," 1910s, 6½" X 13", near-mint, **$2,300.00 (B).**

Courtesy of Chief Paduke Antique Mall

Model, smoking tobacco for pipe or cigarette, with artwork of Model man on front, key lift lid, with 1926 tobacco stamp on lid, good, **$20.00 (D).**

Courtesy of Chief Paduke Antique Mall

National Tobacco Co. National Specialty Mfg. Co., Philadelphia, Pa., cutter, excellent, **$90.00 (D).**

Courtesy of Chief Paduke Antique Mall

Old Gold Cigarettes, flat tin, fair, **$33.00 (D).**

Courtesy of Chief Paduke Antique Mall

Old Gold Cigarettes, the treasure of them all, round vacuum pack tin, 50-count, fair, **$55.00 (D).**

Courtesy of Muddy River Trading Co./Gary Metz

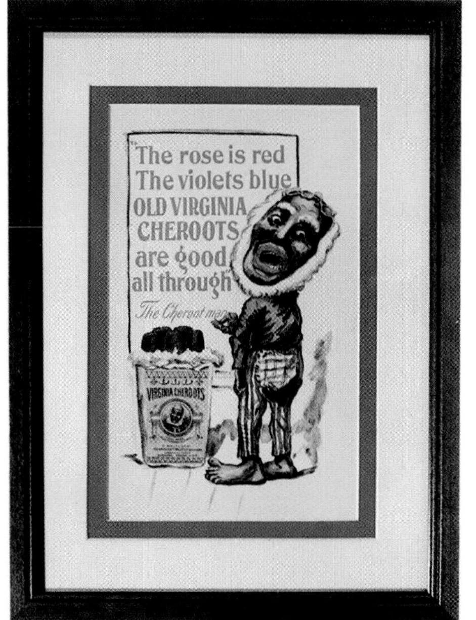

Old Virginia Cheroots, cardboard advertising sign matted, framed, and under glass, 1900s, 6½" X 10½", excellent, **$350.00 (B).**

Courtesy of Richard Opfer Auctioneering, Inc.

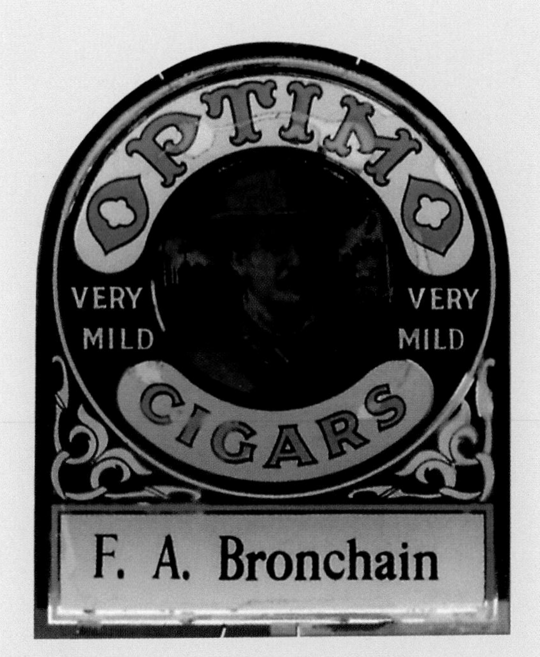

Optimo Cigars, Very Mild, F. A. Bronchain, reverse imaging under beveled glass sign, 11¼" H, excellent, **$170.00 (B).**

Courtesy of Richard Opfer Auctioneering, Inc.

P. Lorillard & Co. Tobacco, store display cabinet, wood with etched glass and brass lettering, great piece, 43" H, excellent, **$6,000.00 (B).**

Courtesy of Wm. Morford Investment Grade Collectibles

Owl Cigars, cardboard double sided die cut string hanger, 7" X 9½", excellent, **$300.00 (B).**

Courtesy of Chief Paduke Antique Mall

Our Advertiser Smoking Tobacco, bag with OCB papers, good, **$8.00 (D).**

Courtesy of Muddy River Trading Co./Gary Metz

Pall Mall Cigarette, tin sign with pin-up girl, same set-up used in Lucky Strike advertisment, 1950s, 15" X 21", excellent, **$230.00 (B).**

Courtesy of Chief Paduke Antique Mall

PALL MALL Menthol 100's, in green, unopened pack, 20-count, excellent, **$8.00 (D).**

Courtesy of Chief Paduke Antique Mall

PALL MALL, wooden counter top display rack, with debossed message on each side, dovetailed joints, excellent, **$115.00 (D).**

Courtesy of Chief Paduke Antique Mall

PALL MALL, wooden counter top display store rack, with paper message at top, Streamlined for better smoking...A Cooler Smoother Smoke, debossed sides, excellent, **$95.00 (D).**

Courtesy of Chief Paduke Antique Mall

Pedro Smoking Tobacco Cut Plug, tin pail, Wm. S. Kimball & Co., The American Tobacco Co., fair, **$35.00 (D).**

Peg Top, The Old Reliable, metal door push, 4" X 12½", excellent, **$150.00 (C).**

Permit to smoke, a good cigar, framed litho advertisment, 1910s, 25" X 31½", excellent, **$250.00**

Courtesy of Pleasant Hill Antique Mall & Tea Room/Bob Johnson

Philadelphia Perfecto, handmade cigar tin, will hold 25 cigars, fair, **$20.00 (D).**

Courtesy of Chief Paduke Antique Mall

Philip Olin & Co., Whol. Grocers (sp. on cutter), Sheffield, Anniston, Ala., excellent, **$95.00 (D).**

Courtesy of Muddy River Trading Co./Gary Metz

Piedmont, the cigarette of quality, featuring artwork of man in moon, framed, matted, and under glass, 1907, 14" X 20", excellent, **$425.00 (B).**

Courtesy of Muddy River Trading Co./Gary Metz

Piedmont, the cigarette of quality, featuring artwork of woman with big hat and fancy hair style, 1910s, 19" X 25", excellent, **$350.00 (C).**

Pinch Hit Chewing Tobacco, sign, embossed painted tin, 14" X 9", poor, **$200.00 (C).**

Courtesy of Muddy River Trading Co./Gary Metz

Piedmont, The Virginia Cigarette, folding wood chair, porcelain sign back, excellent, **$125.00 (B).**

Courtesy of Richard Opfer Auctioneering, Inc.

Pippins 5¢ Cigar, tin litho tip tray, 5½" L, excellent, **$210.00 (B).**

Courtesy of Richard Opfer Auctioneering, Inc.

Pippins Cigar, tin litho advertising sign, 21" L, good, **$250.00 (B).**

Courtesy of Chief Paduke Antique Mall

Plow Boy Chewing and Smoking Tobacco, pail, with side-mounted wire bail handle and paper label, good, **$95.00 (D).**

Plow Boy, chewing and smoking tobacco, round tin with artwork of man smoking pipe sitting on wood-handled plow, paper label, Liggett & Myers Tobacco Co., good, **$50.00 (C).**

Courtesy of Riverview Antique Mall

Red Man, The mild mellow chew, porcelain sign, 22" X 10½", good, **$295.00 (D).**

Courtesy of Chief Paduke Antique Mall

Prince Albert Crimp Cut Tobacco, jar with paper label and original lid, rare, excellent, **$80.00 (D).**

Courtesy of Chief Paduke Antique Mall

S.C.W.W. Co..., Triumph, tobacco cutter, with 1" & 2" measurement at blade, excellent, **$95.00 (D).**

Courtesy of Muddy River Trading Co./Gary Metz

Sir Walter Raleigh Smoking Tobacco, porcelain sign with graphics of pocket tin, 1920s, 36" X 12", excellent, **$825.00 (B).**

Courtesy of Muddy River Trading Co./Gary Metz

Spear Head, plug chew, tobacco tin sign with heavy relief and embossing, 28" X 10", excellent, **$500.00 (B).**

Speedboat mixture, tobacco tin, featuring artwork of 1930s-style boat, 5¾" X 3¼", good, **$200.00 (C).**

Courtesy of Pleasant Hill Antique Mall & Tea Room/Bob Johnson

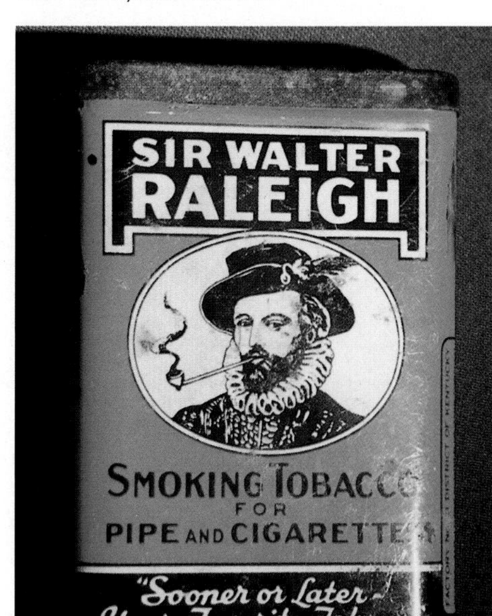

Sir Walter Raleigh Smoking Tobacco, tin, Brown Williamson Tobacco Corp., Louisville, Ky., fair, **$8.00 (D).**

Courtesy of Chief Paduke Antique Mall

Stud Smoking Tobacco, bag with R.J. Reynolds wrapping papers on back, good, **$9.00 (D).**

Courtesy of Wm. Morford Investment Grade Collectibles

Sunset Trail Cigars, tin with strong colors on artwork of cowboys on horseback, 6⅛" X 4⅛", excellent, **$475.00 (B).**

Sweet Cuba, fine cut tobacco metal canister, 8" X 8" X 10", good, **$115.00 (C).**

Courtesy of Chief Paduke Antique Mall

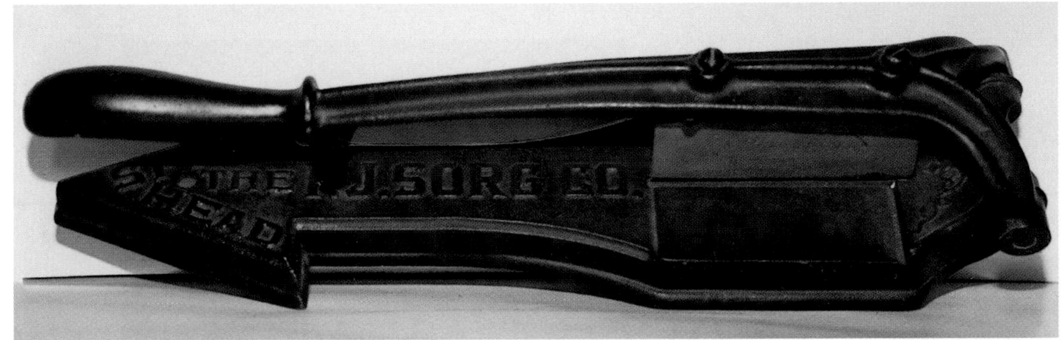

The P.J. Sorg Co., Spear Head, tobacco cutter with arrow-shaped end, excellent, **$150.00 (D).**

Courtesy of Buffalo Bay Auction Co.

Taxi Crimp Cut Tobacco, vertical pocket tin with graphics of early taxi with two men waiting on street in formal attire, near-mint, **$4,900.00 (B).**

Courtesy of Chief Paduke Antique Mall

Tip-Top Sweet Smoke and Chew Tobacco, pail with paper label and 1926 tobacco stamp on lid, good, **$95.00 (D).**

Courtesy of Morford Auctions

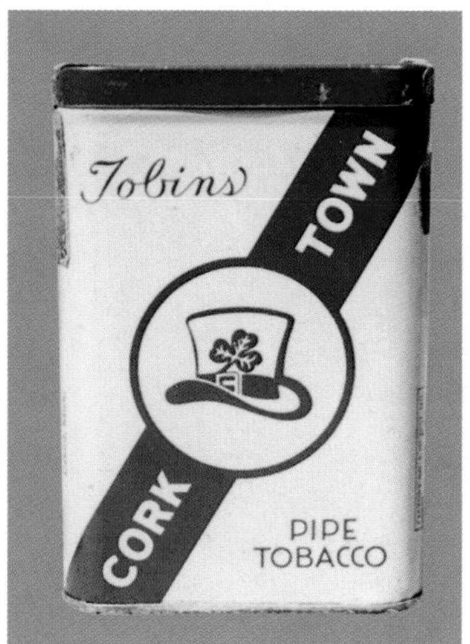

Tobins' Cork Town Pipe Tobacco, rare piece, excellent, **$600.00 (B).**

Courtesy of Morford Auctions

Totem Tobacco, oval pocket tin, with good strong coloring and graphics, excellent, **$1,150.00 (B).**

Courtesy of Buffalo Bay Auction Co.

Touch Down Smoking Tobacco...Fragrant and Mellow with Age, die cut cardboard counter sign with graphics of men at goal line, 9½" X 6", excellent, **$407.00 (B).**

Courtesy of Chief Paduke Antique Mall

Tuxedo Tobacco, specially prepared for pipe or cigarette tin with flip top lid, 1½-oz., good, **$25.00 (D).**

Courtesy of Chief Paduke Antique Mall

Union Leader Redi Cut Tobacco, round tin with Uncle Sam likeness smoking pipe on label, P. Lorillard Company, good, **$15.00 (D).**

Courtesy of Chief Paduke Antique Mall

Union Leader, smoking tobacco paperweight, excellent, **$25.00 (D).**

Courtesy of Pleasant Hill Antique Mall & Tea Room/Bob Johnson

Velvet Smoking Tobacco, cardboard container, 14-oz., fair, **$8.00 (D).**

Velvet Pipe Tobacco, Aged in Wood, Sold Here, porcelain sign, 39" X 12", fair, **$155.00 (C).**

Courtesy of Chief Paduke Antique Mall

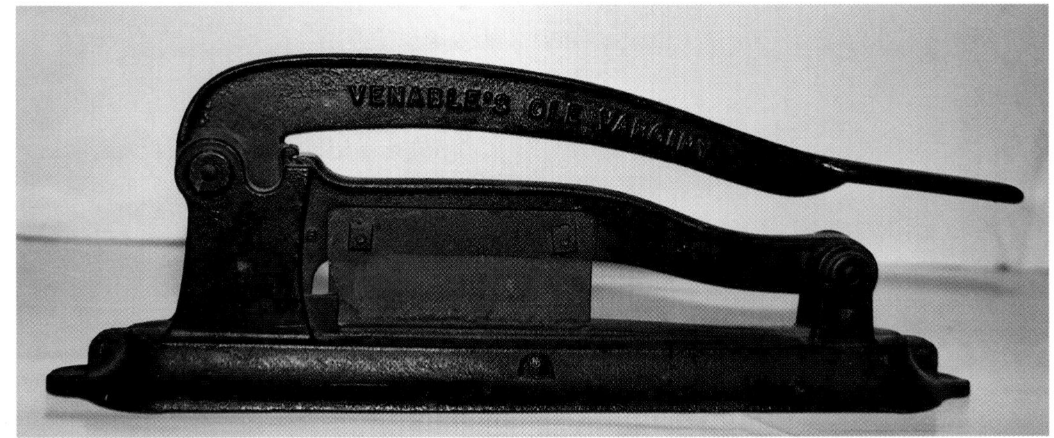

Venable's Ole Virginny Tobacco, cutter, excellent, **$95.00 (D).**

Courtesy of Chief Paduke Antique Mall

Venables Chew Tobacco, cutter, Pat.1875 with 1" & 2" measurements, excellent, **$115.00 (D).**

Courtesy of Muddy River Trading Co./Gary Metz

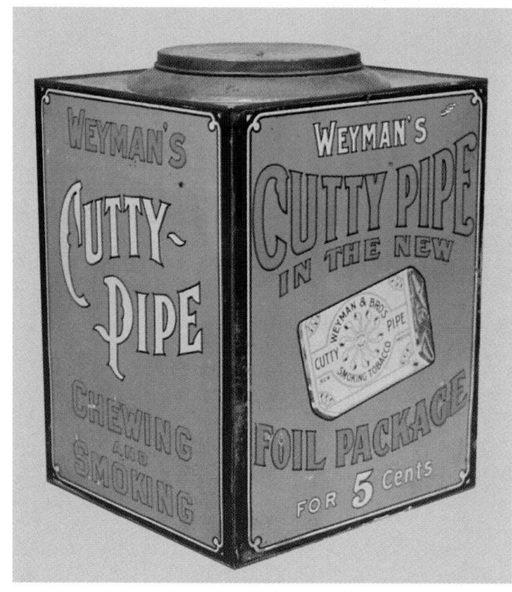

Weyman's Cutty-Pipe Chewing and Smoking Tobacco, store display bin, 9" X 10" X 13½", good, **$400.00 (B).**

Winner Cut Plug, Smoke and Chew, metal pail with wire handle on top, with great graphics of early model race cars, 5¼" X 4" X 8", good, **$155.00 (C).**

Courtesy of Buffalo Bay Auction Co.

Walton, Izaak, 50-count cigar tin, excellent, **$365.00 (B).**

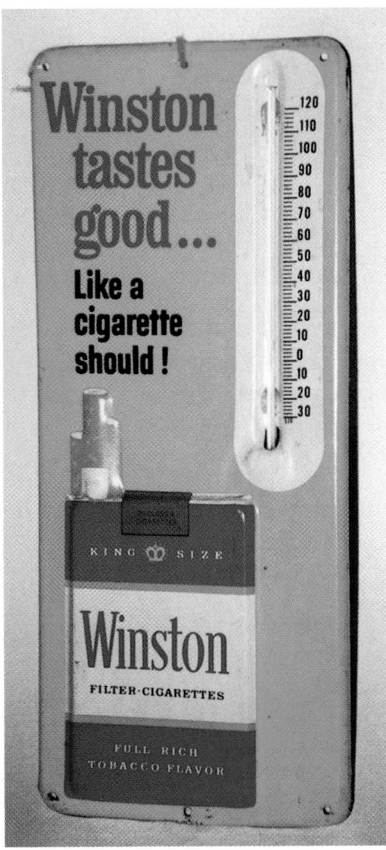

Winston...tastes good...like a cigarette should!, embossed painted metal thermometer with vertical scale at top right and product package lower left, no warning label, 6" X 13½", excellent, **$65.00 (C).**

Courtesy of Creatures of Habit

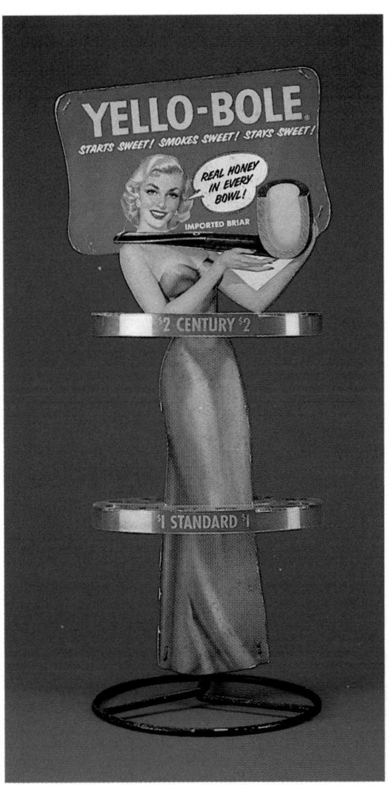

Yello-Bole, pipe store display stand featuring woman in green evening dress holding a sample pipe, metal, plastic, and cardboard, 1950s, excellent, **$135.00 (D).**

NOT PICTURED:

Alonso Rejas...Clear Havana, Made at Key West, Fla., advertising tray with early Vienna-type advertising of woman in center, 10" dia., excellent, **$400.00 (B).**

American Blend, tin litho pocket container, 3⅛" X 4⅜" X ⅞", excellent, **$1,450.00 (B).**

Andrew D. White...Mild and Satisfying, cigar tip tray, 4¼" dia., fair, **$35.00 (B).**

Avalon Cigarettes, You'd Never Guess They Cost Less, with artwork of woman in hat in center and message at bottom, paper on cardboard, 20" X 30", excellent, **$65.00 (D).**

Bagdad Short Cut Smoking, paper on cardboard with graphics of man holding vertical pocket tin, 1909, 20" X 30", excellent, **$233.00 (B).**

Bagley's Old Colony Mixture, John J. Bagley Co., Detroit, Mich., tin litho vertical pocket tin with artwork of woman wearing bonnet, 2" X 3" X ¾", excellent, **$575.00 (B).**

Bagley's Sweet Tips Smoking, tin litho vertical pocket container, excellent, **$65.00 (B).**

Balkan Sobranie Turkish Cigarettes...Handmade of the finest Yenidje Tobacco, cigarette box with great artwork of tobacco on animal-drawn wagons, 6¼" X M⅞" X 1⅛", excellent, **$35.00 (D).**

Beech-Nut Chewing Tobacco, porcelain sign with artwork of product packaging at left of sign, 22" X 10½", fair, **$55.00 (D).**

"Between The Acts," Trihos. Hall Tobacco Co., NY., paper litho advertising, graphics of young girl with bouquet of roses, 1910, 16" X 25", good, **$165.00 (B).**

Black Sheep 5¢ Cigar...A Sanitary Package for 25¢, tin litho cigar container, 3¼" X 5½" X ¾", excellent, **$275.00 (B).**

Blackwells Durham Tobacco Co., Julie Carrs Tobacco, litho tin container for cut plug product, 1½" X 4½" X 3¼", excellent, **$300.00 (B).**

Blue and Scarlet, tin litho lunch pail from Booker Tobacco Co., Richmond, VA, with top wire handle, blue, scarlet, and gold, good, **$125.00 (B).**

Bowl of Roses Pipe Mixture, tin vertical litho tobacco pocket tin with artwork of man smoking pipe in front of fireplace, 3" X 4⅜" X ⅞", excellent, **$325.00 (B).**

British Navy Chewing Tobacco...Strictly Union Made, cardboard advertising sign with graphics of swimming sailors, Canadian product, 9" X 18", excellent, **$69.00 (B).**

Bull Durham...1 oz. bag 5¢, embossed tin litho sign, strong colors with artwork of bull in center, 8½" X 12", excellent, **$1,400.00 (B).**

Camel Cigarettes Sold Here, porcelain flange sign, 12" X 18", yellow on red, good, **$85.00 (D).**

Camel, Smoke...Cigarettes, painted metal sign, with facsimile of product package in spotlight at bottom of sign, 12" X 18", yellow on red, good, $**45.00 (D).**

Canadian Club 5¢ Cigar, cardboard ad sign with graphics of man with product, 21" X 13½", near-mint, **$50.00 (B).**

Castle Hall Cigar, D.S. Erb & Co., self-framing tin litho ad sign, 37½" X 13", excellent, **$220.00 (B).**

Charles Denby...Where cigars are Made...Evansville, Ind., oval metal tip tray with graphics of factory in tray center, 6", excellent, **$30.00 (B).**

Chesterfield, Buy...Here, die cut metal painted flange sign with product package die cut at top of sign, 12" X 15", excellent, **$55.00 (D).**

Chesterfield, Buy...Here, metal die cut flange sign with artwork of product packages under message, 11¾" X 16½", excellent, **$45.00 (D).**

Chesterfield Cigarettes...They Satisfy..., metal tip tray with product image in center of tray, 6⅝" L, fair, **$45.00 (B).**

Chesterfield, flat fifties, hinged cigarette tin, good, **$15.00 (D).**

Chief Oshkosh, wooden cigar box with graphics of Indian on inside cover wearing top hat, 1916, 50-count, excellent, **$70.00 (B).**

Climax-Plug...Chew, litho tip tray with great graphics of flowers, excellent, **$50.00 (B).**

Clown Cigarettes, cast iron product advertising in shape of embossed horseshoe, used to hold papers down at street corner news stands, 6" X 8½" X 2", near-mint, **$102.00 (B).**

Colonist...Up to the Minute...5¢ Cigar...Save The Bands, cardboard litho with artwork of Minute Man type image, 1900s, 13¼" X 19¾", near-mint, **$223.00 (B).**

Cortez Cigars...For Men Of Brains...Made At Key West, metal tip tray, 6⅛" L, good, **$60.00 (B).**

Country Club...Smoking or Chewing Kentucky Long Cut, The Scotten Tobacco Co., Detroit, Mich., lunch pail with top attached metal pail handle, 7" X 4¾" X 4½", excellent, **$325.00 (B).**

Covered Wagon, cardboard cigar box with great graphics of covered wagon scene on inside lid, 50-count, excellent, **$40.00 (B).**

DeNobili Cigar Company, embossed painted tin sign, message of "that different smoke," 3 for 5¢, 19" X 6", excellent, **$25.00 (D).**

Diamond Chewing Tobacco, tin litho advertising thermometer, manufactured by ALLEN & ELLIS, Cincinnati, 5" X 10", excellent, **$400.00 (B).**

Dick Custer Cigars..."Holds You Up," litho container with graphics of Custer on front, excellent, **$741.00 (B).**

Don Remo, change receiver, reverse glass image with cigar cutter on side, 9½" X 6", excellent, **$302.00 (B).**

Duke's Mixture, sign, heavy porcelain with raised metal surface, Belt Enamel Co., featuring artwork of product, drawstring bag, 8¾" X 12", excellent, **$525.00 (B).**

Dutch Masters Cigars, self-framed tin litho hanging sign with image of Dutch pilgrims, 11" X 9", excellent, **$66.00 (B).**

El Gallo cigars, art plate with graphics of rooster, 1905, 10" dia., excellent, **$610.00 (B).**

El Verso...The Sweet & Mellow Cigar, metal tip tray with great graphics of man in easy chair enjoying product, 6⅝" long, excellent, **$75.00 (B).**

Emila Garcia 5¢ Cigar, reverse glass and tin litho cigar holder that slips over a 50-count cigar tin, excellent, **$77.00 (B).**

Forest Stream Tobacco, tin litho slip lid canister with graphics of man fishing in stream in cameo on front, excellent, **$146.00 (B).**

Free Lance...Smoke a...and be Convinced, cardboard cigar sign, 11" X 9½", excellent, **$71.00 (B).**

Game Finecut Tobacco, tin with bird scene, manufactured by "Jno J. Bagley E. Co., Detroit, Mich.," 11½" X 6½" X 8", excellent, **$255.00 (C).**

Garcia Grande Cigar, rectangular metal tip tray with graphics of joker on stool to right of message, 6⅛" L, excellent, **$75.00 (B).**

Half & Half, Burley and Bright Tobacco, tin, 3" X 4¼" X 1", excellent, **$9.00 (D).**

Hand Made Flake Cut, Globe Tobacco Co., Detroit, Mich., small top tin litho tobacco canister, 4⅞" X 6¼", excellent, **$525.00 (B).**

Havana Blossom, cardboard sign with graphics of man promoting product, from P. Lorillard Co., 1910, 12" X 18", near-mint, **$185.00 (B).**

Helmar, rectangular metal tip tray with graphics of Turkish scenes, 6" L, excellent, **$55.00 (B).**

Helmar...Turkish Cigarettes...Quality Superb, cardboard sign on wood, 3½" X 21½", good, **$15.00 (D).**

Hi-Plane Smooth Cut Tobacco, for pipe and cigarettes, die cut cardboard with graphics of airplane in flight, 23" x 22", good, **$66.00 (B).**

Honest Tobacco...Long cut...smoking...chewing, cardboard advertising in frame featuring man at table in hat, 1890s, good, **$1,150.00 (C).**

Indian Crown 10¢ Cigar, McCoy & Co. Makers, New York, embossed tin litho advertising sign with artwork of Indian in full headress to left of product info, 20¾" X 15", excellent, **$975.00 (B).**

Jackson's Best Sweet Navy Chewing Tobacco... "Tole You Chilon," cardboard trade card, from Petersburg, Va., with graphics of old black man, 1890s, 3¼" X 5", near-mint, **$55.00 (B).**

John Weisert Tobacco Co., St. Louis, U.S.A., cardboard container box, with artwork of mule on front, excellent, **$12.00 (D).**

KOOL Cigarettes, advertising fan, images of penguins skating around product package, excellent, **$35.00 (B).**

Kool, menthol magic...Smoke Kool, metal cigarette holder with artwork of Kool penguin and product pack, excellent, **$45.00 (D).**

Kool...Smoke...We Sell Cigarettes, horizontal embossed painted metal sign with Kool penguin to left of message, 25" X 10½", excellent, **$59.00 (D).**

Liggett & Meyers Tobacco Co., Sweet Cuba...fine cut...the kind that suits, store tin with artwork of ocean and lighthouse, fair, **$45.00 (D).**

Liggett & Meyers Tobacco Co., tin tobacco pail with wire bail handle, product information in oval on front, good, **$25.00 (D).**

Liggett & Meyers Tobacco Co., Velvet Pipe & Cigarette Tobacco, round tin container with press on lid, excellent, **$15.00 (D).**

Light Horse Squadron...The Aristocrat of 10¢ Cigars, metal tip tray with camp scene in center, 6⅝" L, excellent, **$95.00 (B).**

Lone Jack...smoke the...seg-ars, etched stained glass advertising sign, 4" X 9¾", excellent, **$900.00 (B).**

Lord Tennyson Puritanos Cigars, Canadian tin litho container, 5" X 5⅛", excellent, **$110.00 (B).**

Lucky Strike, flat fifties cigarettes hinged cigarette tin, Lucky Strike...It's toasted, 5½" X 4½", excellent, **$20.00 (C).**

Mail Pouch...treat yourself to the best...chew...tobacco, porcelain thermometer with messages at top and bottom, vertical scale, 8" X 38¾", blue, orange, and white, excellent, **$175.00 (D).**

Marie Tempest Cigars...B. Newmark & Co., New York, litho on paper of pretty woman with head scarf, 1900s, 16" X 22", near-mint, **$968.00 (B).**

Marvells...the cigarette of quality, painted metal thermometer with artwork of product package at top of vertical scale, message at bottom, blue background, excellent, **$45.00 (C).**

Mascot Tobacco, metal tip tray with scene of animals at water, 5" L, excellent, **$50.00 (B).**

Mayo's Mammy, roly-poly tin litho container of black mammy, good, **$250.00 (B).**

Melachrino...The one cigarette sold the world over, cardboard sign with wooden frame, 28" X 4", excellent, **$45.00 (D).**

Mi Favorita Cigars..."A Solace For Busy Minds"...Clear Havana, metal tip tray, 1⅛" L, excellent, **$130.00 (B).**

Model 10¢ Tobacco, tin litho advertising sign featuring artwork of cigar store Indian, 6" X 15", near-mint, **$127.00 (B).**

Mr. Thomas 5¢ Cigar...None Better, round metal tip tray with graphics of "tom" cat on tray, 4⅛" dia., excellent, **$650.00 (B).**

National Cigar Stands...Our Brands, round metal tip tray with artwork of lady with early off-the-shoulder dress, 6" dia., excellent, **$45.00 (B).**

National Cigar Store, light fixture shaped like cigar store with leaded glass dome, 23" X 22½" X 11", excellent, **$2,700.00 (B).**

OCB...Roll Your Own with...Cigarette Papers, tin paper holder with product message on front, yellow lettering on black, excellent, **$30.00 (D).**

Old English Curve Cut, "A Slice to a Pipeful, It Fits the Pocket," store bin with slanted front with graphics of product on all sides, 13" X 10¼" X 8½", good, **$125.00 (B).**

Old Gold Cigarettes, horizontal porcelain sign, 36" X 12", fair, **$25.00 (D).**

Old Gold Cigarettes, Not a cough in a carload, porcelain sign, 36" X 11", good, **$225.00 (D).**

Old Gold Cigarettes, paper on cardboard, easel back ad sign with artwork of Dick Powell promoting product, 10½" X 13½", excellent, **$18.00 (B).**

Old Gold, die cut easel back cigarette girl with product vendor tray, 14" X 32", excellent, **$140.00 (B).**

Ology Quality Cigar, cardboard die cut easel back sign with graphics of man with golf club, 1930s, 25" X 37", excellent, **$145.00 (B).**

Our Hobby Sliced Plug, Taylor & Co., Burlington, VT, early tin litho pocket tin, rare, 4⅝" X 2¾" X ⅞", excellent, **$300.00 (B).**

Patterson's Recut Tobacco, 10¢ value for 5 cents, paper sign with product image on both sides of message in center, 36" X 18", near-mint, **$55.00 (B).**

Paul Jones Havana Cigars, tin litho, wood grained, self-framing with cameo of Paul Jones in center, also self-framed, this type sign is difficult to find, 20" X 24", excellent, **$725.00 (B).**

Pedro Tobacco, cut plug tobacco bag with graphics on both sides, full opened bags, 2¾" X 4¼" X ⅞", good, **$230.00 (B).**

Peerless Tobacco, canister, tin litho pail with wire handles, factory scene on front, near-mint, **$110.00 (B).**

Pet Cigarettes are the Best, Allen & Ginter, hanging cardboard sign with graphics of young girl at well, 4" X 9½", excellent, **$77.00 (B).**

Pet cigarettes...are the best, die cut easel back store sign with graphics of young girl sitting on tree limb swinging her straw hat, 1905, excellent, **$155.00 (B).**

Peter Schuyler...Get a heck of a cigar, with silhouette of man's head smoking a cigar at top center, porcelain advertising sign, 36" X 12", excellent, **$125.00 (C).**

Peter Schuyler Perfecto Cigars, round tip tray with graphics of Peter Schuyler in tray center, 6" dia., excellent, **$200.00 (B).**

Piedmont...For cigarettes Virginia Tobacco is the best, porcelain sign with product package in center of message, 30" X 49", excellent, **$125.00 (D).**

Popper's Ace Cigar, tin cigar can with litho of bi-plane, 5½" X 3⅛" X 2⅜", excellent, **$1,000.00 (B).**

Postmaster Smokers...2 for 5¢, round tin with artwork of man with cigar on front, 5¼" X 5" dia., good, **$25.00 (D).**

Pride of Virginia sliced plug, rectangular tobacco tin with cameo on front cover, good, **$15.00 (D).**

Prince Albert, crimp cut pipe tobacco round tin with oval outline of Prince Albert, excellent, **$15.00 (C).**

Puritan crushed plug mixture, tin litho vertical pocket tobacco tin, 3" X 4⅜" X ⅞", excellent, **$275.00 (B).**

Recruit Little Cigars, die cut store tri-fold sign featuring scenes on each fold of places to enjoy product, 39" X 29", excellent, **$225.00 (B).**

Red Earl Cigars... 5¢ in price 10¢ in price, round tip tray with graphics of the Red Earl in tray center, 3⅝" dia., excellent, **$80.00 (B).**

Red-Ola cigars...Edward D. Depew & Co., New York, round metal tip tray with artwork of pretty woman in center of tray, 4¼" dia., excellent, **$175.00 (B).**

Rocky Ford...A new high in two for five cigars, 50-count cigar box with graphics of Indian looking with hand over eyes, excellent, **$25.00 (B).**

Roi-Tan...Man to Man...A Real Fine Cigar, reverse glass sign in original brass frame, 13" X 21¼", near-mint, **$687.00 (B).**

Salem...Change To, rubber change pad with astro turf, 10" X 10", good, **$12.00 (D).**

San Alto Cigar, cardboard ad sign with graphics of black servant serving product, 14" X 30", excellent, **$230.00 (B).**

Satin...Turkish Cigarettes, 20 for 15¢, round metal serving tray, 13¾" dia., excellent, **$35.00 (D).**

Scotten Dillon Company, Detroit, Mich., Ojibwa Tobacco, tin litho store bin, originally had 48 five-cent packages, 8½" X 11¼", good, **$325.00 (B).**

Showanda Cigars, paper litho on tin canister with graphics of Indian on front, excellent, **$85.00 (B).**